MUSLIMS IN AMERICAN HISTORY
A Forgotten Legacy

First Edition
(1427AH/2006AC)

© Copyright 1427AH/2006AC
amana publications
10710 Tucker Street
Beltsville, Maryland 20705-2223 USA
Tel: (301) 595-5777 / Fax: (301) 595-5888
E-mail: amana@igprinting.com
Website: www.amana-publications.com

Library of Congress Cataloging-in-Publications Data

Dirks, Jerald.
  Muslims in American History : A Forgotten Legacy/ Jerald
F. Dirks.
      p. cm.
Includes bibliographical references.
  ISBN 1-59008-044-0
  1. Islam. 2. Islam--Essence, genius, nature. I. Title.

BP161.3.D57 2003
297'.02'427--dc22

                                                        2003025598

Printed in the United States of America by
International Graphics
10710 Tucker Street
Beltsville, Maryland 20705-2223 USA
Tel: (301) 595-5999 Fax: (301) 595-5888
Website: igprinting.com
E-mail: ig@igprinting.com

Muslims
in American History
A FORGOTTEN LEGACY

Jerald F. Dirks

amana publications

CONTENTS

Preface

Contemporary scholarship is presently uncovering a vast complex of Muslim-American interaction that stretches chronologically far back into the pre-Columbian era and that has continued unabated to this very moment. In gathering together and summarizing this information, I am only offering a review and synthesis of the scholarly efforts of others. However, such an integrative summary appears to be warranted at this time, as most of the relevant documentation has been scattered here and there in various subspecialty areas of history, with little attempt having been made to bring together this information into a viable historical gestalt.

I hope that by making this material available in one source, this book can serve several purposes. On the one hand, it is my wish that this modest volume may broaden the understanding of the American public with regard to the substantial role played by Muslims throughout American history. On the other hand, I hope that this book may serve as a valuable adjunct to standard high school and college textbooks on American history and as a preliminary textbook for private Islamic high schools and middle schools in America.

As always, I am deeply indebted to my wife of 35 years, Debra L. Dirks. She has selflessly devoted her time to critiquing and proof-reading the various drafts of this book, creating an environment in which I could work, and providing the moral and emotional support that an occasionally self-questioning author needs. In the process, she has willingly sacrificed her own writing time (she is the co-editor of *Islam Our Choice: Portraits of Modern American Women*, available from Amana Publications) in the service of mine.

In addition, I want to thank my former students at Crescent View Academy in Aurora, Colorado, and at Annoor Islamic School in Wichita, Kansas. It was my interaction with them in social studies that first drew my attention to the need for the synthesis of information presented in this book. Each of them was and is both an American and a Muslim. Yet, standard textbooks offered them no hope of claiming their natural heritage within the rich and varied history of Muslims in America. As much as to anyone, this book is dedicated to them.

As a general rule, I have attempted to make this book a fairly informal read. As such, I have greatly limited the use of footnotes, although a complete bibliography of sources consulted may be found at the back of this book. However, some of the material presented may be seen by some readers as fairly controversial. In those places, I have used extensive footnotes so that the reader may know the exact sources that have been utilized.

Jerald F. Dirks, M.Div., Psy.D.
July 15, 2004

1 The Forgotten Story

A. INTRODUCTION

Beginning during the last two decades of the 20th century, a significant body of scholarly work has begun to emerge in the West that calls into question much of our conventional wisdom about American history. This is particularly true for those of us who received our primary and secondary educations during the placid 1950s and turbulent 1960s. Simply put, we our now witnessing a major revision of American history. Long-held beliefs and cherished myths are being relegated to the scrapheap of outmoded thought. In the process, we are learning that there are many legacies within American history that have been inadvertently forgotten or even deliberately suppressed. The present book pays homage to one such forgotten legacy—the role of Muslims in American history.

Islam has typically been seen by most Americans as an exotic, foreign religion that has little in common with the average American and with the vast panorama of American history. Americans of an older generation may first remember Islam in America in association with the so-called Black Muslim movement that gained widespread public prominence during the civil rights era of the 1950s and 1960s. Younger Americans may have first become aware of Islam in America following the spotlight that focused on Islam in the immediate aftermath of the tragedy of September 11, 2001. In reality and in marked contrast to these perceptions, the history of Islam in America can be traced back through the centuries for what appears to be well over 1,000 years.

Unfortunately, the history of Islam in America is a largely forgotten story, a legacy that can be conjured up only through diligent, cross-cultural research and sifting through frequently ignored historical, archaeological, and linguistic details. It is the unraveling of a complex mystery in which the clues are scattered across an area stretching from Turkey, Spain, and West Africa to America. The translation of historical texts from Arabic and Othmanic sources has to be fused with archaeological inscriptions carved into American stone in the Mandinka language of West Africa, linguistic analysis of Native American languages, dimly remembered oral histories, and even epidemiological studies from the field of modern medicine. Needless to say, these widely scattered clues require a multidisciplinary cooperation in order to be laboriously pieced together into a jigsaw puzzle of discovery. Fortunately, a new generation of scholars has begun this arduous task and has started to illuminate a fascinating, if long forgotten, legacy of Muslims in American history.

B. A MILLENNIUM OF MUSLIM-AMERICAN CONTACT

The new picture that is emerging from the scattered pieces of the jigsaw puzzle suggests a complex history of repeated interrelationships between Muslims and America, interrelationships that stretch back into at least the late ninth century when the first documented voyage took place from Muslim Andalusia (contemporary Spain and Portugal) to the Americas. Building on that presumed point of origin, the pre-Columbian history of Muslims in America continues through successive voyages of Muslims to America from Muslim Andalusia, from at least two different sites in Africa, and probably from the Othmanic Empire.

Further, Muslim contact with America did not end with the voyage of Columbus and the subsequent Spanish exploration of the Americas. In fact, Muslims sailed with Columbus and were integral parts of later Spanish exploration. However, contemporary histories seldom bother to report that many of these early "Spanish" explorers were Muslims of Arab and Berber descent.

However, it was not just Muslim explorers, traders, and colonizers who brought Islam to America. The Muslim presence in America was immeasurably augmented by the abominations of the slave trade between Africa and America. Continuing from the early 16th century through the early 19th century, the slave trade deposited millions of African Muslims into bondage on America's shores. Of these millions of enslaved Muslims who were incarcerated and tortured on American soil, perhaps the most famous is Kunta Kinte, a Mandinka Muslim who was immortalized in Alex Haley's *Roots*.

These enslaved Muslims were often ruthlessly persecuted for their religious faith and forbidden to teach their religious beliefs to their children. Nonetheless, certain residuals of their Islamic faith survived generation after generation among their African-American descendants, influencing the development of African-American community and culture. Such Islamic residuals even left their legacy in at least one later church ritual that is unique to African-American Christianity.

An additional group contributing to the Muslim presence in colonial America was a people that have come to be known as Melungeons. Demonstrably present in America by the early 17th century, the Melungeons appear to have been the descendants of a group of Muslims of mixed ethnic background. Centered primarily in the Appalachian region and with their ethnicity and racial background not easily classified, the Melungeons were often the object of discrimination and persecution. As such, they maintained a semi-secretive existence in the more remote parts of the Appalachians. While individuals of Melungeon ancestry can still be identified today, their Muslim roots have largely been forgotten.

The aforementioned Muslim groups of pre-Columbian explorers and traders, "Spanish" colonizers, African slaves, and Melungeons appear to have often intermarried with and occasionally been absorbed into American Indian tribes. While little of Muslim religious practice and belief appears to have survived among those American Indians having Muslim contributions to their ancestry, a surprising number of Turkish, Arabic, and Mandinka words were incorporated into various American Indian vocabularies. In addition, readily identifiable Muslim names can be found among the Cherokee Indians well into the 19th century.

The late 19th century witnessed the first modern wave of Muslim immigration to the United States from the Arab provinces of the Othmanic Empire. These Muslim immigrants were primarily from areas that later became the modern countries of Syria, Lebanon, Jordan, etc. Successive waves of Muslim immigrants from the Middle East, the Indian subcontinent, and elsewhere continued throughout most of the 20th century.

The immigration of Muslims to the United States over the last century or so led to the building of American mosques and to the establishment of a variety of Muslim institutions. For example, the Red Crescent, the Muslim equivalence of the International Red Cross, was established in Detroit in 1920. Moreover, early 20th-century Muslim immigration to America sparked a renewed interest among African Americans in discovering their Muslim roots. While admittedly offering a markedly corrupted form of Islam, organizations such as the Moorish Science Temple and the Nation of Islam sprang up during the first third of the 20th century as African Americans attempted to reclaim their Muslim heritage.

With African Americans beginning to discover and claim their Muslim ancestry, 20th-century America began to experience the phenomenon of native-born Americans converting to Islam in substantial numbers. While conversion has been most prominent among African Americans, Islam has also found a number of converts among European Americans, Latino Americans, and American Indians.

C. THE MUSLIM PRESENCE IN CONTEMPORARY AMERICA

Through conversion and immigration, Islam had become the fastest growing religion and the second largest religion in America by the late 20th century. While exact record keeping does not exist, estimates of the number of Muslims in America variously range from around two to eight million. At least one study indicated that the number of Muslims in the United States doubled between 1990 and 2001. Mosques and Islamic centers can now be found in almost all American cities of any appreciable size. Muslim Student Associations exist on most large college and university campuses. In addition, individual Muslim families often live and work quietly in many small towns across the American heartland, occasionally without their neighbors being aware of their Islamic religious affiliation. As can thus be seen, a Muslim presence has become part of the basic fabric of the melting pot that is America.

D. A BRIEF OVERVIEW

The present, modest volume offers a synthesis of disparate findings relating to the forgotten legacy of Muslims in America. Chapter II looks at the evidence for the presence of Muslims in America prior to the epic voyage of Christopher Columbus in 1492. Chapter III examines the role played by Muslims in the early "Spanish" and "European" explorations of the Americas. Chapter IV reviews the substantial and influential Muslim presence among the African slaves brought to the Americas in cruel and inhuman bondage. Chapter V looks at the Muslim contribution to various American Indian tribes. Chapter VI presents the story of the Melungeons, a largely unknown group of people that has inhabited the Americas for centuries and that has Muslim antecedents. Chapter VII offers some insight into Islamic residuals in African-American life and culture. Chapter VIII focuses on the role of Muslim immigrants to the United States beginning in the 18th century and countinuing throughout the 19th and 20th centuries. Chapter IX discusses the widespread phenomenon of American conversions to Islam during the 20th century. Finally, chapter X presents Islam and Muslims in contemporary America.

2 The Pre-Columbian Era

A. The Mythology

"In fourteen hundred and ninety-two, Columbus sailed the ocean blue..."

Generations of American school children have learned the above ditty as they received their first introduction to the "discovery of America." The Euro-centric bias displayed in such instruction is immediately apparent when one considers that Christopher Columbus did not land on uninhabited rock and soil. The American Indians were already present in America and had been for thousands of years. They had previously developed their own civilizations, their own forms of government, and their own religious and cultural lives. In the process, they had evolved as many as 2,000 different languages, with about 600 in North America and about 1,450 in South America. According to the best estimates of McEvedy and Jones, two specialists in the area of determining the size of ancient populations, there were approximately 14 million Indians inhabiting the Americas at the time of the Columbus voyage, with about half of them being located in North America and the Caribbean and about half located in South America.

Nonetheless, the myth of Columbus discovering America has lived on in the American psyche, and October 12, 1492, the day on which Columbus first landed on the island of San Salvador in the Caribbean Ocean, often continues to be seen as a watershed date in American history. Furthermore, the Columbian myth has remained relatively untouched by the seemingly grudging acknowledgement that he was not the first European to set foot in the Americas. Gradually, elementary school textbooks have begun to include a few words about Leif Erickson's probable voyage to Newfoundland circa 1000 and the establishment of a short-lived Viking colony in eastern Canada.

However, the Columbian myth is now under renewed attack as a new generation of Western scholars has begun to examine a host of ancient Arabic documents detailing a Muslim presence in the Americas as early as the ninth century. Furthermore, this Muslim presence in pre-Columbian American history is not confined to one isolated point in time, nor is it the result of only one Muslim civilization making contact with the Americas. It rather reflects a series of contacts (some of them sustained over considerable periods of time), the establishment of regular trade routes and colonies, and intermarriage and co-mingling with various tribes of American Indians.

Needless to say, such prolonged interchange between American Indians and Muslim explorers, traders, and colonizers was not without effect on American history. Residuals and artifacts attesting to the pre-Columbian Muslim presence in America are relatively numerous but have previously been ignored or misinterpreted by a majority of Western historians. The reader may well ask how this major oversight in understanding American history could have happened.

In part it happened because Western academia has become so specialized. Scholars in one field of study are without a general understanding of other academic disciplines. The typical American historian has never been exposed to various forms of Arabic script and to Mandinka ideograms and writing, and he is thus unable to recognize Arabic and

Mandinka inscriptions carved into the American landscape. Likewise, he is relatively unfamiliar with Islam and Muslim culture and does not recognize them or their residuals when he meets them in unexpected places. Further, he has neither the time nor inclination to sift through mountains of ancient records, documents, and books, often written in Arabic and variously located in Spain and the Muslim Middle East. Yet had he the time, the language skills, and the inclination to do so, he would have found the documentary records that attest to repeated Muslim voyages to the Americas from Andalusia (Spain and Portugal), from West Africa, and apparently from the Othmanic Empire.

In what follows, section B sets the stage by contrasting how the earth was understood in Christian Europe and in the Muslim world. Sections C through E detail the history of and Muslim documentation revealing the pre-Columbian presence of Muslims in America. These sections are divided according to the location (Andalusia, West Africa, and the Othmanic Empire) from which these Muslims traveled to America. Section F examines the surprising amount of confirming documentation that has survived in non-Muslim sources regarding the pre-Columbian presence of Muslims in America, and section G reviews the supporting archaeological evidence. Finally, section H briefly re-examines the Columbus's four voyages to the Americas and highlights the Muslim influence on Columbus's thinking and expedition.

B. THE FLAT EARTH VS. THE EGG

In the centuries prior to the Spanish exploration of the Americas, most Christian Europeans harbored a concept of the earth as a flat object. Sail too far to the west across the Atlantic Ocean and you would drop off the edge of the earth. Sail too far to the east across the

Pacific Ocean and the same thing would transpire. However, "most" is not "all," and the educated elite of Christian Europe, although a relatively small percentage of the total European population, knew that the earth was basically a sphere. After all, as early as the sixth century BCE, Pythagoras suggested that the earth was a sphere. This suggestion was later seconded by Aristotle in the fourth century BCE, by Eratosthenes in the third century BCE, and by Hipparchus in the second century BCE. In the second century CE, Ptolemy had written that the earth was a sphere, and even Christopher Columbus appeared to be acquainted with Ptolemy's work. Nonetheless, the common understanding of the earth in Europe remained that of a flat earth.

Needless to say, this concept of a flat earth where one could literally sail off the edge of the world was a hindrance to seafaring exploration. Common sailors were typically not familiar with Ptolemy and did not have the education to overcome the popular belief in the flat earth theory. What common man of the sea was willing to entrust his life to a theory that the earth was a sphere? Thus prior to Columbus, exploration of the earth by most Christian nations of Europe was limited to overland exploration or to coastal-hugging forays by ship.

In marked contrast, the common understanding among the Muslim population of the world was that the world was roughly a sphere, even if slightly in the form of an egg. For these pre-Columbian Muslims, this belief was not merely one of geography. It was also an article of religious faith. In *Qur'an* 79:30, the earth is described with the Arabic word "*Dahaha*," which is usually translated as "spread" or "expanded." However, a more literal translation would include the concept of being egg-like in shape.

With the *Qur'an* pronouncing that the earth was roughly spherical or egg-shaped, Muslim scientists and geographers quickly began to calculate the size of this sphere. Following the lead of earlier Greek geographers, e.g., Eratosthenes in the third century BCE and Ptolemy in the second century, these Muslim scientists divided the earth into 360 degrees of longitude and then began to determine the size of one degree of longitude at the equator. Using modern techniques, we now know that the distance between adjoining degrees of longitude at the equator is approximately 111.32 kilometers (about 69.18 miles). With this figure in mind, we can admire the precision and accuracy of early Muslim scientists and compare them to earlier Greek attempts to calculate the circumference of the earth. For example, Aristotle's calculations resulted in a proposed circumference for the earth (400,000 stadia) that was almost twice its actual size. Eratosthenes arrived at a figure that was about 15% too large, and Ptolemy underestimated the correct distance by a little more than 16%. In marked contrast, Abu Al-'Abbas Ahmad Al-Farghani (Alfraganus) calculated the distance to be 122 kilometers (off by less than 10%), and the 70 scientists assembled by Caliph 'Abd Allah Al-Ma'mun (ruled from 814-833 CE) calculated the distance at 115.35 kilometers (off by less than 04%). Additional calculations of the length of a terrestrial degree were offered by Muhammad ibn Musa Al-Khwarizmi (circa 780-850), who had been one of the Arab scientists involved in Caliph Al-Ma'mun's project to calculate the circumference of the earth.

However, the role of Muslim scientists in understanding the earth was not limited to calculating the distance between adjacent degrees of longitude at the equator. Between the ninth and 10th centuries, Ibn Yunus and Muhammad ibn Jabir ibn Sinan Al-Battani Al-Harrani

Al-Sabi (Albatenius, Albategnus, Albategnius, or Albategni) invented or improved versions of the compass, quadrant, astrolabe, and sextant, which contributed greatly to man's ability to navigate the oceans. These Muslim inventions and improvements would become the "gold standard" of oceanic navigation for the next several centuries. In addition, Al-Battani, an Arab astronomer who lived circa 858-929, improved Ptolemy's astronomical calculations by replacing geometric computations with trigonometry. Still further, Abu Al-Rayhan Muhammad ibn Ahmad Al-Biruni (973-1048) accurately determined latitude and longitude, calculated the distance between major cities, and suggested that the earth rotated on its own axis. (It would take several hundred years before Galileo reached similar conclusions in Europe.) In the 11th century, Al-Zarqallu invented a single-plate astrolabe (azafea) that worked at all latitudes and that was used by navigators until the 16th century.

Despite the impressively accurate conclusions of Muslim scientists and geographers, Columbus chose to rely on the flawed work of Europeans. For example, Paolo Toscanelli, an Italian physician, incorrectly calculated that it was only 3,000 miles west from Lisbon to Japan. Likewise, Martin Behaim, a German mapmaker, believed China was only about 4,000 miles west of Europe. Compounding the problem, even if Columbus had used the best of the Muslim Arab estimates of the distance between longitudes at the equator (112 kilometers, which was off by less than 01% from the actual distance), he would have been sadly inaccurate because he appears to have used the Italian mile (4,847 feet) for his understanding of the distance between longitudes at the equator, rather than the Arab mile (6,481 feet). This simple confusion between two different lengths of miles would have caused

Columbus to underestimate distances by as much as 25%. Having been guided by these erroneous estimates, it is no wonder that Columbus incorrectly thought he had reached India when he landed on San Salvador on October 12, 1492.

Not only was Columbus wrong regarding the distance from Europe westward to the Orient, he was incorrect in assuming that he had landed in India and that the native inhabitants he met were "Indians." More importantly for our current discussion, he was also not the first Old World explorer to reach the Americas.

C. Andalusian Muslims in America

C1. The Iberian Peninsula Before Islam

The Iberian Peninsula, i.e., what is today Spain and Portugal, has throughout its history been the site of wave upon wave of invading forces. The earliest known settlers of the peninsula were the Iberians, Celts, and Basques. These three groups were then partially displaced by Phoenician, Greek, and Carthaginian invasions. The Phoenicians began settling in the peninsula circa 800 BCE. However, their colonies e.g., Gadir (Cadiz), were basically limited to small coastal areas. By 575 BCE, the Greeks had established two small colonies on the eastern coast of the peninsula. The Carthaginians of North Africa conquered the southern portion of the peninsula beginning in 237 BCE as part of their preparations for the Second Punic War, established a capital city at Cartago Nova in 228 BCE, and continued to rule the southern part of the peninsula until 206 BCE. In response to the Carthaginian threat, the Roman Empire began to impinge upon the Iberian Peninsula in 218 BCE, defeated the Carthaginians in the peninsula in 206 BCE, and established complete control of the peninsula in 19 BCE. Under Roman rule, the peninsula was renamed Hispania, from which the word Spain derives.

However, the invasions of the peninsula were not yet over. By the fifth century, Roman rule was collapsing across much of Europe. Taking advantage of this deterioration in Roman strength and being pushed by Huns from the east, a Germanic tribe known as the Vandals conquered the Iberian Peninsula in 409. The land then became known as Vandalusia, from which the term Andalusia would later derive. However, Vandal rule was relatively short-lived and lasted only until 429, at which time the Vandals left the peninsula and moved across the Mediterranean to North Africa, where they established a kingdom that endured until 534.

In the middle of the fifth century, another Germanic tribe, i.e., the Visigoths, established a kingdom in the south of Gaul (France) and invaded the Iberian Peninsula from the north. In 507, the Franks drove the Visigoths out of southern Gaul, resulting in the Visigoths penetrating more deeply into the peninsula and later establishing their capital at Toledo. The Visigothic kingdom endured until 711.

There were several factors that brought about the destruction of the Visigothic kingdom, a major one of which was religious persecution. With regard to this consideration, it should be noted that the Visigoths were initially Arian Christians, i.e., Christians who rejected the divinity of Jesus Christ and saw him as being the "adopted" son of God. Armed with all the intolerance that religious fervor can generate, King Leovigild of the Visigoths tried to force Arian Christianity on the Roman Catholics and Orthodox Catholics of the peninsula in 570. Needless to say, there was widespread resentment within the non-Visigothic population of the peninsula, and the Arianizing effort produced its own backlash when Leovigild's son, Recared, converted to Roman Catholicism.

However, the religious intolerance and persecutions initiated in the Visigothic kingdom were not limited to Christian vs. Christian conflict. There was also a population of Jews living in the Iberian Peninsula, and these Jews were especially targeted for religious persecution by their Christian rulers. On several occasions, church officials called for the enforced baptism of every Jewish child in the kingdom. The punishment for failure to comply with these edicts was to remove the children from their Jewish homes and parents and to give them to Christian homes. Additional evidence of the religious persecution of the Jews in the Visigothic kingdom can be found in the laws of the *Forum Judicum,* which was codified between 649 and 652. Various ones of these laws stipulated that Jews were forbidden to celebrate the Passover, marry outside of their faith, perform the rite of circumcision, follow Jewish dietary laws, testify against a Christian in court, and in any way aid a Christian in converting to Judaism. Additionally, the laws stipulated that Christians were forbidden to defend or protect a Jew.

A second factor contributing to the fall of the Visigothic kingdom was conflict over monarchic succession. After the death of King Witiza in 710, Duke Roderick of Baetica supplanted Witiza's son, Achila, and seized the throne for himself. The family of King Witiza was not reconciled to these events and plotted its revenge.

As such, two different groups, the persecuted Jews of the Iberian Peninsula and the family of King Witiza, looked southward across the Strait of Gibraltar to the Muslims of North Africa. Both groups sent emissaries to Musa ibn Nusayr, the governor of North Africa for the Umayyad Caliphate of Damascus, asking for a Muslim invasion of the Iberian Peninsula. Musa ibn Nusayr entrusted the task to Tariq ibn Ziyad, and an initial scouting foray was launched in 710. Receiving favorable reports from his scouts and aided by the family of King Witiza, the Jews of the Iberian Peninsula, and the Christian ruler of Ceuta, Tariq ibn Ziyad crossed the Strait of Gibraltar. Upon landing, he is reported to have said, "Behind you the sea, before you the enemy." It was April or May of 711, and the Muslim invasion of the Iberian Peninsula had begun.

In July of 711, the Muslim army and its allies dealt a decisive defeat to King Roderick and the Visigothic army. In short order, the Muslim army of Tariq ibn Ziyad continued north and reached Toledo by the winter of 711. The following year, Musa ibn Nusayr led a second Muslim army into the Iberian Peninsula. By 714, most of the Iberian Peninsula was under Muslim control.

C2. MUSLIM ANDALUSIA

The history of Muslim Andalusia can be divided into seven stages that span the centuries between 711 and 1492. The first three stages correspond to periods of increasing Muslim dominance and strength throughout the Iberian Peninsula, and the latter four stages conform to the political and military decline of Muslim Andalusia.

The period of increasing Muslim strength in Andalusia covers the years from 711 to 1031. Three separate stages of development can be identified within these time parameters. (1) The years from 711 to 756 correspond to the first stage, which is known as the dependent emirate. During this initial stage, Andalusia was a dependent province of the Umayyad Caliphate of Damascus (Syria), even though Muslim expansion in the Iberian Peninsula and Western Europe continued until the defeat of the Muslim army by Charles Martel at the Battle of Tours (France). (2) The second stage, lasting from 756 to 929, is known as the independent emirate. The independent emirate of

Andalusia was founded by *Emir* (prince or commander) 'Abd Al-Rahman I, a member of the Umayyad royal family of Damascus who had managed to flee the Middle East during the civil war in which the 'Abbasid Caliphate of Baghdad supplanted the Umayyad Caliphate of Damascus as the ruling family of the Muslim Middle East. Throughout this second stage, Andalusia was ruled as a monarchy by 'Abd Al-Rahman I and his descendants. (3) The third stage of Muslim Andalusia (929-1031) consisted of the Umayyad Caliphate of Andalusia. This stage was inaugurated when 'Abd Al-Rahman III, a seventh-generation descendant of 'Abd Al-Rahman I, proclaimed himself Caliph and broke the last nominal vassalage between Andalusia and the 'Abbasid Caliphate of Baghdad.

The Umayyad Caliphate of Andalusia ended in 1031, and this event signaled the beginning of the decline of the Muslim political and military dominance of Andalusia. The fourth through seventh stages of Muslim Andalusia can be identified during this period. (4) The years from 1031 through 1086 were marked by intermittent periods of internal conflict and civil war throughout much of Muslim Andalusia. Several small Muslim kingdoms (e.g., Malaga, Seville, and Cordoba) sprang up, and the Christian kingdoms of Leon and Castile began to make territorial inroads into Andalusia. (5) In response to this growing threat from Leon and Castile, the Muslims of Andalusia invited the Almoravid Dynasty of North Africa to invade the Iberian Peninsula. The invasion was successful, and the Almoravids reestablished centralized authority and ruled from 1086 to 1147. (6) The Almoravid Dynasty was in turn displaced by the Almohad Dynasty of North Africa. Almohad rule continued in Muslim Andalusia from 1147 to 1212. (7) In 1212, Almohad rule collapsed, and a variety of petty kingdoms arose and ruled in Muslim Andalusia from

1212 to 1492. Finally, in 1492, the last Muslim rulers in the Iberian Peninsula were defeated by King Ferdinand and Queen Isabella, the royal sponsors of Christopher Columbus.

Throughout its history of growing strength and later decline, Muslim Andalusia was a beacon of intellectual and cultural light in a Europe that was just beginning to emerge from the Dark Ages. Andalusian agriculture, architecture, literature, and science precipitated the later European Renaissance. For example, Cordoba became the largest and most cultured city in Europe during Muslim Andalusia. Its woven silks, intricate brocades, jewelry, and leatherwork were eagerly sought throughout Europe and the Middle East. Its scribes preserved and kept alive in Arabic translation the works of the great Greek authors of antiquity, such as Plato and Aristotle.

Muslim Andalusia was also a monument to interfaith dialogue. Its religious scholars and theologians, whether Jewish, Christian, or Muslim, made significant advances in religious understanding and in cooperative, inter-religious scholarship. With regard to this last point, one need only recall that both Abu Al-Walid Muhammad ibn Ahmad ibn Muhammad ibn Rushd (Averroes, 1126-1198) and Abu Imran Musa ibn Maymun ibn 'Ubayd Allah (Maimonides, 1135-1204) resided in Cordoba during the 12th century. The former scholar represented Islam and the latter Judaism, and each was a towering figure in the advancement of philosophical theology during medieval times. Further, by comparing the eight-point creed of Islam developed by Ibn Rushd with the 13-point creed of Judaism developed by Maimonides, one can clearly see that the former influenced the thinking of the latter.

Additional examples of interfaith fellowship and cooperation in Muslim Andalusia are noted by Harvey Cox, a celebrated Christian theologian. Among these examples, Cox lists the following. (1) Under the auspices of Bishop Raymond of Seville, turbaned Muslim scholars, bearded rabbis, and Christian monks in robes all sat around a table together studying and reading over old manuscripts. (2) Caliph 'Abd Al-Rahman III, the ruler of Andalusia from 912 to 961, appointed Hasai ibn Shaprut, a Jewish scholar, physician, and rabbi, to be his foreign minister. (3) Dante's Divine Comedy was influenced by Arab sources. (4) The theology of St. John of the Cross was heavily influenced by Muslim mysticism.

Given these glories of Muslim Andalusia, it should not be surprising to discover that the Muslims of Andalusia may also have been leading the world in transatlantic navigation, discovery, and exploration. In what follows, three reported voyages from Muslim Andalusia to the Americas are described.

C3. THE FIRST RECORDED VOYAGE[1]

Abul Hasan 'Ali ibn Al-Hussain ibn 'Ali Al-Masudi (871-957) was a famous Andalusian historian, geographer, and scientist. Circa 956, he wrote *Muruj Al-Dhahab Wa Ma'adin Al-Jawhar* (The Meadows of Gold and Quarries of Jewels), which contains the first written documentation of Muslim contact with the Americas. Al-Masudi reported on an epic voyage of discovery made during the reign of Caliph 'Abd Allah ibn Muhammad (888-912), the Umayyad ruler of Andalusia. In 889, Khashkhash ibn Saeed ibn Aswad, a resident of Andalusian Cordoba, sailed west into the Atlantic Ocean with a Muslim crew from Delba (Palos), the same port from which Columbus would launch his three ships

---

1. Information in this section is from Quick AH (1998) and Mroueh Y (1996).

over 600 years later. After a lengthy voyage, Khashkhash encountered a new world, which Al-Masudi referred to in a map as *Ard Majhoola* (i.e., unknown earth). Khashkhash later returned from his monumental voyage, reportedly bringing a wealth of booty, presumably from trade with and conquest in the Americas.

C4. THE SECOND RECORDED VOYAGE[2]

Further documentation of Andalusian Muslim contact with the Americas is to be found in the works of Abu Bakr ibn 'Umar Al-Qutiyya. Al-Qutiyya narrated a story about Ibn Farrukh, a Muslim from Granada, who sailed west into the Atlantic from Kadesh in 999, during what was then the reign of Caliph Hisham II (976-1009). In February of that year, Ibn Farrukh reportedly landed in the Canary Islands, visited King Guanariga, and then continued his voyage westward. After sailing for quite some time, he discovered two islands, presumably in the Caribbean, which he named Capraria and Pluitana. He returned to Spain in May of 999. The three to four month voyage would certainly have allowed enough time to have reached the Americas and returned to Europe.

C5. THE THIRD RECORDED VOYAGE[3]

Yet a third documentary record of Andalusian Muslim contact with the Americas is to be found in *Nuzhat Al-Mushtaq Fi Ikhtiraq Al-Afaq* (Excursion of the Longing One in Crossing Horizons), a 12th-century volume by Al-Sharif Abu 'Abd Allah Muhammad Al-Idrisi (1099-1166), the renown Arab geographer, physician, and advisor to

---

2. Information in this section is from Quick AH (1998) and Mroueh Y (1996).
3. Information in this section is from Quick AH (1998), Mroueh Y (1996), and Irving TB (---).

the court of King Roger II of Sicily. Al-Idrisi wrote that a group of eight Muslim sailors from North Africa sailed west into the Atlantic from Lisbon (Portugal), which was then part of Andalusia. Their ship was stocked with enough supplies to last them for months. After sailing for in excess of at least 31 days, the boat landed on a previously unknown island, again presumably in the Caribbean. The party of Muslim sailors was immediately taken prisoner by a tribe of Indians, bound, and held captive for three days. On the fourth day, a translator appeared who spoke Arabic! He questioned the sailors and apparently arranged for their transfer to another tribe of Indians. This transfer required a three-day canoe ride. They were then freed, placed in a boat, and told that their homeland was two months to the east. They finally arrived back in Andalusia.

One of the fascinating aspects of Al-Idrisi's narrative is the emergence of an Arabic-speaking translator from among the Indians. The presence of such a person suggests a long, if forgotten, history of Muslim-Indian contact. Arabic is a difficult language to master, and the presence of an Arabic-speaking Indian would have necessitated frequent contact between these Indians and Arabic-speaking Muslims, perhaps commercial traders from West Africa.

C6. SUMMARY AND CONCLUSIONS

Aside from the brief narratives noted above, there is little surviving evidence of Andalusian Muslims in America. However, the absence of evidence is not evidence of absence. After all, there is precious little archaeological evidence in the Americas to demonstrate that Columbus was ever actually here, although there can be no doubt that he was.

D. African Muslims in America

D1. A Journey from Morocco

In 682, a Muslim army of Arabs led by 'Uqbah ibn Nafi' marched westward across North Africa into what is now Morocco. They proceeded all the way to the Atlantic Ocean, moving as far south as Sus and Draa in what is now southern Morocco. These events mark the beginning of Muslim rule in Morocco, and by 705 Morocco had become part of the province of Ifriqiyah of the Umayyad Caliphate of Damascus.

Over the next several centuries, Morocco passed through the hands of a variety of Muslim dynasties. In the years after 740, Morocco became part of the principality of the Banu Midrar of Sijilmassah. In the early ninth century, most of Morocco came under control of the Idrisids of Fez, a dynasty claiming descent from Prophet Muhammad. In 921, the Idrisids were conquered by the Fatimid Dynasty of Egypt, which also claimed descent from Prophet Muhammad. The Almoravids began their conquest of Morocco beginning in 1056. Between 1133 and 1147, Morocco gradually passed into the control of the Almohad Dynasty. In the middle of the 13th century, the Marinid Dynasty succeeded the Almohads as rulers of Morocco.

Several Arabic reference works document a voyage taken from southern Morocco to the Americas during the reign of the Marinid Dynasty's King Abu Yaqub Sidi Youssef (1286-1307 CE). According to these accounts, Shaykh Zayn Al-Din 'Ali ibn Fadhel Al-Mazandarani sailed west into the Atlantic Ocean from Tarfaya in 1291. After a prolonged voyage, he landed on "Green Island," presumably in the Caribbean Sea, and later returned to Morocco. Once again, archaeological residual of this specific voyage is either lacking or still undiscovered.[4]

---

4. Mroueh Y (1996).

D2. THE MUSLIM AND MANDINKA KINGDOM OF MALI

Beginning as early as the eighth century, commerce flourished between West Africa and Muslim traders from north of the Sahara. Fueled by a lucrative trade in gold and salt, caravan routes across the Sahara established regular business contact between Muslim traders and their non-Muslim counterparts in Koumbi, the capital of the West African kingdom of Ghana, which was ruled by the Soninke people. However, it was not only gold and salt that were traded in the marketplaces of Koumbi; ideas and knowledge also exchanged hands. For example, Muslim traders introduced the first system of writing and numbers to West Africa, and the Arab writing system was soon adopted by the West African people.

As one would expect, this Arab infusion of knowledge into West Africa was not just confined to writing and numbers. It also included the sharing of religious beliefs and practices, resulting in Islam beginning to find a foothold among new Muslim converts in Ghana. Converts gathered converts, and Islam began its inevitable spread among the native population of West Africa. However, conversion was only one factor contributing to the growth of Islam in West Africa. An additional factor was the immigration of Muslim Arabs from north of the Sahara.

Resulting from the introduction of the Arab writing and numbering systems into West Africa, many Arabs from north of the Sahara were hired by the kingdom of Ghana to serve as government officials, giving Ghana a resident, Muslim-Arab population. By the 10th century, many Muslim traders from north of the Sahara had also established permanent residence in Koumbi, and the city began to be divided into Muslim and non-Muslim districts. With the marketplace of Koumbi located within its borders, the Muslim district of Koumbi quickly prospered. In contrast to the wood and clay houses of the non-Muslim district, houses in the Muslim district of Koumbi were often two-story structures built of stone. At least 12 different mosques soon dotted the landscape.

Throughout this era of rapid Muslim conversion and immigration, the Soninke kingdom of Ghana was officially non-Muslim, with the exception of a brief time when the non-Muslim rule of the Soninke was interrupted by the Muslims of the Almoravid movement between 1076 and 1087. Upon regaining the political upper hand, the Soninke kings of Ghana were severely weakened and found themselves trying to govern some areas that were peopled primarily by Muslim inhabitants.

Just to the east of Ghana, the Mandinka had almost entirely converted to Islam by the 12th century and had gradually grown in wealth and political power. Eventually and inevitably, the Mandinka began to pose a very real political threat to the Soninke. Finally, at the Battle of Kirina in 1203, King Sundiata of the Mandinka overthrew the kingdom of Ghana, established a new capital at Niani on the upper Niger River, and created the Muslim empire of Mali in West Africa. Enriched by prosperous trade routes across the Sahara and along the Niger River, as well as by gold mines at Bure and Wangara, the Mali Empire quickly dwarfed the prior Soninke kingdom of Ghana.

No doubt the most famous city of the Mandinka kingdom of Mali was Timbuktu. Founded as a small settlement circa 1100, Timbuktu had already achieved a substantial measure of size and fame by the time it was conquered by Mali circa 1325. While its economic importance was secondary to its role as a caravan stop, manufacturing site, and nexus of trade and exports, Timbuktu's greatest glory was its status as a scholastic center. Its libraries (even some private libraries held more than 700 volumes), schools (well over 150 during the 16th century), and university (the Jam'iyyah located in the Sankore Mosque) attracted students and scholars from as far a field as Arabia. Within those academic institutions, students were educated in Islamic studies *(Qur'an,* Qur'anic interpretation or *Tafsir,* Islamic theology, the traditions of Prophet Muhammad or the *Hadith* sciences, and Islamic jurisprudence or *Fiqh),* grammar, literary style, rhetoric, logic, history, mathematics, astronomy, and cartography. A liberal scholarship system made sure that education was not denied due to financial difficulties.

Given the economic and scholastic glory of Timbuktu, it is perhaps not surprising to find an Englishman, Richard Jobson, writing in 1620 that in Timbuktu the roofs of houses were covered with plates of gold and the riverbeds glistened and sparkled with gold-reflected sunlight.

D3. MANSA MUSA

Mali reached its height of power and prestige under the rule of Mansa Kankan Musa I, a devout Muslim who governed for 25 years, beginning in either 1307 or 1312 (scholars do not agree on the exact date). The extent of his personal success and that of Mali can be gleaned from the accounts recording details of Mansa Musa's *Hajj* pilgrimage to Makkah in 1324. According to these reports, Mansa Musa was accompanied throughout his pilgrimage by as many as 60,000 people, by over one thousand camels carrying supplies, and by an additional 80 to 100 camels, each of which was loaded with 100 pounds of gold.

Using a contemporary figure of $600 per ounce of gold and assuming that each of 100 camels was carrying 100 pounds of gold, the combined wealth of just the gold accompanying Mansa Musa would equal 96 million dollars in contemporary American currency. Thus, it is little wonder that accounts of this pilgrimage indicate that the economies of many states were radically transformed as Mansa Musa's caravan passed through them.

However, the legacy of Mansa Musa's *Hajj* pilgrimage caravan was not confined to just gold and economic riches. It also disseminated information that is crucial to appreciating the role of Muslims in American history and that was recorded by Shihab Al-Din Abu Al-Abbas Ahmad ibn Fadhl Al-'Umari (1300-1384 CE).

D4. THE MANDINKA VOYAGES[5]

Shihab Al-Din Al-'Umari was a famous Arab geographer who gathered pioneering information from a variety of sources and informants. In his *Masalik Al-Absar Fi Mamalik Al-Amsar* (The Pathways of Sights in the Provinces of Kingdoms), he recorded a fascinating report from Ibn Amir Hajib, the governor of Cairo. Ibn Amir narrated a conversation that he had in 1324 with Mansa Musa, the Mandinka tribal ruler of the West African Empire of Mali, when Mansa Musa was journeying through Cairo to make the *Hajj* pilgrimage to Makkah.

Sultan Musa reported that Abu Bakari, his brother and predecessor on the throne of Mali (1285 to either 1307 or 1312 CE), had authorized two voyages across the Atlantic. The first expedition consisted of 400

---

5. Information in this section is from Smallwood AD (1999), Quick AH (1998), Mroueh Y (1996), Muhammad ANA (2001), Numan FH (---), and Shelton SM (---).

ships, 200 of which were stocked with enough food, water, gold, and supplies to last the crews for several years. This fleet was sent off with instructions to return only when they had reached the farthest extremity of the ocean or when they had exhausted their food and water. After an extended period of time, only one ship returned. The captain of that ship reported that he had been separated from the other ships by an ocean current, quite possibly the North Equatorial or Antilles Current, which would have placed ships sailing from Mali surprisingly close to America at the time the lone ship turned back to Africa.

Sultan Abu Bakari then ordered the construction of a fleet of 2,000 ships, half of which were used primarily for the hauling of supplies. The provisions were so plentiful that they apparently included African elephants, which were taken as work and military animals. The fleet sailed west across the Atlantic in either 1307 or 1311, being personally commanded by Sultan Abu Bakari. The fleet never returned.

D5. THE MANDINKA IN AMERICA[6]

From Mandinka inscriptions reportedly found in Brazil, Peru, and the United States, it can be surmised that Sultan Abu Bakari's voyage was successful and that a sizable group of Mandinka landed in the New World. Plotting a course from these inscriptions, Mandinka linguistic influence on American Indian languages, and other Mandinka artifacts, it appears that the Mandinka initially made contact with Brazil, which was the closest land mass to their West African port of origin. Their presence in Brazil is attested to by inscriptions in Mandinka ideograms that were left at both Bahia and Minas Gerais. From Brazil, they apparently

---

6. Information in this section is from Quick AH (1998).

traversed the rivers of South America before moving overland in both westerly and northerly directions.

Moving west from Brazil, the Mandinka moved into the Lake Titicaca area of Bolivia. There, the Mandinka apparently interacted sufficiently and over a long enough period of time with the Indians of Koaty Island to bequeath the Mandinka writing system of ideograms to the Indians. However, all did not go well between the Mandinka and the Indians of Bolivia, and the Mandinka were apparently attacked at one point, resulting in many of their warriors being killed. Undeterred, it appears that the Mandinka continued moving westward until they reached the shores of the Pacific near Ylo (Peru), where they reportedly left a religious inscription in the Mandinka writing system that refers to the purpose of man being to worship God, to mature, and eventually to die.

Those Mandinka who moved north from South America eventually crossed through Central America and Mexico, where they intermarried with the Carib Indians, for whom the Caribbean is named. For example, some of the Mandinka apparently remained in Panama, where their descendants constituted a distinct tribe of people known as Manding, a rather obvious verbal corruption of Mandinka. Continuing on, the Mandinka moved into what would later become the United States. Within the latter area, Mandinka inscriptions have reportedly been found along the Mississippi River and in Arizona. The former set of inscriptions suggests that the Mandinka used the Mississippi River to explore northwards into the United States and all the way into Canada. This group of Mandinka may have intermarried with and been absorbed by the Iroquois and Algonquin Indians. The latter set of inscriptions, found in a cave at Four Corners, Arizona, describes the heat of the desert and notes that many of the elephants brought by the Mandinka were then sick and angry.

D6. SUMMARY AND CONCLUSIONS

It is difficult to assess the lasting influence of the Mandinka in North and South America. There is little in the way of undisputed archaeological residual of their presence in the Americas, and certainly the Islam that they brought to the New World did not survive into modern times. However, as will be seen later, there is a fair amount of circumstantial evidence in support of their presence in the Americas.

E. OTHMATIC MUSLIMS IN AMERICA

E1. THE OTHMANIC EMPIRE

The founding of the Othmanic or Ottoman Empire is usually credited to Osman I, a nomadic Turkmen chief of the 11th century, who led his Muslim tribe into Anatolia (modern Turkey) in an effort to escape the Mongol hordes that were pushing them westward. Initially only a small tribal area extending from Eskisehir (Dorylaeum) to Nicaea, the Othmanic Empire at its peak ruled a Muslim world that included what is today Hungary, Serbia, Bosnia, Romania, Greece, Ukraine, Albania, Iraq, Syria, Lebanon, Israel, Jordan, Egypt, North Africa as far west as Algeria, and most of the Arabian Peninsula. The Othmanic Empire was finally dissolved in 1922, being replaced by the Turkish Republic and various independent states and European colonies.

During the 15th and 16th centuries, the Othmanic Empire under Sultan Mehmed II (1451-1481) and Sultan Bayezid II (1481-1512) boasted one of the most powerful navies in the world. This Othmanic navy literally controlled the eastern Mediterranean Sea and was known to sail as far west as Spain with some regularity. As such, it is not surprising to discover cartographic evidence that the Muslims of the Othmanic Empire may have sailed much farther west than Spain.

E2. THE PIRI RE'IS MAP[7]

In October of 1929, a most significant and enlightening discovery was made in the Serallo Library in Istanbul, Turkey. Hidden away in the library was a map drawn in March of 1513 by Piri Muhyi' Al-Din Re'is, a Turkish navigator and cartographer. This map portrayed West Africa, the Atlantic Ocean, and the Americas. However, it did far more than that. In its portrayal of the Americas, it revealed geographical features that were not yet known to Christian Europe. For example, the Andes Mountains were clearly portrayed in their correct geographic location, even though they were not discovered by Europe until Pizarro's expedition of 1527. Further, the map demonstrated knowledge of Marajo, an island at the mouth of the Amazon that was not discovered by Christian Europe until 1543. Still further, the map correctly portrayed the bends and turns of the Atrato River of Columbia for a distance of some 300 miles. Finally, the map correctly displayed the Amazon River and the relative latitude and longitude of major topographic features in Africa, the Atlantic, and the Americas.

Piri Re'is wrote that his map was based on earlier source maps, including those of Columbus. However, Columbus never actually explored the mainland of America, and the topographic features recorded for the Americas were still unknown to Christian Europe in 1513. Quite obviously, the earlier information used by Piri Re'is to draw his map of the Americas must have come from Muslim sources, most probably from unknown Othmanic explorers who had traveled inland throughout northern South America.

---

7. Information in this section is from Quick AH (1998), Numan FH (---), and Shelton SM (---).

E3. Conclusions

Clearly, the evidence regarding an Othmanic presence in the Americas before Columbus is circumstantial at best. Perhaps the information recorded in the Piri Re'is map was drawn from Andalusian, Moroccan, or Mandinka voyages to the Americas. However, it seems more likely that the Othmanic Piri Re'is would have been drawing from Othmanic sources. This conclusion is consistent with longstanding, Turkish claims of Othmanic voyages to the Americas prior to Columbus.[8]

F. Confirmation from the non-Muslim Occident

F1. Introduction

There is a surprising amount of confirmation from Western European explorers about the priority of Muslim traders and explorers in the Americas. Unfortunately, Western historians have often chosen to ignore this information because it did not fit with the prevailing theory of the discovery and settlement of the Americas by Christian Europe. However, with the recent publication of Muslim source material documenting a Muslim presence in the Americas well before Columbus, the previously unexplained and discarded information provides significant confirmation of the early Muslim documentation for a Muslim presence in the Americas before the age of Spanish exploration.

Perhaps the most persistent witness among non-Muslims for Muslims being present in pre-Columbian America was no lesser authority than Christopher Columbus himself. In several places in his own writings and in those of his son, Ferdinand, and his nephew, Fernando, Columbus is reported to have directly or indirectly attested to the Muslim presence in the Americas upon his own arrival.

---

8. Kennedy NB, Kennedy RV (1997).

F2. THE WEST AFRICAN PRESENCE[9]

On October 12, 1492, Columbus landed in the Bahamas, which he named San Salvador. However, the original name of the island was Guanahani. The word "*Guana*" is a Mandinka corruption of the Arabic "*Ikhwana*," which means "brothers." The word "Hani" is a common Arabic or Muslim name. Translated from Arabic through its Mandinka corruption to English, the name of the island meant "Hani brothers" and is the first of Columbus's testimonials to the prior presence of West African Muslims in the Americas.

During his second voyage to the Americas, the Indians of Hispaniola told Columbus that black-skinned people had been to the island before him and had left some spears. These spears were tipped with a yellow metal that the Indians called *guanin*, a slightly corrupted form of the Mandinka word (*Ghanin*) for gold alloy. In turn, the Mandinka word is a corruption of the Arabic word (*Ghinaa*) for wealth. Columbus took some of this metal back with him to Europe, where it was found to be 18 parts gold, six parts silver, and eight parts copper, exactly the same ratio as the gold alloy created by the West African metallurgists of Guinea beginning as early as the 13th century!

At the start of his third voyage to the New World in 1498, Columbus noted in his journal that his expedition had encountered a ship that was loaded with goods, presumably for trade. This ship was leaving the coast of West Africa and was headed west in the direction of the Americas. Once again, this appears to indicate that Muslim West Africa was in contact with the Americas at least as early as Columbus.

---

9. Information in this section is from Mroueh Y (1996), Vincent-Barwood A (---), Quick AH (1998), and Smallwood AD (1999).

Writing in his *The Narrative of the Third Voyage*, Columbus attested to a prior Mandinka and West African presence in the Americas when he reported that the inhabitants of the island of Santiago told him that there was an island southwest of the island of Huego in the Cape Verdes to which boats came from West Africa with merchant-traders and goods for trade and barter. The Columbus notation suggests a history of ongoing trade and commerce between the Muslims of West Africa and the Caribbean islands. The only thing lacking in Columbus's report is information regarding just how long such trade had been taking place. Was it a matter of decades or of centuries? As can be seen above in the reports of West African voyages to the Americas, the longer time period cannot be ruled out.

Offering additional circumstantial evidence of a Mandinka presence in pre-Columbian America, Ferdinand Columbus, the son of Christopher, wrote in *The Life of the Admiral Christopher Columbus* that his father had encountered black-skinned people in the area that is now northern Honduras.

Additional Occidental confirmation of the Mandinka in pre-Columbian America can be found in the writings surviving from the expedition of the Spanish explorer, Vasco Nunez de Balboa. Gomara, one of narrators of Balboa's journey, noted that when Balboa reached the Province of Quareca (Panama) in 1513, he encountered the presence of black-skinned people who were slaves of the local king. Gomara wrote that these black-skinned slaves were entirely like the people found along the Guinea coast of West Africa. Peter Martyr, another of Balboa's narrators, recorded that black-skinned warriors were found in the mountains of the Province of Quareca. Martyr described these warriors as being shipwrecked Africans and their descendants who had many years previously journeyed to America. Further confirmation of Balboa's discovery of West African Muslims in the New World is found in Rodrigo de Colmenares's *Memorial against Balboa*. De Colmenares wrote that a captain brought news of a black-skinned people living east of the Gulf of San Miguel. Additionally, several commentators from the 19th and 20th centuries have variously reported that the Garifuna clan of the Carib tribe of Indians has black skin, has a language that is distinct from other clans of the Carib and that appears to be of African derivation, refrains from eating pork (the eating of pork is prohibited in Islam), and prizes crescent-shaped medallions and jewelry (the crescent is often used as a symbol for Islam).

Still further, numerous observers have noted that several of the tribal names of Central America appear to have obvious reference to Mandinka origins. For example, Giles Cauvet's *Les Berberes de l'Amerique* reported that a pre-Columbian tribe in Honduras was known as the Almamys, a corruption of the Mandinka word for the Arabic *Imam* (the Muslim prayer leader). Additionally, a black-skinned tribe that lived at Tegulcigalpa near the Nicaraguan border was known as the Jaras, which appears to be a slight corruption of the Mandinka "Jarra," a clan designation of the Mandinka tribe living in Gambia. As late as 1861, L'Abbe Brasseur de Bourboug wrote in his *Popul-Vuh: le Livre Sacre et les Mythes de l-Antiquite Americaine* that the native people of Darien (Panama) can be grouped under two names according to their distinct origin: Mandingas (Mandinka) and Tule.

F3. General Considerations[10]

On October 21, 1492, writing during his first voyage, Columbus

---

10. Information in this section is from Muhammad ANA (2001), Mroueh Y (1996), Quick AH (1998), and Kennedy NB, Kennedy RB (1997).

recorded that he saw a mosque on a mountaintop. At the time, his ship was sailing near Gibara on the northeast coast of Cuba.

Writing in 1498 during his third voyage to the Americas, Columbus sent some of his crew ashore on the South American continent. His crew reportedly found natives wearing colorful, symmetrically woven cloth that Columbus referred to as *Al-Mayzars*, the Arabic word for a wrapper, cover, apron, or skirt. This type of clothing was a staple of West Africa (although it was also found in Morocco and Muslim Andalusia), and Columbus specifically described the cloth as being like the headdresses and loincloths of Muslim West Africa.

On July 31, 1502, writing during his fourth and last voyage to the Americas, Christopher Columbus recorded that as he was sailing off the coast of Jamaica, he encountered a galley ship that was larger than his own vessel. He described it as being a giant canoe that was about eight feet across and that had a large palm-covered pavilion in the middle. Passing closely enough to see clearly onto the ship, Columbus's son, Ferdinand, reported that the ship contained about 40 men and women, a cargo of tools, copper implements, and forges for working copper. Even more striking, Ferdinand noted that the men and women of this mystery ship wore long, sleeveless shirts that had bright colors and designs. He specifically likened these clothes to those of the Muslims of Granada (Andalusia) and contrasted these clothes with the clothes he had observed worn by American Indians. He then clenched the argument for a Muslim presence by reporting that the women aboard this ship veiled their faces like Muslim women. Surely, this description does not fit with what is known of traditional American Indian dress, although it does conform quite closely to traditional Muslim dress.

Additional testimony from Columbus's fourth voyage suggests a pre-Columbian presence of Muslims in America. For example, upon landing on the island of Guadeloupe, Columbus's crew found an iron pot and the stern post of a ship in a native hut. In describing this stern post, it was remarked that it appeared to come from a European-type ship (Andalusia?) and that it could not have been the stern post from the previously wrecked *Santa Maria*, as the *Santa Maria* had wrecked too far away from the hut for the stern post of the *Santa Maria* to have been brought to it. (The *Santa Maria* had run aground off Haiti during Columbus's first voyage and had been disassembled to provide wood for a garrison on that island. The island of Guadeloupe lies well in excess of 400 miles to the southeast of Hispaniola, and Haiti lies on the western part of the island of Hispaniola.) Further, Columbus's nephew, Fernando, who was present on Columbus's fourth voyage, describes an encounter with "Indians" who tattooed their arms and bodies with Moorish-style designs.

Not long after Columbus's expeditions, Hernan Cortez, the Spanish explorer and conqueror, described the dress of some of the Indian women he encountered as consisting of long veils. He further described the dress of some Indian men as breechcloths and large mantles painted in the style of Moorish draperies. This is consistent with Ferdinand Columbus's description in *The Life of the Admiral Christopher Columbus* of some Indians wearing breechcloths of the same design and cloth as the shawls worn by the Muslim women of Granada (Andalusia).

Additional, although circumstantial, evidence can be found in a map from the French expedition to Florida in 1564. This map details names that suggest earlier Muslim settlements. The map shows a Mayarca

(Majorca), a Cadica (Cadiz), and a Marracou (Marrakesh), all of which are suggestive of Muslim/Arabic names.

F4. Conclusions

Taken together, the above reports and observations of non-Muslim Occidentals provide a consistent pattern of evidence suggesting a Muslim presence in pre-Columbian America. This evidence is particularly strong with reference to the Mandinka of West Africa having predated Columbus's arrival in the New World.

G. Archaeological Confirmation[11]

To date, the archaeological record provides relatively few artifacts attesting to the presence of Muslims in pre-Columbian America. However, the lack of plentiful evidence needs to be evaluated in comparison to the equally small amount of archaeological residual that has been found from Columbus's four voyages to the New World. In short, absence of evidence is not evidence of absence, especially in the face of the large amount of historical information documenting the presence of Muslims in America prior to Columbus. Furthermore, some archaeological residual has withstood the vicissitudes of time and does provide supporting evidence of the Muslim presence in pre-Columbian America.

As has been previously reported, a number of Mandinka ideograms have been discovered in both North and South America. This evidence of Mandinka writing in the Americas prior to Columbus offers convincing evidence of the Mandinka presence in pre-Columbian America.

---

11. Information in this section is from Quick AH (1998).

Furthermore, a shipwreck off the coast of Venezuela has yielded a wealth of ancient coins of Roman and Arabic mintage. The Roman coins were minted between the first through the fourth centuries, and such coins were still in circulation throughout Europe during medieval times. However, the Arabic coins were from the eighth century and were the newest coins found among the numismatic collection. As such, the shipwreck probably occurred in the eighth or ninth centuries and was probably a ship from Muslim Andalusia or possibly Muslim West Africa.

Taken all together, the little archaeological evidence that exists provides support for the extensive documentary record attesting to the pre-Columbian presence of Muslims in America.

H. THE LINGUISTIC EVIDENCE [12]

An additional and particularly intriguing piece of evidence attesting to the pre-Columbian presence of Muslims in America can be found by examining the relationship between certain American Indian words and their corresponding words in the Turkish (Othmanic) and Croatian languages. (Croatian is the language of Croatia and Bosnia, both of which were part of the Othmanic Empire in the century before Columbus's first voyage.) For example, the state of Kentucky is supposedly named for an Indian word (*kain-tuck*) that means "dark and bloody ground." The Turkish *kan-tok* means "saturated with or full of blood." Likewise, the city of Chicago was supposedly named for an Indian word meaning "a nasty, smelly, uncultivated land." The Turkish *chee-kahkah* has the same meaning. Further, the Turkish *tepe* means any pointed or crested building, i.e. a teepee. The following chart provides a brief sampling of these linguistic interrelationships.

---

12. Information in this section is from Katz WL (1997), Kennedy NB (1997), and Kennedy NB, Kennedy RV (1997).

THE LINGUIST EVIDENCE

CHEROKEE WORD/MEANING

ani-yun-wiya=the principal people

atta=father

atta-culla-culla=spiritual father of all chiefs

ana-ta=woman

Duwali=the name of a chief of the
  Texas Cherokees

gatunwali=big mush or hard mush

gunt-sus-kwali=short arrows

tsuniyatiga=naked people

toquo=a turkey

uku=white chief

yuni-winigiski=man-eaters or cannibals

TURKISH WORD/MEANING

ana-youn=the primary people

atta=father

atta-kula-kul=spiritual father of
  the red men

ana-ta= immortal mother

dua-vali=a leader blessed by God

kati-than-vali=leader of hard or
  thick ground grain

guna-saz-kalil=any type of short
  weapon

suna-yat-tikke=to wear only
  a waist-string

tah-wook=chicken or hen

ak-ulu=white leader/rebel

yana-vaham-necis-ki=cooked for
  depraved purposes by the filthy
  or insane

CREEK/SEMINOLE WORD/MEANING TURKISH WORD/MEANING

mico=tribal administrator

hadjo=the wisest and strongest warrior

mico=administrator of a Turkish
  galley

hodja=the wisest priest or leader

ALGONQUIN WORD/MEANING

ina-en-daugwut=permissible

tuckahoe=tubular, potato-like plant

TURKISH WORD/MEANING

igne-an-daʾva=to satisfy the law

tur-kih-ot=round, dirty plant

POWHATAN WORD/MEANING

werewance=a tribal headman

matchcores=skins or garments

moccasins=shoes

tussan=beds

pokatawer=fire

attonce=arrows

aumouhhowgh=a target

tomahawk=a club-like hatchet

pawesacks=knives

pawpecones=smoking pipes

mattafsin=copper

suckahanna=water

noughma=fish

sawwehone=blood

netoppew=friends

TURKISH WORD/MEANING

werra-hahn=religious,
God-fearing leader

makʾad-kar=coverings for snow

mah-kahd-sahn=warm coverings

dosen=to go to bed

pak-ates-vera=holy fire of creation

at taʾn=to throw or shoot a spear
or arrow

ahm-ahch-hawk=carved/drawn/
earthen target

tam-tomak=a short, wooden club
for cutting

pa bicak=a firm or powerful knife

pipo-kan=a blood (ceremonial)
smoking pipe

maʾden-sun=manufactured metal

su-cag-ana=water drained/pulled
from the earth

nun-ma=river fish

su-we-ah-hahn=fluid in the veins
of the king

ne-tap-pu-vid=what adoring,
lasting friendship

marrapough=enemies

maskapow=worst of enemies

mawchick chammay=best of friends

pummahumps=stars

pawcussackes=guns

marre-puc=good for nothing people

ma-asker-puc=good for nothing army/soldiers

macid camia=illustrious community of friends

pa-maad-hum=constant resurrection place in the sky

pa-kiz-sa'ka-kes=powerful, angry thunderbolt that kills

CHIPPEWA WORD/MEANING

bug-o-nay-kishig=hole in the clouds

ndo'odem=I am your friend

sha-hoka=a strong, unmarried warrior

TURKISH WORD/MEANING

bugu-gunu-ne-ki-isik=hole in the clouds

nedim-adim=I am your friend

sah-hoca=great leader of the holy men

Admittedly, some of the above entries show a much clearer and more obvious relationship than others. However, taken as a whole, the chart provides convincing evidence of a Turkish influence across various American Indian languages. Further, it must be kept in mind that the above chart is not exhaustive. Finally, it should be noted that several of the Turkish entries in the above chart represent an ancient form of the Turkish language and are no longer represented in modern Turkish. This suggests that the Turkish influence on various American Indian languages was pre-Columbian and provides powerful linguistic support for the proposition that there was a sustained Othmanic contact with the New World prior to Columbus.

The linguistic evidence for pre-Columbian Muslims in America is not confined to the Turkish language. In 1750, J. C. Pyrlaeus, a Moravian missionary, stayed with the Nanticoke Indians on the eastern shore of Maryland. Pyrlaeus spent a not inconsiderable amount of his time with the Nanticoke Indians compiling a vocabulary of their language. Later linguistic analysis of Pyrlaeus's compilation has revealed that the language of the Nanticoke Indians was basically the same as that of the Muslim Mandinka of West Africa.

How does one account for the Mandinka language of West Africa having basically supplanted the Nanticoke language by 1750? It takes considerable time for one language to take the place of another, and it hardly seems likely that this transformation could have been affected by a few runaway slaves of Mandinka origin having joined the Nanticoke in the 17th and early 18th centuries. As such, one must acknowledge the presence of many Mandinka having joined with the Nanticoke several centuries before Pyrlaeus compiled his Nanticoke vocabulary. One cannot help but posit that this points to the early 14th-century voyages of the Mandinka under Sultan Abu Bakari.

I. COLUMBUS RECONSIDERED

In the light of the preceding evidence suggesting a Muslim presence from Andalusia, Morocco, West Africa, and the Othmanic Empire in pre-Columbian America, it is worthwhile to examine what possible knowledge Columbus may have had of these earlier Muslim visits to America. A sober reassessment of Columbus's life suggests that it is quite likely that he at least had suspicions that Muslims were traveling west across the Atlantic to a distant land well before 1492, even if he might have mistakenly thought that land was the Orient. The following considerations would certainly seem to point in that direction.

Between 1482 and 1485, Columbus engaged in commercial shipping and trade up and down the coast of West Africa, an experience that no doubt later aided his identification of "New World" cloth as being *Al-Mayzars* of West African design. During these years, he may well have encountered stories of prior Mandinka voyages across the Atlantic.

Circa 1485, following the death of his wife, Columbus took a mistress, Beatriz Enriquez de Harana, who was from Cordoba. Cordoba had been a center of Andalusian Muslim learning and culture, and Beatriz may well have heard stories of Andalusian contact with a land across the Atlantic. In turn, Beatriz may have relayed those stories to Columbus.

Columbus himself had at least some contact with Muslim Andalusia, having been present at the fall of Granada, the last Muslim stronghold in the Iberian Peninsula, on January 2, 1492. As such, if not from Beatriz, Columbus may still have heard of the exploits of Khashkhash, Ibn Farrukh, and others who sailed from Andalusia to a world beyond the known Atlantic.

Finally, it has been suggested that Columbus was familiar with and strongly influenced by some of the works of Al-Idrisi, the 12th-century Muslim scholar and geographer, and that Columbus actually had a copy of Al-Idrisi's work on board the *Santa Maria* in 1492 and was thus familiar with Al-Idrisi's account of eight Muslim sailors who sailed west to a new land from Lisbon (Portugal).[13]

While it must remain speculation, it is not too much to ponder whether Columbus's own voyages to the New World were predicated upon prior Muslim contacts with the Americas.

---

13. Muhammad ANA (2001); Rashad A (1995).

J. SUMMARY AND CONCLUSIONS

The historical records of Muslim historians and geographers document repeated contact between the Americas and the Muslim worlds of Andalusia and Africa. These claims are buttressed by the several accounts of early explorers of the Americas from Christian Europe, by name and word analysis from Native American Indian and Mandinka languages, and by a few archaeological artifacts. Taken together, this array of testimony provides far more evidence of Muslims in pre-Columbian America than was available only 50 years ago to support Leif Erickson's now undisputed voyage to the New World circa 1000.

It is perhaps not too much to assume that 50 years from now the textbooks of American schoolchildren will include stories of the exploits of Khashkhash ibn Saeed ibn Aswad, Ibn Farrukh, the eight Muslims who sailed west from Lisbon, Shaykh Zayn Al-Din 'Ali ibn Fadhel Al-Mazandarani, and Abu Bakari and his Mandinka cohorts. Such textbooks of the future may even begin to speculate about, if not actually document, the influence of Muslim seafarers and geographers on the later voyages of Christopher Columbus.

3 The "European" Explorers

A. INTRODUCTION

As was seen in the immediately preceding chapter, there is substantial reason to believe that Muslims from Andalusia, North Africa, West Africa, and the Othmanic Empire had arrived on the shores of the New World prior to Columbus and had done so as early as the ninth century. In some cases, these Muslim voyages may have been isolated occurrences without systematic follow-up. However, in other cases, it appears that these intrepid explorers established systematic trade routes and ongoing contact with the native inhabitants.

With the first of Columbus's voyages in 1492, the way was opened for Spanish exploration of the Americas. Over the next several decades, wave after wave of Spanish explorers and conquerors sailed to the New World, intent upon financial exploitation, conquest, and religious conversion of the masses to Christianity. However, masked by the designation of Spanish explorers were many individuals who were not Spanish Christians at all or were so in name only.

With the fall of Muslim Granada as the last vestige of Muslim Andalusia in 1492, many Muslims remained in the Iberian Peninsula under the rule of their Catholic Majesties, King Ferdinand and Queen Isabella. Some of these individuals continued to practice their Islam openly and publicly. Others, however, were intimidated or forced into "converting" to Christianity, often under threat of death. These latter individuals and their descendants were known as Moriscos (little Moors).

B. THE MORISCOS

B1. THE *RECONQUISTA*

The beginning of the *Reconquista* (reconquest) of Muslim Andalusia by the Christian states of the Iberian Peninsula is usually dated back to the Battle of Covadonga in 718 when the rump state of Asturia held firm against the Muslim advance. However, the *Reconquista* was little more than a name until the 11th century, when Muslim political unity began to dissolve and Muslim Andalusia began to break up into independent rump states. With the fragmentation of Muslim Andalusia into diverse petty kingdoms and principalities, the Christian advance in the Iberian Peninsula gained momentum. Muslim-controlled Aragon fell in 1118, Muslim Valencia in 1238, and by the mid-13th century most of the peninsula was again under Christian rule.

Concomitant with the expansion of Christian control of the Iberian Peninsula, many Muslims began to find themselves under Christian rule. While these Muslims were usually guaranteed freedom of religious practice, at least verbally or on paper, the reality was that they often found themselves subjected to enormous economic, political, and religious discrimination. As a result, some of these Muslims began publicly to convert to Christianity. In some of those situations, the conversions may have been genuine. However, in many cases, the conversions were in name only and were just for public consumption. In private, these individuals continued to practice Islam as best they could, even though under substantial pressure to abandon their religion.

B2. THE UNIFICATION

In 1469, King John II of Aragon (roughly eastern Spain) arranged the marriage of his son, Prince Ferdinand, to Princess Isabella, half sister of King Henry IV of Castile (roughly western Spain). In 1474, following the death of King Henry IV and a bloody civil war over succession rights, Prince Ferdinand assumed the throne of Castile as King Ferdinand V. Four years later, he succeeded his father in Aragon as King Ferdinand II. The unification of Catholic Spain thus began under the twin rule of King Ferdinand and Queen Isabella. This union of Aragon and Castile presented a formidable military presence in the Iberian Peninsula, which would later culminate in the defeat of Muslim Granada on January 2, 1492. At this juncture, the Christian *Reconquista* was completed for all practical purposes.

With the fall of Granada, Ferdinand and Isabella agreed to terms of peace that guaranteed religious freedom to the Muslims of Granada. However, the religious freedom offered by their Catholic Monarchs soon gave way to forced mass conversions that were initiated by Jimenez de Cisneros, Queen Isabella's priestly confessor and later cardinal of the Roman Catholic Church. Faced with the complete eradication of their religious freedom, the Muslims of Granada rebelled in 1499. By 1500, the rebellion had been squashed, and the Muslims of Granada were faced with the choice of conversion to Christianity or forced expulsion from the Iberian Peninsula. Given this choice, many Muslims publicly converted to Christianity while privately maintaining their belief in and practice of Islam.

No doubt, many Muslims were deeply disquieted by the notion of undergoing a public pseudo-conversion to Christianity. However, in many cases, these doubts were allayed by a number of *Fatwas*, i.e., legal opinions or religious rulings, by Muslim scholars of Islam residing in North Africa. These *Fatwas* held that such pseudo-conversions were not a violation of Islam and fell under the concept of the Law of

Necessity, i.e., a person is not held accountable for acts committed under a state of compulsion. In other words, given the persecutions of Muslims then ongoing in Spain, as long as the Morisco continued internally to believe as a Muslim and continued to practice the dictates of Islam secretly and in private, then the Morisco had not in any way abandoned the faith of Islam. Typically, such *Fatwas* were based on verses of the *Qur'an* such as the following.

> Anyone who, after accepting faith in Allah, utters unbelief—except under compulsion, his heart remaining firm in faith—but such as open their breast to unbelief—on them is wrath from Allah. And theirs will be a dreadful penalty.
>
> *(Qur'an 16:106)*

B3. THE SPANISH INQUISITION

In 1478, the year in which they established joint rule of Castile and Aragon, their Catholic Majesties, King Ferdinand and Queen Isabella, received a papal bull from Pope Sixtus IV authorizing the dreaded Spanish Inquisition. The Spanish Inquisition, which was formally constituted under an inquisitor general in 1483, was originally conceived as a means to force Spanish Jews to either convert to Christianity (Jews who did so and their descendants were known as Conversos or Marranos) or be expelled from Spain.

With its creation, the Spanish Inquisition was given a mandate that created the potential for the very worst of abuses and for the negation of basic human and civil rights. (1) By 1483, Pope Sixtus IV had ceded the appointment of all officials of the Inquisition to King Ferdinand and Queen Isabella, and the Roman Catholic Church then lost any modifying influence it might have had on the course of the

Inquisition. (2) The proceedings of the Inquisition were secret. (3) The accused had no right to legal counsel. (4) The accused had no right to confront his accuser in open court. (5) There was no possibility of appeal to ecclesiastical authority or to the pope in Rome, and so there was absolutely no system of checks and balances. (6) The use of torture to extract confessions was routine. (7) Upon conviction by the Inquisition, all of the property of the accused was confiscated and redistributed among the crown, the Inquisition, and the accusers. In other words, there were enormous financial incentives for the crown to refuse any appeal from an accused, for the Inquisition to find an accused guilty, and for individuals to cook up almost any reason to accuse someone else of religious infidelity.

Under the direction of Tomas de Torquemada, the first inquisitor general of the Spanish Inquisition, approximately 13,000 Jews were killed through the torture and execution meted out by the Inquisition. Approximately 2,000 people were publicly burned at the stake. Finally, in 1492, the Jews of Spain were confronted with a royal decree from their Catholic Majesties that stipulated that all Jews must either convert to Christianity and undergo baptism or be forcibly deported from Spain. While some Jews succumbed to this religious blackmail and accepted Christianity, at least outwardly, approximately 100,000 to 170,000 Jews refused to convert and were expelled from Spain.

Hearing of the plight of the persecuted Jews in Christian Spain, Sultan Beyazid II, the Muslim ruler of the Othmanic Empire, sent the Othmanic fleet under the command of Kemal Reis to evacuate the oppressed and persecuted Jews from Christian Spain. He then settled these homeless Jews within the confines of the Othmanic Empire, many around the area of Edirne and Thessalonica, in the spring of

1492. There, within the confines of a Muslim state and government, these Jews were allowed the freedom to practice their religion, their occupations, and a limited self-autonomy in government. In referring to his resettlement of these Jews from Spain, Sultan Beyazid II reportedly stated, "They (Ferdinand and Isabella) impoverished their kingdom and enriched mine." Most of the 25,000 Jews of modern Turkey are the descendants of those Jews who were initially rescued from Christian persecution by the Muslims of the Ottoman Empire.

Not content with the barbarities it was inflicting on Jews, the Spanish Inquisition soon began to target both Muslims and Moriscos. The Muslims and Moriscos of Granada came under attack as early as 1492, and on February 11, 1502, the Spanish Inquisition targeted Muslims and Moriscos throughout all of Spain. Between 1530 and 1609, 3,500 Moriscos were tried in just the single province of Valencia. By the mid-16th century, hundreds if not thousands of Spanish Moriscos had been garroted or burned at the stake for having "relapsed" into Islam, i.e., for having secretly continued to practice Islam in private. It is unknown how many more Moriscos were ruthlessly tortured.

Concomitant with the persecution of Muslims and Moriscos by the Spanish Inquisition, the monarchy of Spain soon passed a succession of laws to inflict ever more severe punishment on Muslims and to restrict the ever-growing number of Moriscos from continuing to practice Islam in private and in secret. For example, the Muslims of Granada were offered the choice of forced baptism or expulsion from Spain in 1502. At the same time, the great Islamic libraries of Granada were publicly burned, and approximately 2,000 Muslim women of Granada were sold into slavery at auction. As a result, many Muslims publicly converted but continued secretly to practice Islam in private.

In 1521, the monarchy issued the *Pragmatica*. This royal decree prohibited Muslims and Moriscos in Castile from having closed windows or doors on Friday, during Muslim holidays, and during weddings and funerals, in order to insure that there was no recitation of Muslim prayers, no religious observance of Islam, etc. The *Pragmatica* also authorized the imprisonment of individuals who were observed to abstain from pork and wine during meals (pork and alcoholic beverages are prohibited in Islam). These imprisoned individuals always had their property confiscated by the state and their wives and children turned into homeless vagabonds. In many of these cases, Moriscos were burned to death for refusing to drink wine, for refusing to eat pork, for throwing sweets at a wedding (a custom of Andalusian Muslims), or for using henna (a custom in vogue among Muslims at that time).

In 1526, like the Muslims of Granada before them, the Muslims of Valencia and Aragon were similarly forced to convert to Christianity. Shortly thereafter, Islam was officially prohibited throughout all of Spain. Suspected of continuing to be practicing Muslims in private, the Moriscos were soon subjected to discriminative taxation, and the government began the wholesale confiscation of Morisco land and property in the early 1560s. In 1566, King Philip II issued a royal decree that forbade Moriscos the use of their Muslim (Arabic) names, their customary dress, and the use of the Arabic language. On September 22, 1609, a royal decree was issued that ordered the expulsion of all Moriscos from Spain.

Between 1609 and 1615, 275,000-300,000 Moriscos were forcibly expelled from Spain, with most of them relocating to North

Africa. However, many Moriscos fled to southern France, where to avoid persecution they claimed to be Huguenots, a newly formed Protestant denomination of Christianity. Subsequently, many of these Muslims who were masquerading as Huguenots made their way to what is now South Carolina.

B4. Muslims and Moriscos in Catholic Spain

It is difficult to know exactly how many Muslims and Moriscos there were throughout unified Spain. However, it has been estimated that 20% of the population of Aragon and more than 30% of the population of Valencia were Moriscos. With each of these areas having a population of about 270,000 individuals in the late 15th century, this would indicate a population of at least 135,000 Moriscos. However, this number still does not include the Morisco population of Castile, Catalonia, and the other small kingdoms comprising unified Spain. As such, it is easy to imagine that there were well over a quarter of a million Muslims and Moriscos throughout all of Spain by the early 16th century. Some researchers place the estimate as high as 500,000. Given a population this large, it is not surprising to find a number of Muslims and Moriscos among the early "Spanish" explorers of the Americas.

B5. Muslims and Moriscos in Portugal

It was not just in Catholic Spain that Muslims and Moriscos met with discrimination and persecution. Concomitant with the Inquisition in Spain, several Portuguese kings (Joao III, Sebastiao, and Phillip III) sanctioned their own Portuguese Inquisition, which was reputed to be far more vicious and lethal than anything that transpired in Spain.

B6. CONCLUSIONS

Given the large number of Muslims and Moriscos in Spain and Portugal and given the state-sponsored discrimination against and persecution of them, it is not surprising that many Muslims and Moriscos elected to leave the Iberian Peninsula. While many of them sought refuge in North Africa and a few in southern France, a fair number of them looked for escape in much more distant lands, including the Americas. Unfortunately, these Muslim and Morisco explorers and settlers of the New World are today often forgotten. Even more regrettably, when they are remembered, it is usually as "Spanish" adventurers. In what follows, a few of these intrepid individuals are briefly memorialized.

C. MUSLIM AND MORISCO EXPLORERS OF THE NEW WORLD

C1. THE PINZON BROTHERS[14]

Martin Alonzo Pinzon was born circa 1441 and died in 1493, both events occurring in Palos, Seville (Spain). His younger brother, Vicente Yanez Pinzon, was born circa 1460 in Palos, and nothing is known of him after 1523. Relatively little information is available on a third Pinzon brother, Francisco. The three Pinzon brothers were of Muslim descent, and the Pinzon family was related to Abu Zayan Muhammad III, the Marinid sultan of Morocco, who ruled from 1362 until 1366. The three Pinzon brothers were wealthy ship owners, ship outfitters, and navigators who played major parts in the early Spanish exploration of the Americas.

Martin Pinzon was part owner of the *Pinta* and the *Nina*, two of the three ships to sail across the Atlantic during Columbus's first

---

14. Information in this section is from Mroueh Y (1996), Muhammad ANA (2001), and — (2003x).

voyage. In addition, he was the ship outfitter for all three ships and was responsible for securing the crews of all three ships. He sailed with Columbus in 1492 as the captain of the *Pinta*. Of note, it was Martin's suggestion to change course that allowed Columbus's fleet to find landfall at San Salvador on October 12, 1492. Subsequently, in a search for gold and spices, Martin and the *Pinta* separated from the other two vessels in Columbus's tiny fleet. He rejoined the other two ships a few months later.

Vicente Pinzon also sailed with Columbus during his historic 1492 voyage to the New World and served as captain of the *Nina*. In late 1499, Vicente sailed a second time to the Americas, landing on the Brazilian coast at Santa Maria de la Consolacion. Sailing northwest from his initial landfall in Brazil, he explored the Amazon River estuary and the Gulf of Paria in northeastern Venezuela. Vicente made two additional voyages to the Americas before 1508. He made his final voyage to the New World in 1508 with Juan Diaz de Solis, apparently explored what is now Central America, and returned to Spain in August of 1509.

Francisco Pinzon was the third of the Pinzon brothers to sail with Columbus in 1492. Francisco served as pilot of the *Pinta*.

C2. Pedro Alonso Nino[15]

Yet a fourth Muslim or Morisco to sail with Columbus in 1492 was Pedro Alonso Nino. Little is known about Pedro aside from the fact that he was an African who helped navigate the Atlantic and map the islands of the Caribbean.

---

15. Information in this section is from Smallwood AD (1999).

C3. Rodrigo De Triana[16]

Rodrigo de Triana, aka Rodrigo de Lepe (Lepe was a town in Andalusia), was another of those intrepid sailors who risked their lives during Columbus's first voyage to the New World. In fact, it was Rodrigo who was the first member of the expedition to sight land. Although a Christian before and during this historic voyage, Rodrigo converted to Islam shortly after his return to Spain in 1493. Given the persecutions of Muslims and Moriscos that were then beginning to take place throughout Spain, Rodrigo's conversion to Islam must have required a great deal of faith. One can only speculate as to what it was that Rodrigo may have encountered during that first voyage of Columbus that contributed to Rodrigo's later conversion.

C4. Nuflo De Olano[17]

Nuflo de Olano was an African who accompanied Vasco Nunez de Balboa on the latter's exploration of Central America. Nuflo was a member of the Balboa exploratory party that first crossed the Americas to see the Pacific Ocean from the shores of America.

C5. Estevanico of Azamor[18]

Estevanico (little Stephen) of Azamor was born in Azamor, Morocco, circa 1500. His name at birth was Mustafa Zemmouri. In 1513, King Manoel of Portugal captured Azamor, and Estevanico was probably enslaved at that time. However, little is known about his life prior to 1527, and the exact time and place of his enslavement remains conjecture.

---

16. Information in this section is from Quick AH (1998).

17. Information in this section is from Smallwood AD (1999).

18. Information in this section is from Katz WL (1997), Smallwood AD (1999), Muhammad ANA (2001), Numan FH (---), and Shelton MS (---).

On July 17, 1527, Estevanico and his Spanish owner, Andres Dorantes, boarded a ship at Sanlucar de Barrameda, Spain, and set sail for the Americas. Arriving in Hispaniola, Estevanico and Dorantes joined the Panfilo de Narvaez expedition to Florida. For the next 12 years, before being killed by Indians in the vicinity of Arizona in 1539, Estevanico explored large sections of North America.

The 1527 expedition of de Narvaez was fraught with a rapid succession of catastrophes. Even before landing in Florida, de Narvaez's fleet of five ships was partially destroyed by a hurricane. Additional members of the expedition were killed by Indians and disease. Upon the death of de Narvaez, command was assumed by Cabeza de Vaca. By the time the expedition had reached the first Indian village they encountered, the expedition's original complement of 500-600 men was down to a mere 80.

For the next nine years, Estevanico served as guide to the remaining party and as the go-between with the Indians they encountered along the way. He led the struggling survivors across what would later become the southern United States, a 5,000 mile journey from Florida, over the southeastern United States and into Mexico as far as the Pacific Ocean, and then eventually to safety at Mexico City. One by one, additional members of the de Narvaez expedition died along the way. By the time the expedition members were captured by Indians, they were down to just four people: Estevanico, Andres Dorantes, Cabeza de Vaca, and one other person. These four managed to escape their captors and continue their journey. Along the way, the Indians told them stories about Cibola, the mythical Seven Cities of Gold.

In 1536, Estevanico finally led his three fellow members of the de Narvaez expedition into Spanish headquarters in Mexico, where they told about their ordeals and about the stories they had heard about Cibola. A reconstruction of Estevanico's travels using modern geographic names suggests a trip that started in the vicinity of Tampa (Florida) and then passed through or close to Mobile (Alabama), Galveston (Texas), Austin (Texas), El Paso (Texas), Rincon (Arizona), Ures (Mexico), Sinaloa (Mexico), and Culiacan (Mexico), before ending up in Mexico City.

His three compatriots left for Spain as soon as they had recovered from their nine-year ordeal. Estevanico was not so fortunate. As a slave, he was sold to the Spanish governor of Hispaniola, Antonio de Mendoza.

Eager to acquire the fabled riches of Cibola, de Mendoza organized a 1538 expedition to discover and plunder the Seven Cities of Gold. He placed Marcos de Niza, a Franciscan friar, in charge of the expedition. However, he chose Estevanico to serve as guide for the expedition and to function as an interlocutor with whatever Indians the expedition would encounter.

In 1538, Estevanico led the expedition from Mexico in search of the fabled Seven Cities of Cibola. During this journey, Estevanico became the first non-Indian to visit the pueblos of northern Mexico. He subsequently discovered Arizona and New Mexico, before reportedly being killed by Zuni Indians in 1539 at an Indian city. At one time or another during his 13 years in the Americas, Estevanico explored Florida, Mississippi, Alabama, Texas, New Mexico, and Arizona. At least two states, Arizona and New Mexico, owe their beginnings to this Muslim.

C6. The Santa Elena Colony[19]

In 1566, the Spanish established a colony at Santa Elena, South Carolina. The colony was defended by a fort, and five satellite forts were also constructed and manned near the modern towns of Rome, Georgia, Greenville, South Carolina, Asheville, North Carolina, and Johnson City, Tennessee. Early colonists, about 200 soldiers in number, were recruited from the Galician Mountains of northern Spain and Portugal by Captain Joao Pardo, a Spanish naval officer of Portuguese descent. This recruitment of colonists from the Galician Mountains is significant in that this was an area of Portugal and Spain that was heavily populated by Berber Muslims and Sephardic Jews. As such, it can be reasonably assumed that many Muslims and Moriscos were among the inhabitants of the Santa Elena colony. In fact, it may well have been than a majority of these colonists were Muslims and Moriscos.

Although seldom mentioned in American history books, this Spanish colony was a viable and thriving settlement which lasted for over 20 years. To bolster the viability of the new colony, Pardo returned two to three years after the initial settlement, bringing additional settlers, probably including Turkish men and women, as well as the wives and families of the original settlers. Thus fortified, Santa Elena and its outlying forts continued to exist until 1587.

In 1587, with the British threatening their continued existence, the Santa Elena colonists burned their colony to the ground. Many of them then sailed south to the Spanish colony at St. Augustine, Florida, abandoning some of the Santa Elena colonists and all of the

---

19. Details on Santa Elena are from Kennedy NB (1997), Campbell H (2001), Kennedy NB, Kennedy RV (1997), Kennedy NB (2003a), and Winkler W (2004b).

colonists at the outlying forts. These abandoned colonists, totaling about 125 men and their families and including Muslims and Moriscos, escaped into the mountains of North Carolina, where some of them appear to have intermarried with the Cherokee, Creek, and Catawba Indians.

C7. THE ROANOKE REFUGEES[20]

In 1584, Sir Walter Raleigh discovered Roanoke Island, which was then part of Virginia but is now part of North Carolina. Part of Raleigh's 1584 mission was to find an area suitable for a new British settlement. Roanoke Island seemed to fit the bill, and one year later Raleigh landed a group of British settlers on the island, establishing the Roanoke Island colony of Ralph B. Layne for the British. However, the settlement was to last a scant one year.

In 1585-1586, Sir Francis Drake, commanding 25-30 English ships, made a series of daring raids against the Spanish and Portuguese in the West Indies, along the coast of Brazil, and on St. Augustine, Florida. In the process, he liberated some 400-500 prisoners, of whom about 300 or more were Moorish and Turkish galley slaves. These galley slaves were Muslims who had been previously captured in battles on the Mediterranean Sea. (Drake subsequently referred to these liberated prisoners as being Turks, Moors, Portuguese, and Greeks who had converted to Islam.)

Having boarded these 400-500 refugees on his ships, Drake then sailed north to Roanoke Island. At Roanoke, Drake was besieged by stranded English settlers who wished to abandon their colony and return to England. In order to make room for his countrymen, Drake apparently left about 200 of the Muslim refugees at Roanoke.

---

20. Details on Roanoke are from Kennedy NB (1997), Campbell H (2001), Hirschman EC (2005), Kennedy NB (2003a), and Kennedy NB, Kennedy RV (1997).

Two weeks later, Sir Walter Raleigh sailed into Roanoke Island but found no trace of the Muslims left on the island by Drake. Apparently, these intrepid Muslims left Roanoke, reached the mainland, and later intermarried with Indians of the Powhatan, Pamunkey, Nansemond, Croatan, and Hatters Indian tribes.

As an addendum to the story of Roanoke, mention should be made of Simon Fernandez, a navigator aboard one of the ships taking colonists to Roanoke Island. Fernandez has been described as having been Portuguese (Morisco?) and as having been a former Barbary Coast pirate. Both designations suggest that Fernandez was actually a Moorish Muslim.

C8. The Karachai and Kavkas Turks[21]

Although seldom mentioned in American history books, the 16th century also witnessed the importation of Turkish silk and textile workers from Karachai and Kavkas in Transcaucasia. These Turkish Muslims were settled by the Spanish in Cuba, Mexico, Florida, and the American Southwest.

The early 17th century also saw two different shipments of Turkish and Armenian silk workers, both men and women, to the British colony at Jamestown, Virginia, from the Othmanic Empire. Almost all of these Turks and Armenians would have been Muslims, and they comprised a substantial percentage of the indentured-servant class at Jamestown. These shipments took place during the mid-1600s, and the earliest written documentation of a Turkish presence at Jamestown is from 1631. These Turks became so numerous at Jamestown that 17th-century Virginia ended up passing a law prohibiting the importation of any more

---

21. Information in this section is from Kennedy NB (1997), Kennedy NB (2002), Kennedy NB (2003a), Kennedy NB (2003b), and Winkler W (2004b).

"Turks" and so-called "infidels" (Muslims) into the colony. Some of these Turks most likely fled their servitude and were taken in by Indian tribes.

As recorded in *The Virginia Carolorum*, among the indentured servants in colonial Virginia were such individuals as: "Mehmet the Turk, Ahmad the Turk, Joseph the Armenian, Sayyan Turk," etc. Additional documentation of a Turkish and Armenian presence in colonial Virginia can be found in the Virginia Assembly authorizing 4,000 pounds of tobacco as an inducement to keep "George the Armenian" in Virginia as a silk producer. A 1652 document refers to a Turk in Virginia who wrote in the Turkish language. In 1652, Governor William Byrd of Virginia referred to a Turkish merchant in a letter.

D. SUMMARY AND CONCLUSIONS

Muslims or Moriscos were part and parcel of most of the early Spanish and some of the early British explorations of the New World. As previously noted, at least four different Muslims or Moriscos accompanied Columbus on his first voyage to the Americas. However, the Muslim and Morisco contribution to the exploration of the Americas did not stop there. When Spain established its first permanent settlement in the New World on Hispaniola in 1494, Muslims and Moriscos of African origin were there as soldiers and explorers. In fact, Muslims and Moriscos traveled as sailors, settlers, explorers, and conquistadors with Columbus, Balboa, Cortes, Valas, Alvardo, Pizarro, Almagro, Valdivia, Alarcon, Coronado, Narvaez, Pardo, and Cabeza de Vaca.

Many of the Moriscos gave up their sham conversion to Christianity upon reaching the New World. Both Muslims and Moriscos began to practice their Islam publicly and began to convert the native Indians to Islam. Fearful of a large Muslim community forming in the Americas, the

Spanish crown soon issued a succession of royal decrees banning Muslims, Moriscos, and even Africans who had been raised by Moriscos from being taken to the Americas, either as free men or as slaves. In some cases, the long arm of the Spanish Inquisition reached into the New World, and there are reports of Moriscos being burned at the stake through the 1700s in what are now Texas and New Mexico.[22]

However, a Muslim and Morisco presence was not confined to the Spanish exploration of the Americas. Numerous Muslims and Moriscos also sailed with the early Portuguese explorers of South America. Many of these Muslims and Moriscos were of Moorish or North African descent, but some of these Muslims were Turkish galley slaves who had been previously imprisoned by the Portuguese. In fact, Muslims and Moriscos were such a prevalent part of the Portuguese explorations that for a time the very word "Portuguese" was used as a synonym for Muslim and Morisco.[23]

---

22. Quick AH (1998) and Hirschman EC (2005).
23. Kennedy NB, Kennedy RV (1997).

4 The Slave Trade

A. HISTORICAL OVERVIEW[24]

The abomination that is human slavery is as old as recorded history. At one time or another, it has been a degradation embraced by almost every culture throughout the world.

Within Asia, human slavery can be traced back at least 3,900 years. For example, the laws of Eshnunna (circa 1900 BCE) and the Code of Hammurabi (circa 1750 BCE) institutionalized and regulated slavery in ancient Mesopotamia (Iraq). China embraced slavery at least as early as the Shang dynasty (18th-12th centuries BCE), by the Han dynasty (206 BCE-25 CE) almost five percent of the population were slaves, and slavery was not abolished in China until an imperial decree of 1906 became effective on January 31, 1910. The ancient Hebrews and Israelites practiced slavery, as attested by several relevant passages in the *Old Testament*.[25] As early as the first century BCE, the Sanskrit Laws of Manu legitimized slavery within India, a country for which it was estimated that there were between eight and nine million slaves in 1841, and a country in which slavery was not made a crime until 1861. Between the eighth and 18th centuries, Korea's slaves numbered between 30 and 50% of the entire population. While slavery was legally abolished in

---

24. Information in this section is primarily from Hellie R (2003).

25. See for example *Genesis* 9:18-29; 12:16; 15:1-4; 16:1-8; 17:12-13, 23-27; 20:14; 21: 8-13; 24:34-35; 25:12; 32:3-5; *Exodus* 13:43-44; 20:10, 17; 21:1-9, 20-21, 26-27, 32; 23:12; *Leviticus* 19:20-21; 25:6, 44-46; *Deuteronomy* 5:14, 21; 12:12, 18; 15:13-17; 16:11, 14; *Judges* 9:18; *I Kings* 9:20-21; *I Chronicles* 2:34-35.

Korea in 1894, it remained a reality of life until 1930. Between 25 and 33% of the population were slaves in 17th-century Thailand and in 19th-century Burma. Examples of slavery can also be found in the history of the Philippines, Nepal, Malaysia, Indonesia, Japan, the Middle East, and the countries comprising Central Asia.

Slavery has also been a prominent feature of European history. In ancient Athens, slaves accounted for about 33% of the population between the fifth and third centuries BCE. Approximately 30% of the people of Roman Italy were slaves between the second century BCE and the fourth century CE. The *Domesday Book* of 1086 documented that 10% of the population of England were slaves as of that date. A history of slavery can also be found in France, Germany, Poland, Lithuania, Russia, and Scandinavia.

Human slavery was also practiced among many of the Indian tribes of the New World. A brief sampling of such tribes would include the Creek, Comanche, Callinago, Tupinamba, Inca, Tehuelche, Klamath, Pawnee, Yurok, and Aztec.

Slavery was especially prominent in certain areas of Africa. For example, slavery thrived in ancient Egypt. During the 19th century, slaves accounted for 65 to 90% of the population of Zanzibar, about 90% of the people of Kenya, and 50% of the people of Madagascar. Between 1750 and 1900, 33 to 67% of the population of the Fulani states of the western and central Sudan were enslaved. During the 19th century, slaves accounted for about 50% of the people of Ouidah (Whydah). Slavery was also rampant in 17th- through 18th-century Kanem, where it contributed to 33% of the population. Between 1580 and 1890, about 40% of the people of Bornu were slaves. The percentage of slaves in Senegambia was around 33%

between 1300 and 1900. As late as the 19th century, slaves accounted for almost 50% of the population of Sierra Leone. Further, slavery was not abolished in Liberia and Ethiopia until the 1930s.

Common to almost all of the above historical examples was the fact that the slave was an object of the law, not its subject. In other words, the slave was a type of property or chattel who belonged to someone else. He lacked personal liberty and most, if not all, civil rights. He was usually not free to choose his occupation or spouse. Further, he was generally seen to occupy the lowest rung of human society, a position that he inherited by entering slavery through being captured in war, by being kidnapped, by being convicted of a crime, by having a debt he could not pay, by being sold into slavery by his family, or by selling himself into slavery as a way of escaping poverty.

Despite the similarities to be found across the world's many and diverse institutions of slavery, important differences developed over time and location. One important difference had to do with the function of the slave. In what is variously called household, patriarchal, or domestic slavery, slaves basically did domestic and personal services for their owners. Their primary duties involved the performance of basic household duties, and they were rarely used for productive labor. In such a situation, slaves were usually a drain on their owner's assets, as their service did not produce income that covered the cost of their upkeep. As such, these slaves were basically status symbols who were primarily owned by the wealthy.

In contrast, productive slavery was an institution that used slaves to produce income for their owners. This type of slavery was most common in areas emphasizing such labor-intensive activities as mining and certain types of agriculture. It was this type of slavery that came to dominate the transatlantic slave trade and slavery in the Americas.

B. The Transatlantic Slave Trade

B1. Origins of Slavery in European America

The transatlantic slave trade began with none other than Christopher Columbus. Columbus began by enslaving 10 Arawak Indian men and women and sending them to Seville, Spain. He followed that up by later enslaving 1,100 Taino Indian men and women, whom he sent back to Spain on four Spanish ships. Overcrowding, inclement weather, and exposure to European diseases resulted in only 300 of the original 1,100 Taino Indians surviving their journey to Spain. Undeterred, Columbus wrote to King Ferdinand and Queen Isabella about America being an untapped motherlode of potential slaves: "From here, in the name of the Blessed Trinity, we can send all the slaves that can be sold."[26]

As the early Spanish conquistadors began to colonize in the New World, they continued human bondage in the Americas by enslaving American Indians to work in their mining operations. However, this early foray into slavery did not work out for the Spanish, in part secondary to the high death rate among enslaved Indians who lacked any natural resistance to the European diseases to which they were being exposed for the first time. This consideration created an initial demand for the importation of slaves from elsewhere. This demand was soon met by importing African slaves, most of whom had already been exposed to most European diseases. The first shipment of African slaves to the Americas occurred in 1501.

The initial demand for imported slaves from Africa was then significantly enhanced by European colonists turning to agricultural pursuits in the New World. Two of the earliest crops to be cultivated

---

26. Katz WL (1997).

by European colonists in the Caribbean were tobacco and sugar cane. Over time, sugar and tobacco production were supplemented with other mainstay crops such as rice, indigo, and cotton. These five crops gradually evolved into the primary exports shipped from the Americas to Europe. Common to all five crops was that the planting, growing, and harvesting of these crops were extremely labor-intensive and created a booming demand for additional slaves. That need was met by shipping increasing numbers of African slaves to the Americas.

Of these five crops, tobacco was initially the mainstay crop in what is now the United States. However, with the invention of the cotton gin by Eli Whitney in 1793, cotton production became far more feasible and profitable, and the era of "King Cotton" was initiated. By 1860, the export of cotton from the United States accounted for 191 million dollars, a dollar amount that equaled 57% of all U.S. exports. The sorry side-effect of the "King Cotton" era was a dramatically increased need for slaves. As such, about 67% of all plantation slaves in the United States were engaged in the production of cotton by 1850.

B2. THE AFRICAN CONNECTION

The various African kingdoms and peoples were not the totally blameless and innocent victims of the transatlantic slave trade. They were also necessary participants in the slave traffic. Either willingly or through economic and indirect military coercion, they entered into a collusive relationship with the European slavers.

By and large, European slave traders were reluctant to journey inland into Africa, which they saw as a dark, forbidding, dangerous, and unknown land. Largely fabricated tales of cannibalism and other exotic dangers were told by the native Africans to keep the European slavers confined to the relative safety of coastal areas. As such, these European merchants of human flesh had to rely on African middlemen to drive slaves to the coast, where they were traded to the Europeans.

The Africans certainly had other things of value to trade with the Europeans besides human slaves. Africa produced great quantities of gold, gum, ivory, skins, palm oil, cattle, grain, fabrics, and wood, all of which were in much demand in Europe. However, the European traders would barter only their lesser merchandise for such material. When it came to such articles as guns, ammunition, and certain kinds of cloth, the only goods the Europeans would accept in trade were slaves.

Obviously, the Africans could elect not to trade for guns, ammunition, and cloth. However, to keep the first two of these articles of trade in the category of necessities for the Africans, the Europeans were quite adept at fomenting wars between neighboring African kingdoms and tribes. Once the war was started, it was relatively easy to trade guns and ammunition with one or the other side for slaves. The trade having been made with one side, the very existence of the other side could soon become contingent upon trading slaves to the Europeans so that it could secure its own guns and ammunition. In short, the Europeans took advantage of existing conflicts and provoked other conflicts in order to generate an arms race that left the various African tribes and kingdoms caught between losing a war and trading slaves for military supplies.

While slavery had existed in Africa before the onset of the transatlantic slave trade, its existence as an institution was relatively modest when compared to what transpired with the advent of slavery in the Americas. In traditional African society, slaves had been used principally as domestic servants and to broaden the lineage possibilities of chiefs, kings, and princes. As such, the institution of slavery in Africa primarily conformed to the household, patriarchal, or domestic version. In contrast, slavery in the Americas was primarily one of productive slavery.

This dichotomy between the patriarchal slavery to be found in Africa and the productive slavery championed in the Americas produced a gender-based difference between slaves retained in Africa and slaves shipped to the New World. The demand for slaves in Africa was basically one for women who would serve as domestic servants and as mothers to extend the lineage of various potentates. In contrast, the demand for slaves in the Americas was for men who would function as agricultural workers. As such, about 65-70% of the slaves sent to the New World were men.

B3. THE MIDDLE PASSAGE

As previously noted, the initial capture of slaves in Africa was done almost exclusively by Africans. Once captured, these slaves were marched overland to the coast, a journey that could take several weeks. Along the way they were chained, bound, and made to carry heavy loads (sometimes trade goods, but other times merely rocks) in order to insure that they were too exhausted to attempt to escape. Once they had reached the coast, they were confined to holding pens until traded to the European slave merchants. Having finally fallen into the custody of the Europeans, the slaves were first branded with a hot metal rod and then subjected to transatlantic shipping, a process that has become known as the Middle Passage.

The horrors of the Middle Passage almost defy verbal description. Slaves were stripped naked (in part to prevent the slaves from hanging themselves and in part as the start of the process of dehumanization that would theoretically result in their eventual docility and acceptance of their slave status), chained to each other, and packed like sardines into the holds of the ships. Once sailing was under way, the slaves were given inadequate rations and water, and such food and water were often carelessly distributed. In addition, the slaves were occasionally brought to the deck and made to dance and sing to entertain the European sailors, were frequently beaten, and otherwise remained confined in their chained and often prone positions. Further, sanitation facilities in the ships' holds were basically non-existent. Throughout the entire journey, the slaves were allowed to wash only twice, the second time being right before docking in the Americas.

Needless to say, the lack of sanitation facilities and the frequent beatings endured by the slaves resulted in numerous illnesses and injuries. As such, occasional inspections would single out the sick and injured among the slaves. Those who were deemed too frail to bring a good sale price in the New World were summarily thrown overboard along the way, in order to save the pittance that would otherwise have been spent on their bare sustenance. In those cases where pregnant women delivered their babies aboard ship, the babies were often immediately cast overboard.

Given the above conditions and given that the typical Middle Passage voyage could take several weeks to a few months, it is not surprising that it has been estimated that 10% to more than 20% of the shipped slaves died in transit to the Americas. In at least one instance (the voyage that transported a slave known only as Ball's Muslim), 33% of the slaves who had initially boarded their ship failed to reach the New World alive.

B4. AFRICAN SLAVES IN THE AMERICAS

Arriving in the New World, the African slaves were soon sold to the highest bidder at large slave auctions, usually in the Caribbean, Brazil, and the southern United States. Once sold, the slaves were immediately put to work and underwent a period of survival testing to see whether or not they would survive the disease environment of the Americas. Many slaves died during this first year of survival testing. Most slaves who were sold in the slave markets of the United States prior to the 18th century had first undergone their period of survival testing in the Caribbean islands.

The exact number of African slaves shipped to the New World is unknown. The records are incomplete, and documentation is often lacking. As such, historians continue to debate this point. Confounding the discussion is the fact that the shipment of slaves from Africa to the United States was technically illegal after January 1, 1808. However, a contraband slave trade, for which we can expect no reliable records, continued until the early 1860s.

What is now generally accepted is that earlier estimates of around 9.5 million Africans being shipped to the Americas as slaves were misleadingly low. With additional information being discovered and analyzed over the intervening years, more contemporary estimates suggest that the number was closer to 15 million and may well have been as high as 20 million.[27] Of these, approximately 10 million or more appear to have been shipped to what is now the United States, with the first shipment being consigned by Lucas Vasquez de Leon in 1526.[28]

Whatever the total number of slaves shipped to the Americas, they accounted for a substantial percentage of the population. When looking at the Caribbean islands, we find that approximately 33% of the popula-

---

27. Diouf SA (1998).

28. Ahmed Z (2003).

tion of 18th-century Cuba were slaves. However, compared to other Caribbean islands this was hardly remarkable. About 90% of the population were slaves in Jamaica by 1730, in Antigua by 1775, and in Grenada by 1834. Looking at South America, about 50% of the population of Brazil consisted of slaves by 1800. Within the United States and its predecessor colonies, 64% of the population of South Carolina were slaves in 1720. Mississippi's population was comprised of 55% slaves in both 1810 and 1860. About 40% of the population of the American South were slaves during the 19th-century heyday of "King Cotton," and more than 36% of all New World slaves were located in the southern United States by 1825.[29]

C. RACE AND SLAVERY

Before turning our attention to those African slaves who were Muslims, it pays to digress for a moment to reflect on the intimate relationship that existed between race and slavery in the transatlantic slave trade.

Throughout recorded history, human slavery has typically been an exogenous institution. With the exception of enslavement for debt and for crimes, slaves have typically been drawn from a population considered to be "outside" the population of the slave owners. As such, slaves were typically acquired from a different tribe, country, ethnic group, or religious affiliation from that of the owner. However, such a process did not exclusively limit slavery to just one ethnic group or to just one race.

The slavery practiced by Europeans had basically conformed to the above scenario. Slaves were exogenous to the owner's population,

---

29. Hellie R (2003).

but slaves were not exclusively drawn from one race; there was no inherent equation between slavery and race. By the dawn of the 16th century, this pattern had changed throughout Europe, and European slavery was practiced only on Africans. In part, this change reflected the papal bulls of Pope Nicholas V in 1454 and Pope Calixtus III in 1456. Both papal rulings exonerated and justified Portugal's growing slave trade by championing it as a crusade for Christianity against the heathens and Muslims of Africa. In part, this change also reflected a literal interpretation of the following Biblical passage from the *Old Testament.*

> The sons of Noah who went out of the ark were Shem, Ham, and Japheth. Ham was the father of Canaan. These three were the sons of Noah; and from these the whole earth was peopled. Noah, a man of the soil, was the first to plant a vineyard. He drank some of the wine and became drunk, and he lay uncovered in his tent. And Ham, the father of Canaan, saw the nakedness of his father, and told his two brothers outside. Then Shem and Japheth took a garment, laid it on both their shoulders, and walked backward and covered the nakedness of their father; their faces were turned away, and they did not see their father's nakedness. When Noah awoke from his wine and knew what his youngest son had done to him, he said, "Cursed be Canaan; lowest of slaves shall he be to his brothers." He also said, "Blessed by the Lord my God be Shem; and let Canaan be his slave. May God make space for Japheth, and let him live in the tents of Shem; and let Canaan be his slave."
>
> (*Genesis* 9:18-27)

There are many aspects of the above Biblical story that will make absolutely no sense to any discerning reader: a prophet of God becoming drunk, a grandson being cursed for a son's accidental viewing of Noah's alleged nakedness, perpetual slavery for the descendants of one man because of an unintentional action on his part, etc. Despite these absurdities, this story was long a matter of belief by the adherents of the Judaeo-Christian tradition, and this belief has a direct bearing on understanding the roots of racial prejudice and injustice in the European-American subculture and in the transatlantic slave trade.

To understand this connection, two additional pieces of information are needed. Firstly, in the so-called Table of Nations reported in *Genesis* 10:1-32, Ham is reported to be the progenitor of the African peoples. Secondly, although there is no Biblical support for such a concept, popular Christian thinking in past centuries often maintained that Noah's alleged curse resulted in the descendants of Ham having black skin. This Judaeo-Christian basis for racial prejudice, intolerance, and injustice was still being perpetrated as late as the mid 20th century, and I can well remember being taught as a young boy in vacation *Bible* school that Ham and his descendants were turned black as a result of Noah's curse. Let me hasten to add that, despite the isolated voices of some individual Christians who still preach this doctrine, I know of no Christian church that would publicly embrace such a concept today.

In short, racial injustice in American history and the atrocities of the transatlantic slave trade were not just the result of European-American cultural practices, but were in essence a matter of popular religious doctrine and dogma. It was part of the very fabric of the Judaeo-Christian tradition in American history, and the story of Noah's curse of the Hamitic people allowed many Christian churches to opine that the slavery, degradation, and dehumanization of African Americans were divinely ordained. Furthermore, with the community of the church being seen as the new Israel, even as Jesus Christ was seen as the new Abraham,[30] some Christian churches once posited that the European-American Christian was inherently superior to all others, not only by his non-Hamitic descent, but also by virtue of his religious affiliation.

Needless to say, under this frame of reference, African slaves who were Muslim in their religious affiliation were doubly cursed. On the one hand, they were the descendants of the cursed Ham and Canaan, descendants who were supposedly "divinely" ordained to be the slaves of others. On the other hand, they were not only non-Christians, but Muslims, a group that most pre 20th-century Christians saw as being worse than pagans.

D. MUSLIMS SLAVES IN THE AMERICAS

D1. MUSLIMS IN SUB-SAHARAN AFRICAN

Muslim contact with Africa began as early as 615, when Prophet Muhammad authorized either 14 or 16 of the early Muslims to seek religious refuge in the African kingdom of Abyssinia (Ethiopia and Eritrea). By the late seventh century, most of northern Africa was ruled by the Muslim caliphate, and most of the inhabitants of northern and Saharan Africa had converted to Islam. Over the next few centuries, Muslim traders initiated and furthered the spread of Islam from North Africa to sub-Saharan Africa. Early in the 11th century, Islam gained a prominent foothold in West Africa, following the conversion of two

---

30. See, for example: *Romans* 4:16; *Galatians* 3:15-18, 22-31; *Hebrews* 8:1-13.

prominent rulers, War Diaby and Kosoy. The former ruled the region now known as northern Senegal, while the latter ruled what is now Mali. By the 14th century, much of West Africa had converted to Islam. Between 1725 and the middle of the 19th century, Islam spread into what is today Gambia, Guinea, and southern Mali. In addition, Arab traders had also been instrumental in spreading Islam far down the coastline of East Africa.

During the time of the transatlantic slave trade, numerous tribes in West Africa were basically Muslim. A listing of these Muslim tribes would include the: Fulbe, Fulani, or Tukolor; Mande or Mandinka; Serahule or Soninke; Hausa; Taureg; Songhai; Kassonke; Kanuri; Mandara; Wolof; Vai; Nupi; Susa; Ashanti; and Yoruba or Nago. The extent of the Islamic influence in these tribes can be illustrated by the fact that about 50% of the Yoruba are Muslims, about 90% of the Hausa and Mandinka are Muslims, and about 95% of the Fulani are Muslims.[31]

D2. The Demographics of Muslim Slaves in America

As noted previously, there is no documentary evidence to support definitive conclusions as to exactly how many Africans were brought to the Americas as slaves. Scholars and researchers are left to estimate and hypothesize from what evidence does exist, with contemporary estimates of the number of slaves brought to the New World ranging between 15 and 20 million.

The issue becomes even muddier when trying to determine what percentage of these African slaves were Muslims. Ships' manifest lists typically did not record the religious affiliation of the slaves being

---

31. Austin AD (1997); Diouf SA (1998); Lo M (2004); Quick AH (1998).

transported. Likewise, slave auction sales lists and slave ownership records in the Americas are usually silent when it comes to an individual slave's religion.

Given the above, contemporary scholars must make inferences based upon three considerations. Firstly, some slaves had demonstrably Muslim names. As non-Muslim Africans did not use Muslim names, the presence of a Muslim name in a ship's manifest, an auction sales list, or a plantation's slave list is a clear and unequivocal indication that the individual slave was a Muslim. However, as many slaves were renamed in the Americas with Christian names and as not all African Muslims had identifiable Muslim names, one cannot just rely upon this first consideration. A second and quite important consideration has to do with the slave's tribal affiliation. Tribal affiliation was occasionally noted in various written records pertaining to the slaves. Thus, if a slave was a member of the Mandinka, Hausa, Fulani, or another one of the known Muslim tribes, it can be reasonably inferred that the slave was probably a Muslim, with the probability varying according to the percentage of Muslims in that particular tribe. Finally, in some cases neither a slave's African name nor his African tribal affiliation is known. In such cases, the general location in Africa from which the slave was taken is frequently known. If the slave was taken from West Africa, the probability of the slave being a Muslim would be higher than if the slave came from the Congo region.

Based upon these three considerations, scholars have offered a variety of estimates as to the percentage of African slaves who were Muslims. As was the case in estimating the total number of African slaves brought to the New World, earlier estimates tend to be lower than more contemporary ones. For example, writing in 1984, Austin estimated that as many as 10% of all slaves transported from West Africa (from where over half of all slaves in North America originated) were Muslims. Writing about 14 years later, Diouf estimated that 15-20% of all imported African slaves were Muslims. In part, Diouf had revised the estimate upward based upon such considerations as: (1) 29% of the Africans living in Mexico in 1549 were from such tribes as the Wolof, Tukulor, or Mandinka, all of which were known to be heavily Muslim; (2) 15% of the African slaves in Peru between 1560 and 1650 were from the Wolof, Mandinka, Fulani, and Susu tribes; (3) 30% of the slaves imported into South Carolina between 1733 and 1807 were from Muslim-dominated West Africa; (4) 58% of the slaves brought to Virginia between 1710 and 1769 were from West Africa; (5) about 67% of the slaves imported into Louisiana by the French were from Senegambia in West Africa; and (6) just over 46% of all slaves brought to North America appear to have originated in areas of West Africa with a significant Muslim presence. However, just five years after Diouf's scholarly analysis, Ahmed revised the estimate upward, suggesting that 30% of all imported African slaves were Muslims.

At the present time, it appears safe to conclude that 20-30% of all African slaves imported to the New World were Muslims. Given an estimated 15-20 million African slaves brought to the Americas, this suggests that somewhere between three and six million African Muslims were enslaved in the Americas.

As previously noted, approximately 65% of the African slaves brought to the Americas were men. However, it appears that among the Muslim slaves, the percentage of women was far less than the 30-35% found in the imported slave population as a whole. In part, this finding reflects the traditional Islamic attitude concerning the protection of women at all costs. For example, Diouf has estimated that only 15-20% of the Muslims enslaved in the Americas were women.

D3. WHO WERE THE MUSLIM SLAVES

An unfortunate stereotype has long existed in the United States that the African slaves brought to this country were simply illiterate, uneducated savages who were devoid of any civilization. In part, this erroneous stereotype may have been perpetrated to bolster the equally erroneous claim that the African slaves were actually better off living in American slavery than in African freedom. However fallacious this stereotype was in portraying African slaves in general, it was even more misleading and malicious when applied to Muslim slaves.

Consistent with the basic teachings of Islam, education was highly emphasized throughout Muslim West Africa. As previously reported in chapter II, Timbuktu was one of West Africa's great academic centers. Located in present-day Mali, Timbuktu was graced with numerous libraries (even some private libraries held more than 700 volumes), a multitude of schools (well over 150 during the 16th century), and a famous university (the Jam'iyyah located in the Sankore Mosque) that attracted students and scholars from as far away as Arabia. Between the 14th century and the end of the transatlantic slave trade, the academic institutions of Timbuktu trained literally thousands upon thousands of students in Islamic studies, the Arabic language, literary style, rhetoric, logic, history, mathematics, astronomy, philosophy, and cartography.

However, Timbuktu was hardly the only educational star dotting the sky of Muslim West Africa. Kano, Nigeria, had about 3,000 teachers at the end of the 15th century. The Fulani tribe of Bundu (in contemporary Senegal) had established schools in every city. By the end of the 19th century, 60% of the people of Senegal were literate in Arabic. In fact, throughout the period of the transatlantic slave trade, a clear majority of the Muslims of West Africa were literate and educated, including an estimated 20% of Muslim females. Further, almost all members of the Mandinka tribe could read and write.

In contrast to the successful state of education in Muslim West Africa during the 16th through 18th centuries, the vast majority of Europeans and Americans were totally illiterate. Further, the literacy rate among European and American females was almost non-existent and was substantially lower than the 20% literacy rate found among Muslim females in West Africa. While a liberal financial aid system assured the Mandinka of Timbuktu a free or nearly free education for those among them who could not afford to pay for their own learning, the United States did not emphasize mass education and literacy until the beginning of the 19th century. Even as late as 1828, it was estimated that more Africans in Senegal were literate in Arabic, which was for them a second language, than were French peasants in French.

In summary, the enslaved Muslims who were brought to the Americas were as a group a highly educated people for the times. Most of them were literate in at least Arabic, and it has been estimated that the percentage of literacy in Arabic among African slaves in America was actually higher than the percentage of literacy in English among their owners. Most of the Muslim slaves were at least bilingual (Arabic and their native African language). Some of them were even trilingual or better, having previously learned Turkish or one or another of the European languages.

Prior to their enslavement, almost all of these African Muslims had previously studied the *Qur'an*, and some had even become familiar while yet in Africa with major sections of the *Bible*, specifically including the *Pentateuch*, *Psalms*, and *New Testament* gospels. In addition, some of these African Muslims had previously studied Plato, Aristotle, and Hippocrates during their educations in Africa. Finally, it should be noted that several museums in the American South continue to house Arabic manuscripts written by these African Muslims. A perusal of those manuscripts reveals parts or all of the *Qur'an* and even whole books of Islamic jurisprudence that had been previously memorized when these Muslim slaves were studying in Africa. Years later, some of these Muslim slaves had still retained enough of their education to pen these volumes from memory!

So, who were these highly educated, Muslim slaves in America? To answer that question, one needs to appreciate which people were the most vulnerable to being captured as slaves in Africa. This entails a brief look back into Africa and to the African people who were most at risk for enslavement

As a general rule, there were two groups of people who were most at risk for being enslaved. Given that one of the primary pathways to enslavement was being taken as a prisoner of war, it should come as no surprise that many of the enslaved Muslims taken to America were professional military officers, government officials, and princes of their realms. As a group, they were highly trained and educated personnel. The other group that was at high risk was comprised of those people who were engaged in extensive and often solitary travel. Given the nature of the West African educational system, those most likely to be engaged in extensive, solitary travel were scholars and professional educators. These academics frequently traveled long distances to acquire additional knowledge and to teach what they had already learned. Among this group of enslaved Muslims, one finds numerous individuals who had a college education and not a few who had the equivalence of an advanced university degree (master's degree or doctorate). Within their ranks were lawyers, teachers, professors, and *Imams* (Muslim prayer leaders and religious scholars).

As noted earlier in this chapter, only about 15-20% of the African Muslims enslaved in the Americas were women. In contrast, about 30-35% of all African slaves in America were women. It has been suggested that one reason for this relatively low percentage of Muslim women being enslaved had to do with the traditional Islamic attitude concerning the protection of women. Having now reviewed the two primary pathways to enslavement in Africa, one can now also note that it would be highly unlikely for Muslim women to be engaged in actual warfare or to be engaged in solitary travel over significant distances. These factors also contributed to the relatively low percentage of Muslim women who were enslaved in the Americas.

D4. LIFE FOR MUSLIM SLAVES IN AMERICA [32]

Upon reaching the shores of America, Muslim slaves from Africa were subjected to all the degradations, humiliations, and hardships as other African slaves. Whether an African slave was a Muslim or a pagan, he lived a dangerous, precarious, and often unnaturally brief existence in America. However, as a Muslim, an African slave in the Americas also suffered from several hardships not shared by his non-Muslim counterparts. In addressing this two-pronged attack on the Muslim slaves in the New World, we will begin by focusing on what

32. Much of the information in this section is from Hellie R (2003) and Diouf SA (1998).

life was generally like for most, if not all, African slaves in the Americas, regardless of religious affiliation. Having completed that review, we will then look at those special hardships that were reserved for African Muslims.

We can begin our review of slave life by considering the legal structure governing slavery in the Americas. For most of the colonies in the Americas, the laws governing slavery were based upon existing slave laws in the colonists' home country back in Europe. Thus, the Spanish colonies in the New World based their slavery laws on the Siete Partidas of 1263-65 and the Spanish Slave Code of 1789. Likewise, the French colonies could look back to the 1685 Code Noir of Louis XIV.

However, there were no laws governing the institution of slavery in England, and thus the English colonies of the New World were free to create their own laws out of whole cloth. In fact, there were no laws governing the institution of slavery in the English colonies until the island of Barbados enacted its first code in 1688, fully 187 years after the European powers first brought slaves to the Americas. Until then, slave owners in Barbados were completely free to treat their slaves in whatever way they desired. Fifty-two years later, in 1740, South Carolina based its slave laws on that of Barbados. Each of the remaining 13 colonies of what would later form the United States was left to its own devices to create its own laws governing slavery.

To understand the nature of these slave laws and to appreciate the horrors they inflicted upon the enslaved, one needs only to review a few laws and court decisions emanating out of the American South. (1) South Carolina laws stipulated that a slave was outside the "peace of the state." Therefore, the "peace of the state" was in no wise disturbed or broken by any physical assault and battery upon a slave. One can only cringe at the license this sort of reasoning gave to one set of humans to abuse another set of humans. (2) In the 1860 Alabama case of Creswell's Executor v. Walter, the court ruled that a slave had no legal mind or will that the law could recognize and that a slave was inherently incapable of performing civil acts. (3) The Louisiana Code of 1824 specifically noted that a slave had no right to be married. (4) Throughout the American South, a slave had no legal right to own any sort of property (as all a slave possessed was automatically the property of his owner) and was forbidden to marry outside his or her own race. (5) Manumission or the freeing of a slave was actually legally prohibited by South Carolina in 1820, Mississippi in 1822, Arkansas in 1858, and Maryland and Alabama in 1860. (6) Finally, in the American South prior to 1830, the various laws governing slavery typically failed to address such crucial issues as how long at a time an owner could work his slave and whether a slave had any right to food and clothing.

Having noted the above, it must be admitted that the Louisiana Black Code of 1806 made it a crime to punish a slave in a cruel and unusual manner. Further, across the American South, 10 different slavery laws prescribed forced sale to another owner or emancipation of a maltreated slave. Unfortunately, these laws were seldom enforced and were worth very little more than the paper on which they were written. Thus, the 1839 case of North Carolina v. Hoover and the 1843 case of Alabama v. Jones were considered sensational, because the courts had the temerity to punish the slave owners for beating their slaves to death. The reaction to these two court cases illustrates that a slaveholder could kill his slave at any time and for any reason in many parts of the southern United States.

Given that slaves in the American South were forbidden to marry outside their race, the preponderance of male slaves, about 65-70% of the slave population, had no chance to marry. Additionally, even in those cases where slaves did marry and have families, the slave owners in the American South would often destroy the marriages and nuclear families of their slaves by selling off a spouse, parent, or child. Still further, the raping of female slaves by their white owners and white overseers was a not uncommon phenomenon that added still more difficulties to the establishment of marriages and families among the slaves. Finally, with the legal end of African slave importation to the United States on January 1, 1808, southern slaveholders had to find new ways to maintain and increase their supply of slaves. This they often did by breeding their slaves together as though their slaves were merely herds of cattle. Just as the slave owner would select prize bulls to be mated to cows, he might select the strongest of his male slaves to impregnate the owner's "herd" of female slaves. That this procedure was effective can be demonstrated by turning to official United States census figures, which show that the slave population of the American South rose from 657,327 to 3,838,765 between 1790 and 1860.

As noted previously, there were generally no laws in the American South stipulating the limits of how hard a slaveholder might work his slaves. Thus, slave owners often literally worked their slaves to death, reasoning that it was cheaper to buy new slaves than to limit their work load and to pay for their slaves' basic and reasonable sustenance. This was especially the case with field hands who had passed the prime of their working lives.

Given the very real danger of being worked to death, a definite hierarchy existed in the slave work force in the southern United States. Slaves with the easiest jobs, and thus the best chance of continuing to live, were domestic servants. Next in line were those slaves who worked as carpenters, masons, tailors, etc. Lowest on the totem pole and with the lowest life expectancy were the field hands. Among the field hands, those who worked growing tobacco were still substantially better off than those who toiled in the more labor-intensive sugar and cotton industries. However, no matter the skills and abilities of those slaves held in the American South, slaves were prohibited from performing various jobs that would allow any demonstration of their true capabilities and intelligence.

A slave was generally allotted only two sets of clothing per year. Such clothing was almost always made from the cheapest fabric, which was invariably coarse, uncomfortable, and ill-suited for the slave's climate and working environment. However, some slave owners simply refused to dress their slaves at all, thus lowering the financial cost of their upkeep. That such conditions existed with some frequency can be attested to by the number of runaway slave notices that described the fugitives as having absconded either entirely naked or with only a rag tied around their waists. In the face of such conditions, the slaves either went naked or bought their own clothes with money earned from: hiring themselves out at night; selling the results of their nighttime gardening, hunting, and fishing; etc. In at least one instance, a slave owner justified his refusal to clothe his slaves by arguing that it made no more sense than it would to clothe cattle, donkeys, and dogs.

Charles Bell, a slave born in the Americas, vividly described the dress of some of his fellow slaves. He described an elderly man whose only clothing was an old shirt that hung in tatters from his neck and arms. Two young girls were dressed only in petticoats. An adult female's clothing only consisted of a frontless shirt and a piece of an old cotton bag tied around her loins. A boy was entirely naked.

The degradations experienced by slaves through the lack of proper clothing were not always just the reflection of the individual slave owner's greed, sadism, and/or sexual vice. At times, these degradations were a matter of law. For example, several locations in the Americas prohibited slaves from wearing their owner's cast-off clothing or any clothing whose fabric, colors, and shape suggested clothing suitable for whites. In 1830, Surinam even went so far as to pass a law that prohibited female slaves from wearing any clothing above the waist.

Overworked, underfed, under-clothed, and occasionally undergoing punishments that could include up to 1,000 lashes with a whip and being burned at the stake, the African slaves held in the Americas, especially those who experienced the barbarities of the slave system in the American South, were treated as little more than highly expendable beasts of burden. To illustrate that point, consider the following facts and figures. At the end of the 18th century, the typical slave in the southern United States made about $257 a year for his owner. In exchange, the owner generally spent only about $13 a year on the food, clothing, and general upkeep of his slave. Given the sum total of the above, it should come as no surprise that the average life expectancy of a slave was only 15 years. If the slave labored in harsh climates and under a particularly heavy work load, his life expectancy could fall to as low as six years.

D5. Special Hardships for Muslim Slaves

Those slaves who were Muslims experienced all of the same depravities as their non-Muslim counterparts. However, as Muslims, they were also afflicted with some discrete hardships that their fellow slaves were spared. In what follows, a few of those burdens that were often unique to Muslims are examined.

Islam prescribes five pillars of religious practice: the *Shahadah* or testimonial of faith; saying the five daily prayers at their appointed times; *Sawm* or fasting during the lunar month of *Ramadan*; paying *Zakat* (obligatory charity) out of one's economic surplus; and making the *Hajj* pilgrimage to Makkah during its appointed time at least once during one's lifetime, if one is financially and physically capable of performing this act. Typically, slavery did not interfere with saying the testimonial of faith upon accepting Islam. Likewise, slavery did not prevent the paying of obligatory charity, as a slave had no economic surplus from which to pay it. However, slavery in the Americas did infringe upon the other three pillars of religious practice.

The five mandatory times of prayer in Islam are just before sunrise, shortly after true noon, shortly after the halfway point between true noon and sunset, shortly after sunset, and after the fullness of night. Furthermore, a Muslim must make ritual ablution before saying these prayers. The work schedule of a slave in the Americas drastically curtailed a Muslim slave's ability to say the second, the third, and sometimes the fourth daily prayers. One can well imagine the fury of the Muslim slave's white, Christian overseer or owner upon being informed by the slave of the need to take a 10-minute break in the middle of the cotton harvest in order to make ablution and to offer a non-Christian prayer! Even today, Muslims often experience difficulty in the American workforce with finding time to or with being allowed to say their prayers. Just imagine the difficulties faced by the Muslim slave.

Fasting during the lunar month of *Ramadan* is another pillar of religious practice that was particularly difficult for Muslim slaves in the Americas. Throughout the entire month, Muslims are to fast between the start of dawn and sunset. During this time, they are neither to eat nor drink. (Various exceptions to the *Ramadan* fast exist for children and for those who are ill, pregnant, nursing, or traveling. However, unless the exception is a chronic condition, those days of fasting that were skipped are to be made up later in the year.) Given the physically demanding nature of slavery and the meager rations typically given to slaves in the first place, the Muslim slave could literally endanger his own life by fasting during *Ramadan*. While this risk could grant the slave a legitimate exception from fasting, having to forego the *Ramadan* fast was yet another assault on the Muslim slave's practice of his religion.

The pilgrimage to Makkah and the performance of the rites of the *Hajj* pilgrimage is a pillar of religious practice that is conditional on the individual Muslim having the economic and physical wherewithal to make the pilgrimage. Obviously, an enslaved Muslim in America had neither the physical freedom nor the financial means to make the *Hajj* pilgrimage. As such, he was relieved of the obligation to perform the *Hajj*, but at the cost of being denied one of the most spiritually uplifting experiences any Muslim may encounter.

However, it was not just in the performance of the five pillars of religious practice that the Muslim slave encountered hardships not shared by his non-Muslim counterparts. Nor was it the case that the Muslim slave only experienced an infringement upon his religious life when it came to performing three of the pillars of Islamic religious practice. Islam is not just the performance of five religious rituals; it is an all-encompassing way of life that Muslim slaves were often prevented from practicing.

For example, all Muslims are enjoined to read and study the *Qur'an*, Islam's book of revealed scripture. For those Muslim slaves who had memorized the entire *Qur'an*, enslavement in the Americas had little impact on their ability to reflect and meditate on the divine message contained in the *Qur'an*, so long as they were not so fatigued from overwork that they could not refrain from falling asleep. However, most Muslim slaves in the New World had not memorized the entirety of the *Qur'an*. For them, securing a copy of the *Qur'an* was a major issue. Some of them were able to get a fellow slave to write out the *Qur'an* from memory, but that meant securing the finances to be able to buy the requisite pen, ink, and paper. Some of them, especially those in parts of South America, were able to buy a copy of the *Qur'an* from merchants who traded with Muslim West Africa. However, that meant having the financial resources to make the purchase. In a very few instances, Muslim slaves were given copies of the *Qur'an* by sympathetic Christians. As for the rest of the Muslims enslaved in the Americas, they were forced to rely on their recollections of those parts of the *Qur'an* that they had previously memorized in Africa. In short, most of the Muslims enslaved in the Americas were prevented from having access to their primary religious guide and source of spiritual inspiration. For them, this loss would have been impossible to overestimate.

A further interference in the Muslim slaves' practice of Islam concerns dietary restrictions. As previously noted, slaveholders fed their slaves a very meager ration in an effort to minimize costs. As a result, slaves received little meat in their diet. When meat was given to them, it was typically the cheapest meat available, which was invariably pork. Just as does Judaism, Islam prohibits the eating of pork.

> He hath only forbidden you dead meat (carrion), and blood, and the flesh of swine, and that on which any other name hath been invoked besides that of God. But if one is forced by necessity, without willful disobedience, nor transgressing due limits—then is he guiltless. For God is oft-forgiving, most merciful.
>
> (Qur'an 2:173)

> Forbidden to you (for food) are: dead meat (carrion), blood, the flesh of swine, and that on which hath been invoked the name of other than God...But if any is forced by hunger, with no inclination to transgression, God is indeed oft-forgiving, most merciful.
>
> (Qur'an 5:3)

> Say: "I find not in the message received by me by inspiration any (meat) forbidden to be eaten by one who wishes to eat it, unless it be dead meat (carrion), or blood poured forth, or the flesh of swine—for it is an abomination—or what is impious, (meat) on which a name has been invoked other than God's." But (even so), if a person is forced by necessity, without willful disobedience, nor transgressing due limits—thy Lord is oft-forgiving, most merciful.
>
> (Qur'an 6:145)

He has only forbidden you dead meat (carrion), and blood, and the flesh of swine, and any (food) over which the name of other than God has been invoked. But if one is forced by necessity, without willful disobedience, nor transgressing due limits—then God is oft-forgiving, most merciful.

(Qur'an 16:115)

As can be seen, all four of the above Qur'anic passages forbid the eating of pork, but each of them allows an exception in the case of real necessity. Certainly, the conditions in which most Muslim slaves were kept would appear to meet the "necessity threshold test." Nonetheless, some Muslim slaves refrained from eating the occasional pork allotted to them and instead supplemented their diets by fishing and hunting at night, thus depriving themselves of much needed sleep. Even for those Muslims who ate the pork under the stipulated exception of necessity, the very act of eating the pork was often experienced as shameful and disgusting.

Another hardship for Muslim slaves was the conditions of nudity or near nudity in which many slaves were kept. Islam mandates modesty in dress for both men and women. The lack of adequate clothing to cover oneself was thus an especially heavy burden for Muslim slaves to bear. As such and where possible, Muslim slaves were once again driven to doing extra work or to gardening or hunting on the side, in order to raise the money to buy enough material to insure modest dress. Where acquiring some money was not possible, Muslim slaves had to endure the special indignity of exposing themselves in ways that are specifically forbidden by their religion.

As previously noted, Muslim slaves who were imported from Africa to America enjoyed an exceptionally high rate of literacy and education. One the one hand, they had the opportunity to use their knowledge and intelligence to try to secure slave jobs that were less physically demanding. As such, their education could be a distinct advantage to them. On the other hand, literacy by a slave was often illegal and was almost always strongly discouraged. Therefore, Muslim slaves often had to be extremely careful in how much of their knowledge and education they displayed. As these Muslim slaves were often much better educated than their owners, too much of a show of education and literacy could easily be perceived as an arrogant affront or threat. It could even be seen as a direct refutation of the "Biblically-sanctioned" theory of inherent white superiority in which their owners believed. In either case, the end result could be severe and debilitating punishment or even death.

It has already been noted that only about 15-20% of all the Muslims sent to the New World as slaves were women. This presented major problems for enslaved Muslim males who wished to marry, as Muslim males are only permitted to marry other Muslims and "People of the Book," i.e., basically Jews and Christians.

> (Lawful unto you in marriage) are (not only) chaste women who are believers, but chaste women among the People of the Book.
>
> *(Qur'an 5:5)*

With women accounting for only 15-20% of all Muslim slaves in the Americas, with no known Jews to be found among the African slaves in the New World, and with African slaves converting to Christianity only after some prolonged existence in America, this left the vast majority of Muslim males without a potential spouse acceptable to the teachings of Islam. As such, the loss of marital potential was a burden disproportionately carried by Muslim slaves.

For those Muslim slaves who were able to marry, an issue confronting them was how and if they were going to be able to educate their children in the basic tenets of Islam. Throughout certain parts of South America, such education was possible at times. In pre-1835 Bahia, a semi-autonomous Muslim community in Brazil, former African schoolteachers and religious leaders were sometimes able to educate Muslim youth in Arabic, *Qur'an*, and the fundamentals of Islam. Known Muslim teachers in Bahia include: (1) Dandara, an emancipated Muslim and former schoolteacher from the Hausa tribe; (2) Aprigio, a free Muslim; (3) Sanim, an enslaved member of the Nupe tribe and former schoolteacher, who gave lessons in the home of Belchior da Silva Cunha, a bricklayer and freed Muslim of the Nago tribe; and (4) Dassalu (Mamadu), Nicobe (Suleyman), and Gustard (Ibrahima), three enslaved members of the Nago tribe. From what is now known, it appears that these homemade schools were equipped with written texts, writing slates, and other classroom paraphernalia. These Islamic schools were able to function until 1835 in Bahia, even though the practice of Islam was technically illegal in Brazil.

In marked contrast to what had been achieved in Bahia, very little educational opportunity was available to Muslim children enslaved in the American South. Both enslaved adults and children were overworked, and there was precious little free time for Muslim parents to engage in the education of their children. Complicating the process still further, teaching a slave to read and write was illegal throughout much of the South, and basic school supplies were next to non-existent. Thus, Muslim parents had to think long and hard about bringing children into the world, knowing that they would probably not be able to educate their children in their Islamic faith. This dilemma may help account for the fact that about half of the well-known Muslim slaves in the Americas did not have children.

As can be seen from the above, African Muslims enslaved in the Americas had a whole range of special difficulties confronting them when it came to the maintenance of their Islamic faith. Mosques had to be secretly constructed, maintained, and staffed. Lunar calendars had to be kept to keep track of *Ramadan* and Islamic holidays, all of which are based on a lunar calendar not used in the New World. Circumcisions, weddings, and funerals had to be conducted according to Islamic traditions, while remaining hidden from the awareness of those non-Muslims who might report the proceedings. Dietary restrictions and fasting had to be maintained where possible. Mandatory prayers had to be said. All of these requirements placed special burdens on enslaved Muslims with regard to the maintenance of their Islamic heritage.

One final hardship faced the enslaved Muslims in America. While manumission or emancipation was always difficult to achieve and was almost impossible to get in many parts of the American South, conversion to the slave owner's Christianity was almost a requirement for any hope of being freed. This placed enormous pressure on the enslaved Muslim to convert to Christianity, at least publicly. As a result, the Americas produced their own equivalents of the Moriscos of Spain, i.e., Muslims who continued to practice their Islam in privacy and in secret, but who publicly professed to be Christians. The need to maintain this public façade placed even more burdens on the Muslim parent when it came to the issue of educating his children.

D6. Conclusions and Summary

Despite the enormous pressures placed on Muslim slaves in the Americas, the available historical records indicate that almost none of them actually left their Islamic faith. However, in many cases, these devout Muslims were unable to pass along their Islam to their descendants. As such, it has been estimated that the true Islam brought to the Americas from Africa did not outlive the death of the last of the emancipated Africans circa 1920-1930. Nonetheless, as will be seen in chapter VII, Islamic residuals from these enslaved Muslims left a significant residual within the African-American community, culture, and religious life.

E. The Muslim Role in Slave Revolts

E1. Introduction

Given the conditions in which slaves were kept in the Americas, it is small wonder that these slaves would occasionally rise up in revolt against their owners. Despite the overwhelming odds against the success of any slave rebellion, there are several examples of slave rebellions occurring in both North and South America. Common to most of these slave rebellions was the prominent role of Muslim slaves.

To have any chance, however remote, of being successful, a slave rebellion had to be properly organized and coordinated across the slaves of many owners. Further, some basic military knowledge was needed. These considerations necessitated a great deal of organizational skill on the part of the slaves, a military background, and the ability to communicate secretly with each other across long distances. With regard to meeting these three requirements, the role of Muslims was absolutely crucial.

As noted previously, many enslaved Muslims in the Americas had been professional soldiers back in Africa. These Muslim slaves had the requisite military background and experience to lead a slave army in revolt. Further, both as former military personnel and as former religious leaders and teachers, highly educated Muslim slaves were a crucial part of the organization and coordination needed in any slave rebellion. Finally, having become literate in both oral and written Arabic while in Africa, Muslim slaves played an indispensable part in achieving the needed level of secret communication across long distances.

With regard to the role of Muslim slaves in maintaining secret communication prior to and during a slave rebellion, the benefits of their skills in oral and written Arabic cannot be overstated. Two issues come into play when considering this point. (1) The various African slaves in the Americas came from a variety of tribal backgrounds, each with its own distinct dialect or language. The only common language that could unite these slaves while still remaining unintelligible to their white owners and overseers was Arabic. (2) Through the medium of written Arabic penned on scraps of cloth or paper, the slaves of one plantation were able to communicate, plan, and coordinate their efforts with slaves of a different plantation. If the written message was intercepted by non-Muslims, it would remain indecipherable and would probably be seen as the illiterate scribbling of some African charm or incantation.

In what follows, the role of Muslim slaves in several slave rebellions is presented. In each case, the slave revolt is briefly reviewed, and then the role of Muslim slaves in that rebellion is highlighted.

E2. The *Amistad* Revolt

The *Amistad* slave revolt was largely popularized by Steven Spielberg's 1997 movie of the same name. While a box office hit, the movie was a highly fictionalized account of the slave revolt that occurred onboard a Spanish schooner, the *Amistad*. Among the movie's most glaring errors was the short shrift given to the role of Muslims in the slaves' successful revolt.

In March or April of 1839, a shipment of African slaves aboard the *Tecora* began the long and painful journey from the slave holding center at Lomboko to Cuba. The shipment was unusual in that so many of the Africans were women and children. However, there was at least one thing the enslaved inhabitants of the *Tecora* had in common with almost all other slave shipments. Along the way, the unspeakable brutalities of the Middle Passage were inflicted upon the enslaved Africans. For most of the voyage, they were kept shackled to each other below deck in a hold that was only four feet high. They were beaten and flogged, and some of them had vinegar and gunpowder rubbed into their wounds. While they were given more than ample supplies of rice to eat, they were given very little water and were tormented by constant thirst. Moreover, they were forced to eat all the rice they were given upon pain of whippings. At times they were forced to eat to the point of vomiting. Many of the Africans died during the *Tecora*'s crossing of the Middle Passage.

Upon reaching Cuba in June, the Africans were unloaded from the *Tecora* at a small village near Havana under the cover of night, as Spain had technically outlawed the transport of slaves from Africa in 1820. Having been covertly landed in Cuba, 49 African men were quickly purchased for working in the sugar cane fields by a Jose Ruiz at a price of $450 per person, and four children (three girls and a boy) were purchased by a Pedro Montes. These 53 slaves were then taken through Havana in the dead of night to the *Amistad*.

During the night of June 26, 1839, Montes, Ruiz, three Spanish crewmen, two slaves owned by the captain of the *Amistad*, and the 53 African slaves boarded the *Amistad*, which set sail on June 27th for the three-day journey to Puerto Principe, Cuba. Over and above the 53 enslaved Africans, the *Amistad* carried a cargo of dishes, cloth, jewelry, etc., all of which was insured for $40,000. Ruiz insured his 49 enslaved Africans for $20,000, while Montez insured the four enslaved children for $1,300.

The 53 Africans were immediately placed in chains and were shackled about the hands, feet, and neck. Shortly after setting sail, the *Amistad* encountered adverse winds that threatened to more than double the expected length of the trip. As such, strict rationing of an already meager food supply was begun for the African slaves. Short of water and food and subjected to continuing whippings, the frightened Africans pondered their fate.

On July 2, 1839, Cinque, one of the slaves, managed to extract a loose nail from the ship. Using the nail, he picked the lock on his shackles and then freed his fellow slaves. Using stealth, the slaves liberated a quantity of sugarcane knives from the ship's hold and then attacked the crew. The captain and cook were killed, one of the captain's slaves and the two slave owners were taken prisoner, and the two Spanish crewmembers fled overboard into a small boat and escaped. Two of the previously enslaved Africans were killed in the liberation of the *Amistad*.

In exchange for their lives, Montes and Ruiz promised to sail the slaves back to Africa. However, they deceived the slaves by sailing generally eastward during the day, but sailing north and west at night. The navigational deceit of Montes and Ruiz was also aided by a gale that blew up along the way and that drove the *Amistad* northeast along the coast of the United States. A trip that was supposed to have been one of only three days gradually became one that lasted for almost two months. Already short of food and water before the slave revolt, the situation quickly became intolerable, and an additional eight Africans died during this phase of the journey.

On August 26, 1839, the U.S. Coast Guard survey brig, the *Washington*, under the command of Lt. Commander Thomas R. Gedney, intercepted and captured the *Amistad* off Culloden Point, Long Island, New York. Rather inexplicably, the *Washington* did not deliver the *Amistad* to New York authorities but took the *Amistad* to the much more distant New London, Connecticut, where the slaves were arrested for piracy and for murdering the two crew members. (Of note, slavery was not legal in New York but was in Connecticut. The insured market value of the 53 African slaves was $21,300, and the officers of the Washington put in a salvage claim on the value of the African slaves in the Connecticut court system.)

Civil and criminal trials soon followed. In mid January of 1840, Judge Hudson found in favor of the defendants, i.e., the African slaves, and ordered that they be returned to Africa as free men. This decision was immediately appealed. In September of 1840, Judge Thompson of the Circuit Court upheld the District Court decision. This decision was also appealed. Finally, in February and March of 1841, the *Amistad* case was argued before the U.S. Supreme Court, with the Africans being represented by Roger Baldwin and Congressman John Quincy Adams, the former sixth president of the United States. On March 9, 1841, the Supreme Court upheld the lower court decisions and ordered the Africans to be freed immediately.

Throughout their imprisonment, the Africans had been tutored in the basics of the English language and in Christianity by students from the Yale Divinity School. All of the Africans were made to read the four *New Testament* gospels. This process did not end upon the rendering of the Supreme Court decision. Before the Africans were returned to their homes in West Africa, they were made to endure a further course of studies in the English language and in Christianity and to do public speaking to help raise money for their passage home. This additional period of instruction lasted from March into November of 1841. In November, the 35 surviving Africans (several of those apprehended off Long Island had died in prison captivity) were finally boarded onto the *Gentleman* for the return trip to Africa. Their passage had been at least partially paid for by a Christian missionary society, which sent along missionaries to establish a Christian mission in West Africa and which expected the Africans to work with the missionaries in converting other Africans to Christianity. In January of 1842, the *Gentleman* arrived at Freetown, Sierra Leone. Most of the Africans immediately deserted the missionaries and returned to their prior way of life and religion.

There is substantial evidence that many, if not most, of the Africans aboard the *Amistad* were Muslims. For example, one of the *Amistad* Africans, Ba-u, reported that his father was a *Marabout* (a West African term for a Muslim teacher, religious leader, and "holy" man) back in Africa. He further noted that it was customary in his country for men to have to pay a dowry for their brides and that he had paid 10 cloths, one goat, one gun, and numerous mats for his wife. The use of a dowry system was seconded by another of the *Amistad* Africans, Ndzha-gnwaw-ni or Nga-ho-ni, who noted that he had given 20 cloths and one shawl as a dowry for his wife. Both of these statements appear to be examples of the Islamic practice of *Mahr*, the dowry that must be paid to the bride by a Muslim husband upon their marriage.

Additional confirmation of a significant Muslim presence aboard the *Amistad* comes from Richard Robert Madden. A native of Ireland who had previously served the British government in the Gold Coast area of West Africa, in Kingston, Jamaica, and in Havana, Cuba, Madden testified in Connecticut on behalf of the *Amistad* Africans on November 11, 1839, and later reported that several of the Africans were familiar with such Arabic greetings and statements as "*Salam 'Alaykum*" (peace be upon you) and "*Allahu Akbar*" (God is greater). This in itself is ample testimony to the fact that Muslims were part of the *Amistad* uprising. However, Madden went on to note that when he began to recite what he referred to as a "Muslim prayer" in Arabic, he was immediately joined in that recitation by one of the *Amistad* defendants.[33]

To the above information supporting an ample Muslim presence aboard the *Amistad*, one can add the following details supplied in a September 9, 1839, letter written by Lewis Tappan, the chief abolitionist in helping to free the *Amistad* slaves. Tappan reported that he visited the African prisoners in their cells after they had been provided with Western clothing. He noted that: the three females, two of whom were Mandinka, wore calico frocks and had tied the little shawls given them into turbans;

---

33. Diouf SA (1998).

most of the men had been circumcised, according to the report of the physician who examined them; and most of the slaves were Mandinka.[34]

All three of Tappan's observations indicate a substantial Muslim presence aboard the *Amistad*. Firstly, the reference to the turbans is most enlightening, as Diouf has noted that the only women in Africa who wore turbans were Muslims. Secondly, male circumcision is mandatory among Muslims. Thirdly, as previously established in this chapter, almost all of the Mandinka were Muslims.

E3. THE HAITIAN AND DOMINICAN REVOLTS[35]

With Haiti now situated on its western side and the Dominican Republic now on its eastern side, the island of Hispaniola was one of the earliest European colonies in the Americas. Christopher Columbus first saw the island of Quisqueya on December 6, 1492, and renamed it La Isla Espanola (the Spanish Island), from which we get its current name of Hispaniola. The Spanish initially colonized Hispaniola in 1494, making it their first permanent settlement in the New World.

When the Spanish first arrived on Hispaniola, there was a population of between 100,000 and several million Indians of the Taino and Ciboney tribes. The Spanish quickly enslaved these Indians and forced them to work for them in mining for gold. The working conditions of these enslaved Indians can only be described as brutal beyond belief. By 1514, only 20 years after the Spanish had initially colonized Hispaniola, barbaric working conditions and exposure to European diseases had reduced the Indian population to around only 30,000. Throughout the remainder of the 16th century, the Indian population was almost totally exterminated.

---

34. Tappan L (1839).

35. Information in this

Given the high morbidity rate among the enslaved Indians, the Spanish quickly began importing African slaves to fill the void. Even though the gold mines rapidly played out, the slave trade continued unabated. African slaves were used to clear the forest to make way for new sugar fields and to raise the livestock that the Spanish and later French colonists brought to the island. In fact, the island of Hispaniola became so dependent upon African slaves that a 1789 population estimate concluded that Saint-Dominique (the western third of the island, corresponding to modern Haiti, which was transferred from Spain to France in the Treaty of Rijswijk in 1697) housed 32,000 European colonists, 24,000 freed mulattos or blacks, and 500,000 African slaves.

The huge disparity in numbers between Europeans and enslaved Africans helped make Hispaniola a particularly fertile breeding ground for slave revolts. However, two other factors were also at play. On the one hand, the African slaves on Hispaniola appear to have had an unusually high percentage of Muslims among them, which greatly aided the slaves' ability to organize and communicate secretly with each other through oral and written Arabic. On the other hand, beginning as early as the start of the 16th century, the European colonists had specifically requested the importation of slaves who had a background in handling livestock.

This latter consideration was unusual in the course of the transatlantic slave trade. While many African slaves were used throughout the New World in agricultural pursuits, those pursuits were typically ones that involved raising crops. Unlike white slaveholders elsewhere in the Americas, the European colonists of Hispaniola wanted slaves who had experience working with cattle and horses. The slave traders fulfilled that specific demand by sending wave after wave of Africans who had been enslaved as prisoners of war and who were captured cavalrymen of the Muslim kingdoms of West Africa. Thus, Hispaniola was soon stocked with a contingent of African slaves who had extensive military training and who had the requisite knowledge to deal with cavalry attacks.

One of the ways that the early European colonists were able to hold a much larger population of slaves in bondage was through the use of cavalry. A fierce cavalry charge by the Europeans was usually all that it took to instill absolute panic in a numerically superior force of rebelling slaves. Needless to say, such would not be the case when the slaves being charged were predominantly comprised of professional cavalrymen.

With this background in mind, we can better appreciate the events of the first of a series of Haitian slave revolts. In 1522, the enslaved Wolof, a predominantly Muslim tribe of Africans, rose up in revolt on the plantation of Don Diego Colon, the son of Christopher Columbus. The enslaved Wolof quickly defeated the Spanish forces at Colon's plantation and then spread their revolt from one plantation to another. When the Spanish tried the usually successful tactic of sending a cavalry charge into the midst of rebelling slaves, the Wolof did not panic and flee. Instead, as trained cavalrymen who knew the ins and outs of a mounted military engagement, they simply stood their ground, opened their ranks to allow the cavalry to pass through them, and then closed ranks and did an about face to meet the coming countercharge.

The Spanish were never completely able to subdue the Wolof rebellion. While they were eventually able to reestablish their control over the sugar plantations, the Wolof simply withdrew to the mountains of the interior, where they established their own independent communities in relative freedom. These communities and the Africans who lived within them came to be known as Maroons. Using horses captured from the Spanish, the Wolof Maroons established their own cavalry to serve as a defense for their oases of freedom in the New World. Over the next several decades, the Wolof Maroons continued to raid and plunder the plantations of the Spanish colonists. In writing to his Spanish king, one colonist described these Wolof Maroons as being constantly on horseback and as being skilled and daring in both the cavalry charge and the use of the cavalryman's lance.

While the Wolof revolt of 1522 was the first slave rebellion to shake the European grip on Hispaniola it was hardly the last. A second series of slave revolts began in the middle of the 18th century and eventually led to the formation of an independent Haiti on January 1, 1804. However, this time it was not Spain who bore the brunt of the slave rebellion. Spain had ceded the western third of Hispaniola to France in the 1697 Treaty of Rijswijk and the remainder of Hispaniola in the 1795 Treaty of Basel. Thus, it was from the French army of Napoleon Bonaparte that the slaves of Haiti won their independence.

Following the transfer of the western third of Hispaniola to France in 1697, Saint-Dominique, as the French third of Hispaniola was then called, quickly became France's most lucrative colony. However, massive turmoil and ongoing slave rebellions were always present. Maroon communities had existed ever since the revolt of 1522 and were constantly being enlarged by escaping African slaves, many of whom were Muslim. From advertisements and notices about runaway slaves, it can be concluded that an average of 1,000 African slaves was escaping every year. In perusing these advertisements, one is confronted by numerous Muslim names, e.g. Ayyoub, 'Ali, Sulayman, Yahya, Bilali, Fatima, etc. Further, some of these notices specifically mentioned that the slave in question was fluent in Arabic.

Beginning in the mid 18th century and continuing up until the time of the Haitian Revolution (1791-1804), numerous Muslims led Maroon uprisings against the French. Prior to his execution in September of 1787, a Muslim Maroon named Yahya (also called Gillot) led a group of Maroon rebels in rebellion throughout the parishes of Trou and Terrier Rouge. An African Muslim named Halaou led an army of thousands of Maroons in the Cul-de-Sac region. However, the most feared of the Muslim Maroons in the mid 18th century was Francois Macandal.

Macandal was an African Muslim, had been born in Guinea, and appears to have been a member of the Mandinka tribe. He had been highly educated in Arabic while in West Africa and was probably a *Marabout* (a West African term for a Muslim teacher, religious leader, and "holy" man). In 1740, having previously lost a hand in a sugar mill accident, Macandal escaped from his owner and fled to the Maroon communities of the mountainous interior. Not content with just living out his life as a free man, Macandal sought to free all the enslaved Africans on Hispaniola. His long term plans called for an independent Haiti ruled by Africans and their descendants. To this end, he organized a group of Maroons, taught them the making and use of poison, and led his cohorts out of the mountains to make frequent and devastating raids on the European plantations. He was so successful as a revolutionary leader that it has been estimated that Macandal and his followers were responsible for the deaths of 6,000 of his enemies just during the last three years of his life. Macandal was finally captured and burned at the stake on January 20, 1758. To this day, Macandal remains a figure of near mythic proportions in Haitian history.

Another Muslim who became a legend in the Haitian drive towards independence was a slave known only as Boukman (man of the Book, a West African description of a Muslim whose book is the *Qur'an*). Very little is known about Boukman and his origins, and he has often been misidentified as being a voodoo priest. However, it is known that he was imported to Haiti from Jamaica. During the night of August 14, 1791, Boukman gathered a large number of slaves together in the forest in the area of Bois-Caiman. In an impassioned speech, Boukman rallied Maroons and his fellow slaves to fight for freedom and independence by denouncing the Europeans' god, a god who inflicted tears and suffering on the enslaved Africans. In contrast, he noted that the God of the slaves was good and had ordered the slaves to seek their freedom in armed combat. Within one week, Boukman and his followers had laid waste to 200 sugar plantations and 1,800 coffee plantations. Approximately 1,000 slave owners had been killed. Boukman continued to lead his army of Maroons until being shot and killed in November of 1791.

E4. The Bahia Revolts[36]

Bahia is a large province in eastern Brazil that was first visited by Portuguese explorers on the Christian holiday of All Saints' Day, November 1, 1501. The Portuguese sailed into the bay on which the city of Salvador now stands and named it Baia de Todos os Santos or All-Saints' Bay. Up until 1823, Bahia was ruled by Portugal. The

---

36. Much of the information in this section is from Diouf SA (1998).

independent Empire of Brazil had been declared one year earlier, but forces loyal to Portugal continued to control Bahia until July 2, 1823.

From the 16th through parts of the 19th century, Bahia was a major importer of African slaves. Beginning around the start of the 19th century, enslaved Muslims became an increasingly numerous part of the transatlantic slave trade with Bahia. Especially large numbers of enslaved members of the Hausa, Fulani, and Yoruba or Nago tribes, all of which were primarily Muslim, began entering Bahia around that time. For example, 8,307 members of the Hausa, Nago, and Ewe tribes were imported into Bahia as slaves in just the single year of 1807. With the number of enslaved Muslims in Bahia growing rapidly, the stage was set for a series of slave rebellions.

On December 26, 1808, a large number of Hausa and Nago slaves escaped from their sugar plantations. They were soon joined by a second group of escaped slaves, and together they attacked the town of Nazare das Farinhas. Although the slave rebellion received a defeat at Nazare das Farinhas and about 100 slaves were taken prisoner, the survivors among the escaped slaves continued to launch guerilla warfare attacks against the European colonists for several months.

A second slave revolt began on February 28, 1814. Under the command of a *Marabout* from the Hausa tribe, about 600 Africans attacked the town of Itapoan. Although poorly armed, the Africans killed 14 whites while losing 58 of their own men, mostly members of the Hausa tribe.

In March of 1814, yet a third slave rebellion was launched. Between 1816 and 1830, at least 17 slave revolts transpired in Bahia, with Muslims being the leaders in five of these revolts and being participants in all of them. For example, on April 10, 1830, 20 members of the Yoruba or Nago tribe attacked a hardware store and equipped themselves with swords and knives. Although poorly armed, the Nago rebels immediately attacked a slave market, freeing the Africans who were to be auctioned off. Now fortified with these new additions to their ranks, the rebels numbered over 100 members and attacked a police station. Eventually, the rebels were attacked by men with rifles, and the rebellion came to an end.

On January 25, 1835, the month of *Ramadan* in the lunar calendar of Islam, over 500 Africans dressed in white with the turban head coverings of African Muslims took over the urban corridors of the city of Bahia. They were primarily armed with knives, lances, and swords, but a few had managed to acquire pistols. Having gained temporary control of the streets, they attacked the city jail and national guard and police barracks and fought against cavalry. By the end of the day, 70 Africans and about six whites were dead. Within the next few months, over 500 Africans had been tried for their part in the rebellion—199 from the Nago tribe, 31 from the Hausa, 10 from the Ewe, 13 from the Bornu, etc. Of these, 18 were sentenced to death, but only four members of the Nago tribe were actually executed. These four were executed by a military firing squad. The other 14 were not killed, because the ruling whites of Bahia could not find any slaves willing to carry out the hangman's task on them, regardless of the rewards offered or the punishments threatened. Another 45 Africans were sentenced to the awful brutality of 1,000 lashes, 50 per day across 20 scattered days. One of these 45 died from the whippings he received.

The post mortem that was conducted by the ruling whites after the January 25, 1835, revolt indicated that the enslaved Muslims of Bahia had been exceptionally well organized. They had previously created mosques and Islamic schools about which the whites of Bahia had no knowledge, and they had been secretly educating the young and those not previously educated in Africa in Arabic, Qur'anic studies, and Islam for quite some time.

E5. Summary and Postscript[37]

As the educated, professional, and military elite among the enslaved Africans sent to the Americas, Muslims comprised a key component of the best organized and most successful of the slave revolts. They were also frequently the leaders of those revolts. Examples such as the *Amistad* revolt, the Haitian revolts, and the revolts in Bahia help to illustrate those facts.

As a postscript, it should be noted that the European colonists and colonial powers soon came to recognize that highly educated African Muslims presented their own unique set of difficulties as slave labor. As noted previously, these enslaved Muslims were prone to uprisings and rebellions, which threatened the security of the European colonies and the safety of the European slaveholders. Furthermore, escaped Muslim slaves were seen to present a substantial risk of interfering with Christian missionaries' efforts among the American Indians. There was a very real fear that runaway Muslim slaves would be successful in preaching Islam to the Indians and that the Indians would elect to become Muslims instead of Christians. Finally, the Europeans were afraid that escaped Muslim slaves would incite the Indians to rebellion against the Europeans.

These fears of Muslims inciting the Indians to rebel were well grounded in fact, as illustrated by joint African and Indian revolts in Hispaniola between 1522 and 1532, in Mexico in 1523, in Cuba in 1529, in Panama between 1550 and 1582, in Venezuela in 1550, in

---

37.. Most of the information in this section is from Diouf SA (1998).

Peru in 1560, in Ecuador in 1599, in Guatemala in 1627, in Chile in 1647, in Martinique in 1650, and in Florida in 1830-1840. While each of these revolts was eventually quelled, the Spanish consistently blamed the Muslims for their incitement. As such, the Spanish quickly made it a major crime for an African to be among the Indians. Just how serious of a threat did the Spanish consider a Muslim to be when with the Indians can be illustrated by the case of Pedro Gilofo, an enslaved Wolof who joined up with the Indians. When found in an Indian village in Costa Rica, he was sentenced to death on September 1, 1540, by being boiled alive.

As can be seen, the Spanish colonists of the New World were threatened in multiple ways by the African Muslims they enslaved. Slave rebellions led by Muslims, Muslims interfering with Christian proselytizing among the American Indians, and escaped Muslim slaves inciting the Indians to rebellion were all very real concerns to the European colonists. Not surprisingly, these considerations quickly led to a series of successive and ineffective attempts to limit the immigration of additional Muslims to the Americas.

The first such attempt to limit the importation of enslaved Muslims to the New World occurred on September 16, 1501. On that date, King Fernando issued a royal decree to Sir Nicolas Ovando, in which the king ordered Ovando not to allow any Muslims to enter the Spanish colonies. More specifically, the king's decree stressed that the only African slaves that should be allowed into the colonies were those who were not Muslims. This royal decree was for all intents and purposes ignored.

On May 11, 1526, having experienced the 1522 rebellion of Wolof Muslims in Hispaniola, a Spanish royal decree singled out the Wolof

Muslims as being especially difficult to keep enslaved, noted how prone to rebellion they were, and thus prohibited their future import to the New World. This royal decree also forbade the importation of African slaves from the Middle East, slaves from Guinea, and slaves that had been raised with Moors (North African Muslims). In short, the decree attempted to stop the flow of Muslims to the Americas.

Unfortunately for the named groups of Muslims, this royal decree was also basically ignored, and the transatlantic slave trade of African Muslims continued. As such, another Spanish royal decree was issued in 1531. This decree labeled the Muslim Wolof as being disobedient and rebellious, and the importation of the Wolof, Moriscos, and other Muslims to the Americas was once again banned. In particular, the decree singled out the Moriscos as being especially dangerous.

This royal decree from Spain was also consistently violated. The economics of the slave trade were just too lucrative an enticement to slave traders, and the flow of African Muslims imported into the New World as slaves continued unabated. In response, Spain issued yet another law on August 14, 1543, and again another law on July 16, 1550, both of which prohibited the importation of Muslims and Moriscos to the Spanish colonies. Again, these laws were largely ineffective in stemming the flow of enslaved Muslims to the Americas.

F. SOME BRIEF BIOGRAPHIES

F1. INTRODUCRION

As can be imagined, the institution of slavery in the Americas was not conducive to the preservation of detailed, biographical information on enslaved African Muslims. Nonetheless, as many of these Muslims were highly educated and literate individuals, some left autobiographical sketches, and others came to the attention of whites who chose to write a brief account about them. All in all, a surprising amount of information has survived to the present time, although one always has to remember that these enslaved African Muslims were writing and talking in an environment that was hostile both to themselves and to their Islamic religion. As such, one suspects that they were quite circumspect about some topics and were under constant pressure to portray themselves as more Christian and less Muslim than they actually were.

In what follows, a series of brief biographies is presented. In each case, the biography is of an African Muslim who was once enslaved in the Americas. In some cases, the available information is quite minimal. In other cases, the information is more extensive. Unless otherwise referenced, the information contained in these biographies is taken from Austin's *African Muslims in Antebellum America: Transatlantic Stories and Spiritual Struggles* and from Diouf's *Servants of Allah: African Muslims Enslaved in the Americas.*

F2. BALL'S MUSLIM

Known only as Ball's Muslim, the little information available on him is that found in a short, nineteen-page biography written by Charles Ball in 1854 and entitled *The Man Who Prayed Five Times A Day.* From this brief biography, we know that Ball's Muslim was an enslaved African and that he came from a desert country with no trees or grass—probably Mali. He appears to have been a member of the Tuareg tribe.

Ball's Muslim reported being captured in war and marched to the Gambia River early in the 19th century. Reaching the Gambia, he saw white men for the first time and was placed on a boat where he witnessed three babies being thrown overboard, their desperate mothers jumping in after them. He also noted that many of his fellow enslaved Africans died from heat and inadequate food on the boat ride down the river and during the Middle Passage. According to his report, about 33% of the enslaved Africans aboard his ship died before reaching Charleston, SC. His own ordeal on the ship had been one of such crowding and confinement that upon arriving in Charleston, SC, circa 1807, he was unable to stand or to straighten his arms and legs for a week. Despite being enslaved in South Carolina, he continued to perform his five obligatory prayers every day.

F3. KUNTA KINTE[38]

Kairaba Kunta Kinte was a member of the Mandinka tribe and a *Marabout* (West African term for a Muslim teacher, religious leader, and "holy" man) who migrated within West Africa from Mauretania to Gambia. His family lineage stretched back to the old Mandinka kingdom of Mali. Late in the 17th century, he arrived in the village of Juffure along the Kamby Bolongo (Gambia River) to discover the village suffering from an acute drought that had left many villagers dead. The *Marabout* immediately began the Muslim prayers for rain and continued praying for five straight days. At the end of that time, the skies opened and the rains began.

Kairaba remained in Juffure and married twice. He had two sons by his first wife and one son, Omoro, by his second wife, Yaisa. Omoro Kinte married Binta, and they had four successive sons: Kunta, the oldest and born in 1750; Lamin, the second; Suwadu, the third; and Madi. All four sons were born and raised in Juffure, and all received their education in Arabic and the *Qur'an* at the local village school.

---

38. Information relating to Kunta Kinte is from Haley A (1976).

One day in 1767, when he was only 16 years old, Kunta Kinte left the village and entered the jungle to cut wood to make a drum. While thus engaged, he was jumped by four men. Kunta was restrained and marched to a British ship, the *Lord Ligonier*, commanded by a Captain Davies. The *Lord Ligonier* sailed out of the Gambia River on July 5, 1767, and docked at Annapolis, Maryland, on September 29, 1767. This Middle Passage voyage had been long and gruesome. Out of the 140 enslaved Africans who had began the journey in the hold of the ship, only 98 were still alive when the ship reached Annapolis, a fatality rate of 30%.

Kunta Kinte was soon sold at the slave auction in Annapolis to a John Waller of Spotsylvania County, Virginia, and was given the slave name of Toby. As a proud Mandinka Muslim, Kunta did not take easily to being enslaved and ran away four times during his first year of captivity. Alone and not speaking English, he was quickly recaptured after each escape. After the fourth escape, he was given a choice between two punishments, castration or amputation of a foot. He chose the latter.

With one foot ruthlessly amputated, Kunta was kept alive by the kindly ministrations of Dr. William Waller, the brother of Kunta's owner. Enraged at the maiming of Kunta, Dr. Waller purchased Kunta from John Waller on September 5, 1768. Kunta was then moved to Dr. Waller's plantation on the Mattaponi River. Having only one foot, Kunta was given the relatively easy work of tending to the plantation's vegetable garden.

As an enslaved Muslim in the American South, Kunta did his best to maintain the performance of his five obligatory prayers every day, and he continued to practice his Arabic by scratching Arabic phrases in the dirt. Eventually, he married a woman known as "Bell, the bighouse cook." The marriage produced a daughter, Kizzy, who received some instruction from her father in the Mandinka language and in the basics of Islam.

At age 16, Kizzy was sold to a Tom Lea in North Carolina. Having been raped by her owner, Kizzy had a son, George. George later gained some renown as a trainer of fighting game cocks and thus received the nickname of Chicken George. A surviving photograph of Chicken George in the archives of the Collections and Stories of American Muslims depicts an African-American male in what can only be described as typical Muslim dress. Apparently, the Islam of Kunta Kinte survived into at least his second generation of descendants.

F4. MHOMET (MUHAMMAD)[39]

All that is known about this enslaved Muslim is the information obtained from an advertisement in the *Savannah Georgia Gazette* on September 7, 1774. The brief runaway notice stated that Mahomet ran away from a plantation on Augustin's Creek in 1771. He was described as being short, well made, and pitted with smallpox scars. It was further noted that a runaway slave matching his description had been observed by a settlement near the Indian Line on Ogechee. A reward of 10 pounds sterling was offered for his return, and a reward of 20 pounds was offered for information leading to the arrest and conviction of those who might have been harboring him.

F5. THE MOOR

Known to us only as The Moor, this enslaved African Muslim was the son of a Muslim prince on the Niger River and was perhaps a member of the Fulbe (plural = Fulbe or Fulani; singular = Fula) tribe. He was

---

39. Information on Mahomet is from Muhammad ANA (2001).

captured in war, enslaved, taken to the coast of West Africa, and transported on a Spanish ship to New Orleans in 1812, four years after the last slaves legally entered the United States. The Moor lived and worked along the Mississippi River. Interviewed in 1822, he wrote the first *Surah* (chapter) of the *Qur'an* in Arabic and commented that the people in his home country in Africa were more literate and educated than Americans were. He reported having a wife, bitterly protested having to eat pork in order to survive, and denied ever using alcohol. As can be seen by his statements, The Moor did his best to continue practicing his Islamic faith even while being enslaved in the American South.

F6. S'QUASH

S'Quash was an enslaved African Muslim who arrived aboard a slave ship in Charleston, South Carolina, in December of 1807, the last month for the legal importation of slaves into the United States. He was said to have been a large and muscular man and to have been removed from the ship hog-tied and heavily guarded. S'Quash was purchased by Joseph Graham and later rose through the ranks of the Grahams' slaves to become the overseer of the Grahams' plantation in South Carolina. As such, he ascended to the highest level to which a slave could aspire in the American South. Later, he helped relocate the Grahams and their slaves to Mississippi.

It was noted that other slaves on the plantation paid great respect to S'Quash, but he held himself above them and refused to live with them, probably because they were not fellow Muslims. Likewise, he refused to marry until he found a woman whom he felt was a suitable bride, who was said to have been a Dinka (probably a Mandinka and a Muslim). S'Quash was said to have been an excellent horseman and literate in both Arabic and Greek! He was described as having been extremely dark, although not a "Negro."

This latter description of S'Quash reflects the prejudices of the ante-bellum American South. Southerners felt that Africans were inherently inferior to whites. As such, when they encountered an African slave who was literate, was educated beyond their own abilities, and demonstrated superior intellectual and moral qualities, they were quick to maintain that the slave could not possibly be an African but had to be an Arab or a Moor.

F7. PHILIP THE FULA

Little is known about this enslaved African Muslim. He was briefly remembered by Joseph LeConte as having been an old African and a practicing Muslim. LeConte described Philip as going through the various positions of a Muslim's five daily prayers and as having been a very intelligent man. LeConte further recorded Philip's manner of counting from one to twenty. The words employed for these numerals identify Philip as having been a member of the Fulbe (Fula = singular; Fulbe or Fulani = plural).

F8. SAMBO

In 1805, an otherwise unknown slave named Sambo (probably Samba, i.e., the second son in a family) was said to be able to write Arabic and to have runaway with three other slaves. His literacy in Arabic identifies him as having been a Muslim.

F9. MAHOMMAH GARDO BAQUAQUA

Mahommah Gardo Baquaqua's father was a member of the Songhai (later called Dendi) tribe, and his mother was from the Hausa tribe. Mahommah was born circa 1830 in Djougou, a large city in northern Dahomey (contemporary Benin). He was indulged as a child, had been a disinterested student at best, and had failed to learn and practice his Islamic faith as a devout Muslim. Nonetheless, he had managed to learn to read and write some Arabic.

As a youth, he was apprenticed to a maternal uncle who was a blacksmith. However, the uncle soon died, and Mahommah apparently benefited little from his brief education in the blacksmith trade. Subsequently, he was captured during a war in Daboya, released through the efforts of his brother, and became the servant of a minor, non-Muslim chief through the efforts of his mother. While in the service of the non-Muslim chief, Mahommah began to violate the Islamic prohibition on alcohol and developed a taste for palm wine, a weakness that caused his later enslavement.

Circa 1846, while on a journey to visit his mother in Djougou, he fell in with a bad lot, became drunk, and awoke to find himself shanghaied as a slave. He was sold three times before completing the 350-mile journey to the African coast and was forced to march in long slave caravans, in which each slave's neck was fastened with tree limbs and iron bolts to the slave's neck in front of him. Arriving at the African coast, Mahommah saw a ship for the first time and mistakenly thought it was an idol that the white man worshipped. Before being boarded on the ship, Mahommah and his fellow slaves were herded into a pen, made to sit with their backs to a roaring fire, and were then branded with a white hot iron so that each slave could be readily identified as the property of a particular slave trader. He was then shaved, stripped completely naked, and forced into the hold of the ship.

Over the length of the voyage, Mahommah and his fellow slaves had to share their hold, which was too low for them to stand, with the ever accumulating amounts of human excrement and vomit from the seasick slaves. They were only allowed to go on deck and wash twice, the second time right before making port. Food and water were scarce, consisting only of small servings of some boiled grain and one pint of water per day, and beatings and death were a daily occurrence. Needless to say, Mahommah's recollection of his Middle Passage was a loathsome memory that remained with him throughout his life. The ship finally docked in Pernambuco in northern Brazil. Mahommah later recalled that he didn't even care that he was a slave, because he was just so glad to have escaped alive from the filth and brutality of the ship.

Mahommah's initial owner in Brazil was a baker. Mahommah initially tried to be a serious and conscientious worker, helping to build a stone house, hawking his owner's breads, and avoiding alcohol. However, he soon found out that this brought him little profit, and he tried to runaway. Quickly captured, he then began backsliding, worked less, and reacquired his taste for alcohol. Having become a less industrious slave, Mahommah was then beaten. He then attempted suicide by jumping into a river, but he was pulled from the river, given another beating for his efforts, and sold to a plantation owner.

Almost immediately upon his arrival at his new owner's Brazilian plantation, Mahommah and his fellow slaves were lined up behind the owner's family, both family and slaves facing clay statues. They were then forced to kneel, chant Christian rituals in a tongue they did not understand, and cross themselves repeatedly at set times. Any inattention to or disinclination to perform this forced Catholic ritual was met with an immediate lashing by the owner's whip. In short, Mahommah and his fellow slaves were forcibly "converted" to Christianity without even knowing what was transpiring.

Mahommah's stay with the plantation owner was short lived, and he was sent to Rio de Janeiro, where he was purchased by a sea captain. He began his service to the sea captain as a brass polisher but then rose through the ranks to under steward and then to steward. Despite his promotions, Mahommah was often severely punished by the captain and the ship's mate, with one beating leaving him barely clinging to life.

Mahommah's last voyage with his owner/captain was in 1848. The ship docked in New York City with a load of coffee, and Mahommah escaped into the city. He was quickly captured and returned to the ship, but his escape had come to the attention of some New York lawyers who had him hauled off to jail. Once in jail, he was physically rescued by some apparent abolitionists who smuggled him off to Boston, where he was given the choice of finding safety in either England or Haiti. Mahommah chose the latter.

In Haiti, Mahommah experienced significant difficulty, because he did not know the local language. Eventually, he came to the attention of some Christian missionaries, Mr. and Mrs. William L. Judd, who helped him. In what appears to have been an opportunistic conversion at best, Mahommah was baptized into the Baptist faith in 1849, claiming that he wanted to be a Christian missionary to Africa. Perhaps, it was the only way he knew to obtain passage back to his home.

In any case, the Judds bought into Mahommah's claim and sent him off to Central College in McGrawville, New York, where he was sponsored by the American Free Baptist Missionary Society and where he was ostensibly studying to become a Christian missionary. From around 1850 to 1853, Mahommah continued his studies at Central College. He subsequently journeyed to Canada and then moved to

Detroit, Michigan, where he wrote his autobiography in 1854. By February of 1857, he was in England, apparently still seeking a way back to his native Africa. Thereafter, he is lost from the pages of history.

The backsliding of Mahommah from his Islamic faith and heritage appears to have been unusual among African Muslims enslaved in the Americas. Perhaps, it was simply a reflection of his poor understanding and mastery of Islam as a student back in Africa. However, before rushing to an overly quick and harsh judgment, it should be noted that in his October 26, 1853, letter to George Whipple, the secretary of the American Missionary Society of the Congregational Church, Mahommah inexplicably penned three words in Arabic, which appear to be a poorly written and half forgotten rendition of the *Bismillah*, i.e., in the name of Allah, the Most Gracious, the Most Merciful. The actual Arabic words written by Mahommah correspond to "Allah, Allah, most ever."

Perhaps, Mahommah, like some other African Muslims, had simply undergone a sham conversion to Christianity in order to find sponsors to pay for his return to Africa.

F10. LAMINE KEBE

Lamine Kebe's father was a member of the Serahule or Soninke tribe, and his mother was from the Mandinka. Following his father's lineage, he was born into the Jakhanke clan of the Serahule tribe of Futa Jallon circa 1765-1775. The Jakhanke clan of the Serahule was known for its scholars, schoolteachers, and anti-militaristic interpretations of Islam. His childhood family was fairly affluent and consisted of many schoolteachers, both men and women.

Between the ages of seven and 14, Lamine attended his hometown school with 55 to 57 other pupils. During this phase of his education, he received instruction in Qur'anic studies (both memorization of the Arabic text and translation and commentary in his native Serahule language), Arabic, and 30 handwritten textbooks, the latter of which included books of grammar, *Fiqh* (Islamic jurisprudence), *Sunnah* (the sayings and actions of Prophet Muhammad), theology, poetry, etc. He noted that his education was thoroughly bilingual and that the Serahule schools were provided by the government, with separate classes for boys and girls. He apparently was an exemplary student and memorized the entire *Qur'an* by age 14.

He was then sent to Bundu, over 900 miles away from his hometown, where he spent an additional seven years completing his higher education. Whether in his hometown primary school or at Bundu, he received instruction in the *Bible*, later stating to an American interviewer that he studied a handwritten copy of the *Torah*. He supplemented his formal education by traveling rather extensively during his youth, undertaking at least two journeys to the Jaliba or Niger River

After completing his education, he served as a schoolteacher for five years in the city of Kebe or Kaba. He subsequently married and had three children.

When he was about 30 years old and while he was on the return portion of a paper-buying trip to either Timbuktu (Mali) or Timbo (Guinea), he was surrounded while he slept one night, placed in shackles, and enslaved. Details about his voyage to America are basically lacking. However, he probably was shipped out of Africa from the Kaba River of Guinea. Later, he once referred to the Middle Passage as his journey over the "bitter water."

Upon reaching America, he was bought and sold several times by multiple owners. He ended up spending 30 to 40 years in American slavery across three Southern states, including Georgia. Throughout his enslavement, he was known by the slave name of "Old Paul." In 1834, he was finally freed by his last Christian owner and moved to New York to seek help in paying for his return passage to Africa.

In New York, he apparently hooked up with the American Colonization Society (ACS), an organization dedicated to sending freed Africans and African Americans back to Liberia, Africa. Later that year, he was referred to in *The African Repository* as a scholar who was literate in Arabic and familiar with the *Bible* in his own (Arabic?) language. (His familiarity with the *Bible* must have been gained during his Islamic education in Africa, because the article went on to say that he was unaware that the printing press had ever been invented, suggesting that his knowledge of the *Bible* was from the handwritten, Arabic manuscripts that he had studied during his youth.) Over the course of the next year, he occasionally spoke at various fundraising meetings organized by the ACS and similar organizations. During this time, he also carried on an Arabic correspondence with 'Umar ibn Said, whose own biography is presented later.

Despite his efforts on their behalf, the American Colonization Society did not send him back to Africa until he began making statements in 1835 that he wanted to bring Christianity back to Africa. Finally, the ACS sent him to Liberia, which was about 500 miles from his original home. In an apparent reference to him, the August, 19, 1835, list of passengers immigrating to Liberia on the *Indiana* includes the name of a 60-year-old "Paul A. Mandingo." (Old Paul was Lamine's slave name, and his mother was a Mandinka.) The list goes on to say that he had been born free, was literate, and was from Georgia, one of the southern states in which Lamine had been enslaved. Upon reaching Liberia, he quickly left for Sierra Leone, and nothing else is known about his later life.

Before closing this section on the life of Lamine Kebe, two brief postscripts are in order. (1) An 1835 description of Lamine by Theodore Dwight noted that he was six feet tall, friendly, dignified, simple in his demeanor, and a devout Muslim, belying Lamine's report that he wished to be a Christian missionary in Africa. Unfortunately, feigning to be a Christian who wished to proselytize in Africa was often the only recourse open to an enslaved African Muslim who wished to be emancipated and to return back home to Africa. (2) Lamine's instructive observations on the comparative teaching methods utilized in America and in West Africa were recorded by Theodore Dwight and later published in 1836 in *The American Annals of Education and Instruction*. They provide an enlightening look into the educational system of the Serahule in the late 18th century.

F11. MUHAMMAD KABA[40]

Muhammad Kaba was born circa 1758 in Bouna (Bouka), a short distance east of Timbo in Futa Jallon (Guinea). He was a member of the Mandinka tribe and was obviously well schooled as a youth in Africa. His teachers were his father, 'Abd Al-Qadir, and an uncle, Muhammad Batul. His father was quite wealthy and owned cows, horses, extensive farm lands, and about 140 slaves. His uncle was a locally famous lawyer or *Al-Faqih* (scholar of *Fiqh*, i.e., Islamic jurisprudence). Under their tutelage, he gained fluency in both Arabic and his native language, completed

---

40. The information on Muhammad Kaba from Austin AD (1997) and Diouf SA (1998) has been supplemented by information contained in Curtin PD (1968).

his primary education, and had entered higher education, where he was studying to be an *Al-Faqih* like his uncle. Like many other enslaved African Muslims, he was a highly educated individual.

He was kidnapped at age 20 in 1778 by a band of robbers, taken to the coast, and sold to Europeans. He was then shipped to Jamaica and given the slave names of Robert Tuffit and Robert Peate. He eventually married and spent the next 56 years as a slave. Circa 1814, after around 36 years of slavery and being about 56 years old at the time, he publicly converted to Christianity. For the remainder of his life, he presented the outward appearance of being a Christian, a facade which undoubtedly lightened the burdens his Christian owners placed on him as he entered old age. However, the reality of his religious affiliation can be seen in his 1834 correspondence from Manchester Parish, Jamaica, to Abu Bakr Al-Saddiq, whose biography is presented later, upon the latter's emancipation.

Having heard that Abu Bakr had gained his freedom, Muhammad took pen in hand to write him a letter in Arabic. He then entrusted the letter for delivery to a B. Angell, a European Christian, stressing that the letter was meant to convince Abu Bakr to renounce Islam and to accept Christianity. However, a translation of the actual text of the letter begins "In the name of Allah, the Merciful, the Omnificent, the blessing of Allah, the peace of His prophet Muhammad." Within the text of the letter, there is absolutely no mention of Christianity or of Abu Bakr abandoning Islam.

In referring to this letter, Richard Robert Madden, a British magistrate in Jamaica and a witness for the defense in the famous *Amistad* court case, noted that Muhammad's conversion to Christianity had obviously been a sham, which was designed to lighten the burdens that his owner placed on him. While outwardly pretending to be a Christian, he used his ability to write Arabic to maintain an Islamic correspondence with a fellow Muslim, a correspondence that would remain undecipherable if it fell into the hands of almost all Christians on the island.

F12. ANDERSON'S SLAVE

Very little is known about this enslaved African Muslim. Both his African and slave names have been lost to recorded history. What is known is that he was a Muslim from the Mandinka tribe, that he received an education in Arabic and Qur'anic studies while in Africa, and that he was owned by a Captain David Anderson in South Carolina. In 1768, Anderson's slave wrote two pages in Arabic, which came to the attention of American whites. The pages contained *Surat* (chapters) 1, 112, 113, and 114 from the *Qur'an*.

F13. LAMINE NDIAYE[41]

Lamine Ndiaye was a Muslim from the Wolof tribe and was originally from Futa-Toro, Senegal. In Africa, he worked both as a merchant-trader and as a linguist or translator. Given these occupations, it appears that Lamine was fairly well educated.

In 1730, he was doing some trading on the lower Gambia River when he was employed as a translator by Ayuba ibn Suleyman ibn Ibrahim Diallo, whose biography is presented later. Lamine and Ayuba were subsequently kidnapped on the south bank of the lower Gambia, sold to a Captain Pike, who was in the employ of a William Hunt, a merchant in London, England. The transaction took place on February 27, 1730, and Lamine and Ayuba were shipped to America within a week of their purchase on the *Arabella*.

---

41. The information on Lamine Ndiaye provided by Austin AD (1995) and Diouf SA (1998) has been supplemented with information from Curtin PD (1968).

Arriving in Annapolis, Maryland, in 1730, Lamine first came under the control of Vachell Denton, the slave agent in Maryland for William Hunt. He was then purchased by a southern plantation owner. He was apparently given the slave name of Lamine Jay and was sent out to work as a common field hand, one of the lowest and most back-breaking jobs in the hierarchy of slave labor. For the next seven years, he toiled in that capacity.

However, all was not lost. Lamine's former employer Ayuba gained his freedom in 1734 and traveled to England, preparatory to his return to Africa. While in England, Ayuba exerted what influence he had to get the Duke of Montague to provide the money for Lamine's purchase. Using the funds provided by the Duke of Montague, Thomas Bluett managed to locate Lamine on a Maryland plantation, purchased him, and then emancipated him in 1737. After journeying from America to England, Lamine returned home to Gambia in February of 1738. In Africa, Lamine briefly traveled with Melchior de Jaspas of the Royal African Company on the latter's journey to Bundu. Thereafter, nothing is known about him.

Ayuba's efforts on behalf of Lamine illustrate a theme that will be more fully developed later, i.e., that of formerly enslaved Muslims helping other Muslims to obtain their freedom from slavery.

F14. YARROW (YORO) MAMOUT

Yarrow Mamout was born in Africa, either circa 1686 (his own self-report) or circa 1707 (his one-time American owner's report). In either case, he arrived in Maryland circa 1731 and was purchased by the Bell family, for whom he worked making bricks. After helping to build his owner's home in Georgetown, Yarrow was emancipated by the Bells.

As a freed African Muslim living in Catholic Maryland, Yarrow was of some interest to several of his white neighbors and associates. It is chiefly through their observations that we know him. According to their reports, he was a diligent worker and successful businessman, despite having limited skills in English. He even managed to own his own home. Although some historians have maintained that he never married or had children, the 1820 census for Washington, DC, lists a "Yarrow Marmood" as having a family.[42]

Of more importance than his economic success was his character, personal conduct, and continued adherence to his religion of Islam. He was known for his honesty, sobriety, good temper, jocularity, and cheerful conduct. He reportedly was well liked by everyone who knew him. Even though living in the midst of an ocean of Roman Catholicism, he was often publicly observed singing praises to Allah. No matter where he was, even in the public street, and no matter what he was doing, he would stop to perform the five obligatory prayers of Islam every day. To the end of his life, he followed Islamic dietary restrictions and avoided all pork and alcohol. Further, he advised others to do the same.

In 1819, Yarrow came to the attention of Charles Wilson Peale, the renowned portrait artist. Yarrow agreed to sit for Peale, and the resulting portrait is currently owned by the Historical Society of Pennsylvania. An examination of that portrait reveals an ancient and modestly attired gentleman wearing a typical head covering for a West African Muslim. At the time of the portrait, Yarrow claimed to be 133 years old, although his former owner thought that he was only about 112!

---

42. Muhammad ANA (2001).

F.15. WILLIAM RAINESFORD

William Rainesford was a Muslim from the Mandinka tribe. He was enslaved and taken to Jamaica, where he was forcibly baptized in the Christian faith. Later, he was to write portions of the *Qur'an* in Arabic from memory.

On October 2, 1834, he was one of four Mandinka in Jamaica who sent a letter to the Irish abolitionist, Richard Robert Madden, one of the British magistrates in Kingston, Jamaica. The letter offered a comparison between Christianity and the Islamic religion of the Mandinka. Needless to say, the four Mandinka Muslims were particularly scathing in drawing their comparisons. Among other things, they observed that Islam honors freedom of religious choice and all of the books of revelation sent by Allah to mankind, including the *Torah*, gospel, and *Qur'an*. In contrast, they perceived Christians to be intolerant of revelations and religions other than their own, their own forcible baptisms being a case in point. In addition, they noted that Islam teaches charity and compassion to the poor, while the Christians they had observed were prone to exploiting the poor.

F16. CHARLES LARTEN

Charles Larten, his slave name, was a Mandinka who had been highly educated in Arabic and Qur'anic studies while in Africa. By the time he had completed his education, he had memorized the entire *Qur'an* in Arabic. He was enslaved and forcibly baptized into the Christian faith in Jamaica. Nonetheless, he remained a Muslim and later wrote the complete *Qur'an* in Arabic from memory. He was one of the four signatories to the October 2, 1834, letter to Richard Robert Madden (see under the entry for William Rainesford).

F17. ANNA MUSA (BENJAMIN COCHRANE)

Anna Musa was born into a prominent family of the Kassonke tribe of Mali. His father was a dignitary and leader who was referred to as "a lord in the (Kassonke) nation." Anna Musa was highly educated and was trained as a medical doctor in Africa. In addition, he had extensive experience as a soldier in Africa, having been a member of several military campaigns.

He was captured, enslaved, and shipped off to the Caribbean, where he was given the slave name of Benjamin Cochrane and forcibly baptized into the Christian faith in Jamaica. Anna Musa quickly discovered that a Muslim slave might enjoy some benefits from his owner by pretending to be a Christian, and he thereafter typically maintained a Christian façade in public. Throughout his enslavement, he variously served owners in Tortola, Barbados, and Jamaica. In addition, he fought for British West India regiments and on British battleships. By 1834, he was a practicing physician in Kingston, Jamaica, but was denied admission to the college of medicine.

He was one of the four signatories to the October 2, 1834, letter (see under the entry for William Rainesford) to Richard Robert Madden, the British magistrate in Kingston, Jamaica. Of note, Madden narrated a particularly insightful encounter that he had with Anna Musa, the publicly professed Christian. One day when he was being visited by Anna Musa and two other African slaves who professed publicly to be Christians, Madden happened to repeat the *Shahadah*, i.e., the Islamic testimonial of faith, which when translated from Arabic into English may be rendered as "I testify that there is no god but Allah and that Muhammad is His messenger." Madden later wrote that he no sooner had gotten those Arabic words out of his mouth than he was surrounded by three Muslims fervently chanting Islamic prayers in Arabic. In particular, he noted that Anna Musa excitedly began to recite the entirety of the *Qur'an* to him in Arabic. The public charade had been stripped away, and a devout Muslim had been revealed.

F18. *CHARNO* THE FULA

Very little is known about this enslaved African Muslim. Even his actual name is lost to history, although he was called *Charno*. As *Charno* means *Marabout* in the Pulaar language of the Fulani, we can safely infer that he was a Fula (plural = Fulbe or Fulani; singular = Fula) and that he was a *Marabout* (West African term for a Muslim teacher, religious leader, and "holy" man). Aside from the above, all that is known about him is that he wrote the first chapter of the *Qur'an* in Arabic at the request of a white man.

F19. LONDON

London was a Mandinka and had learned Arabic in Africa. The latter consideration identifies him as being a Muslim. While enslaved in Savannah, Georgia, in 1857, he attempted to write the *Gospel of John* and some Christian hymns in the English language, but using Arabic letters.

It is doubtful that the content of London's writing represents any true adherence to Christianity. As noted repeatedly in these brief biographies, many enslaved Muslims in the Americas feigned a conversion to Christianity in order to receive better treatment from their owners. There is no reason to believe that London's situation was any different.

F20. AYUBA IBN SULEYMAN IBN IBRAHIM DIALLO[43]

As his name declares, Ayuba was the son of Suleyman, the son of Ibrahim, of the Diallo (Jallo) clan of the Fulbe tribe (plural = Fulbe or

---

43. The information on Ayuba in Austin AD (1995) and Diouf SA (1998) has been supplemented with information from Curtin PD (1968).

Fulani; singular = Fula). He was born circa 1702 in the Bundu area of eastern Senegal, and his father was an *Alfa* (West African term for the Arabic *Al-Faqih*, i.e., a scholar of Islamic jurisprudence, but in West Africa it can also refer more generally to a Muslim religious leader) and *Imam* (Muslim prayer leader). His mother was Tanomata, the first wife of Suleyman.

During his youth in Africa, Ayuba was well educated by his father in Arabic, in Qur'anic studies, and in 30 handwritten manuscripts. Ayuba memorized the entirety of the *Qur'an* in Arabic by the time he was 15 years old and was in training to become an *Imam* like his father. Over the course of his education, he apparently gained fluency in at least three languages: the Pulaar language of the Fulbe, the language of the Wolof tribe, and Arabic.

By age 15, Ayuba was already assisting his father as *Imam* at their local mosque. At about the same time, he married the daughter of the *Alfa* of Tombut (Bambuk). He had three sons ('Abd Allah, Samba, and Ibrahim) by this wife. Approximately 12 years after his first marriage, he took the daughter of the *Alfa* of Tomga as a second wife, with whom he had one daughter (Fatima).

Early in 1730, Ayuba was sent by his father on a trading venture to the north shore of the Gambia River on the African coast, which was approximately 200 miles away from his home. He was accompanied by two servants, entrusted with two slaves to sell, and was instructed to buy paper and other items from an English ship. However, his father stressed to him that he shouldn't cross south of the Gambia River, as he would then be entering the territory of the Mandinka people, enemies of the Fulbe at that time.

Arriving on the north bank of the Gambia River, he attempted to sell his two slaves to a Captain Pike, who was in the employ of Mr. William Hunt, a merchant in London, England. After some haggling over price, the deal fell through. At this point, Ayuba sent his two servants back home, engaged the services of Lamine Ndiaye as a translator, and crossed into the area south of the Gambia River. He was then able to sell his two slaves for about 20 to 30 cows. The trade transaction being completed, Ayuba and Lamine rested at the house of an old acquaintance of Ayuba before beginning their journey back to the north side of the Gambia.

While they were resting and were thus unarmed, about seven or eight men jumped Ayuba and Lamine and took them captive. Their heads and beards were shaved to make them appear to be prisoners of war, and Ayuba vigorously objected to this treatment, probably because wearing a beard is part of typical Islamic grooming for a male Muslim. They were then marched back to the Gambia River. Ironically enough, having reached the Gambia, Ayuba and Lamine were sold to the same Captain Pike with whom Ayuba had tried to strike a deal only a few days before, the purchase being completed on February 27, 1730.

Recognizing Ayuba, Captain Pike agreed to allow Ayuba's family to ransom him. However, after a week of waiting for the ransom payment to arrive, Ayuba and Lamine were shipped off to Annapolis, Maryland, as slaves. Irony piling up upon irony, just days after Ayuba's ship, the *Arabella*, departed on the Middle Passage, his family arrived at the coast with slaves to trade for his freedom.

Arriving in Annapolis, Maryland, with Lamine, the two were placed in the control of Vachell Denton, the slave agent in Maryland for Mr. Hunt. However, the two were soon separated, sold to different owners, and lost track of each other. Ayuba was sold by Vachell Denton to a Mr. Tolsey of Kent Island, Chesapeake Bay, Maryland, who gave Ayuba the slave name of Simon. At Kent Island, Ayuba was initially assigned duties preparing tobacco for market. He apparently hated this work and began to malinger and perform his duties slowly. As such, he was reassigned to duties working with cattle. While this was a slightly better job in the hierarchy of slave occupations, Ayuba remained unhappy. Despite the fact that the public performance of Muslim prayers could easily expose him to severe punishment, Ayuba poured out his despair in ceaseless prayer to Allah. On one occasion as Ayuba was thus praying in the woods, a white boy threw mud in his face as he began to prostrate in prayer.

Having been enslaved for only a few months in America, Ayuba had taken all that he was prepared to take. Desperate for the taste of freedom, he ran away from his owner at Kent Island, Maryland, and made it as far away as southeastern Pennsylvania (now Kent County, Delaware) before he was captured by a local sheriff and imprisoned.

In June of 1731, Ayuba was visited in prison by Thomas Bluett. While Ayuba could not speak any English and while Bluett was not conversant in any of the languages known by Ayuba, Bluett somehow managed to discover that Ayuba could write in Arabic. Further, Bluett recognized Ayuba's pronunciation of the words "Allah" and "Muhammad" during Ayuba's attempts to communicate with him. Given this information and the additional observation that Ayuba refused to accept wine when it was offered to him, Bluett correctly surmised that Ayuba was a Muslim.

Despite Bluett's limited success in identifying Ayuba as a Muslim, the authorities still did not know who Ayuba was or who his owner was. Thus, Ayuba languished in the prison until he was confronted with an old slave who could speak the language of the Wolof tribe, a language that Ayuba had learned in childhood. Once communication was established, Ayuba explained who he was and that he belonged to Mr. Tolsey. Along with this information, Ayuba imparted some specific complaints against his owner. These complaints apparently centered on Mr. Tolsey not having been sensitive to Ayuba's need to perform the five obligatory prayers of Islam on a daily basis.

Armed with this information, the authorities returned Ayuba to Mr. Tolsey and explained the nature of Ayuba's complaints against him. Rather remarkably, instead of responding with punishment, Mr. Tolsey provided Ayuba with a place to pray. Ayuba's condition had thus improved, but he was still a slave.

In early 1733, Ayuba wrote a letter in Arabic to his father back in Africa. He sent the letter to Vachell Denton, requesting that the letter be sent on to William Hunt for eventual forwarding to his father. When the letter reached Hunt in England, it came to the attention of James Oglethorpe, the founder of the colony of Georgia. Mr. Oglethorpe became interested in Ayuba and arranged for his purchase from Mr. Tolsey by the Royal African Company. Though still technically a slave, Ayuba's days of slave labor were over after less than three years of slavery. He was on the verge of once again becoming a free man.

It took some time to arrange for Ayuba's passage to England, and during the interim he stayed in the home of Vachell Denton and was taken care of by some local ministers and lawyers in Annapolis. In exchange for their hospitality, Ayuba taught them some rudimentary Arabic. Finally, in March of 1733, Ayuba sailed for England on the *William* in the company of Thomas Bluett, who had first visited him in prison in June of 1731 and who was impressed by Ayuba's devotion to his Islamic faith, his public performance of the five daily prayers of Islam, and his adherence to Muslim dietary restrictions. With regard to this last point, Bluett noted that Ayuba avoided all alcoholic beverages, pork, and all other meat that he or another Muslim had not personally slaughtered, excepting fish.

The voyage to England took about two months, and during this time Ayuba managed to learn enough English from Bluett and the ship's captain to converse. Arriving in England in late April of 1733, Ayuba continued to gain mastery over the English language, wrote three copies of the *Qur'an* in Arabic from memory, and translated some Arabic documents for Sir Hans Sloane and others. During his more than year-long sojourn in England, he was presented with an Arabic translation of the *New Testament*. After much study of it, he rightfully concluded that there was no basis for a belief in the trinity to be found within the *New Testament* itself. He also disputed respectfully with members of the Christian clergy, met the royal family, was elected a member of the Spalding Gentlemen's Society, and made several important friends and contacts over the next year. These people then put together the money to buy Ayuba's technical freedom from the Royal African Company, which had placed a high price of 59 pounds, six shillings, and 11 pence on his head. Over and above receiving his freedom, Ayuba also received gifts (valued at more than 500 pounds by Bluett) from Queen Caroline of England, the Duke of Cumberland (the third son of the king and queen of England), the Duke of Montague, the Earl of Pembroke, and others.

As a brief digression, some minor speculation is in order regarding other activities in which Ayuba might have been engaged while in England. Firstly, George Sale's English translation of the *Qur'an* was initially published in 1734, and it is tempting to hypothesize that Ayuba might have had a hand in this translation. This hypothesis gains some credibility from the fact that Ayuba later sent greetings to a "Mista Sail" in a letter written to his English secretary from Gambia in 1736. Secondly, Ayuba's membership in the Spalding Gentlemen's Society might well have placed him in contact with Sir Isaac Newton, the English physicist, and with Alexander Pope, the renowned poet.

In 1734, after having spent over one year in England, Ayuba returned home to Africa on the *Dolphin*, a trip that lasted seven weeks. Arriving back in Africa on August 8, 1734, he served as a commercial representative for the Royal African Company and was given the authority to ransom fellow Muslims who were destined for slavery in America. Unfortunately, it is not presently known how many African Muslims he was able to save from having to undertake the Middle Passage voyage to slavery in the Americas. However, it is known that during his stay in England he was able to use his influence with the Duke of Montague to have the latter ransom his one-time translator, Lamine Ndiaye, from his enslaved status in Maryland. Throughout his tenure with the Royal African Company, he continued to correspond with friends in England via letters in Arabic.

Not everything was sunny for Ayuba once he was back in Africa. A bitter war was raging in his home area of Bundu, and he was not able to return home until June of 1735. His father had died before his return, and his first wife had remarried, thinking that Ayuba was dead. Within a short time of his return home, Ayuba was held prisoner by the French for about a year before being released. He continued working for the Royal African Company until its demise in the early 1750s. Thereafter, little is known about Ayuba other than a note that appeared in the Spalding Gentlemen's Society records stating that he had finally died in 1773.

Ayuba's story was immortalized in a brief, 54-page biography written in 1734 by Thomas Bluett. The biography presents us with Bluett's personal observations of Ayuba. These observations were based on Bluett's sporadic contact with Ayuba, beginning with Bluett's initial meeting with Ayuba in June of 1731 and continuing until Ayuba's departure for Africa in 1734. Bluett described Ayuba as being about 5 foot, 10 inches tall and as having long, black, curly hair. He further noted that Ayuba was exceedingly pleasant, compassionate, polite, composed, absolutely faithful to his Islamic beliefs, and quite intelligent. With regard to this last observation, Bluett noted that Ayuba demonstrated good judgment, a ready memory, an ability to disassemble and reassemble a plow, grist mill, and clock, and the capacity to argue for his religious beliefs forcefully and objectively even though English was still a new language for him. Ayuba's arguments must have been powerful indeed; for despite the fact that Bluett was a Christian missionary, even Bluett had to conclude that the Muslim Ayuba held reasonable beliefs about God and the next life.

F21. MUHAMMAD 'ABD ALLAH

Muhammad 'Abd Allah was a Pulo from Kano, a city in northern Nigeria on the Jakara River. Over 1,000 years old at present, Kano was the capital of the old Hausa kingdom of Kano and since the 15th century has been surrounded by a city wall that has 14 gates and is over 12 miles in circumference, 30 to 50 feet high, and 40 feet wide at the base. At the end of the 15th century, Kano boasted 3,000 teachers. Coming from this environment, it is not surprising that

Muhammad was highly educated in Arabic and in Qur'anic studies and that while living in Africa he had served as a *Marabout* (West African term for a Muslim teacher, religious leader, and "holy" man) and had completed the *Hajj* pilgrimage to Makkah.

Muhammad was enslaved and taken to Bahia, Brazil, circa the early 19th century. He somehow managed to become fluent in both spoken and written Portuguese and to gain his freedom from slavery. He then spent his life working as a carpenter in Bahia. As an elderly man in the mid 19th century, he had worked briefly for Count Francis de Castelnau, a French official stationed in Bahia. As ample testimony to Muhammad's continuing practice of Islam as a devout Muslim throughout his life in Brazil, Count Castelnau subsequently reported that Muhammad was constantly trying to convert him to Islam

F22. ABU BAKR AL-SIDDIQ[44]

Abu Bakr Al-Siddiq was born into the Mandinka tribe in Timbuktu circa 1790-1794. Two years later, the family moved to Jenne, which was on the upper Niger River and which was located about 250 miles southwest of Timbuktu. His father was Kara Musa, an expert in Qur'anic exegesis and a *Hajji*, i.e., a Muslim who had completed the *Hajj* pilgrimage to Makkah. Abu Bakr's paternal grandfather was 'Umar ibn Sahid Al-Malik, who has been variously described as being a *Mar* and an *Al-Qa'id* (both titles may be translated as "prince"). As can be seen, Abu Bakr's paternal family was part of the ruling Mandinka aristocracy, in part because they were *Sherif*, i.e., descendants of Prophet Muhammad. As for his maternal lineage, Abu Bakr's mother was Hafsah (Naghodi in the Hausa language), the daughter of Muhammad Tafsir, a *Hajji* from Bornu and Katsina in northern Nigeria.

---

44. The information on Abu Bakr is taken primarily from Curtin PD (1968).

Abu Bakr was part of a large nuclear family. While he reported having only one full brother (Salih) and one full sister (Aminah), he had nine paternal half-brothers and four paternal half-sisters. His paternal half-brothers included 'Umar, Sa'id, Musa Baba, Mu'min, 'Abd Allah, Suleyman, Mustafa, Yusuf, and 'Abd Al-Rahman. His paternal half-sisters consisted of 'Aishia, Salimah, Hawa, and Keltum.

Abu Bakr's father died while trading in Bouna when Abu Bakr was only about four years old. As a result, Abu Bakr was educated by a tutor, who taught him Arabic and Qur'anic studies. Upon reaching the age of nine, Abu Bakr, his tutor, and several of his tutor's other students started traveling to supplement their education and to eventually visit the grave of Abu Bakr's father in Bouna. The first year of these travels was spent in the Dyula trading center of Kong (the modern Ivory Coast), which was located about 330 miles south of Jenne and in which was located Abu Bakr's paternal uncle, 'Abd Rahman. Following their stay in Kong, Abu Bakr and his tutor moved about 60 miles east to Bouna, which was a great center of learning, a home to many scholars from a variety of nations, and the residence of another paternal uncle, Mahmud, who was married to a daughter of the king of Bouna. At Bouna, Abu Bakr began taking more advanced Qur'anic studies, including the study of *Tafsir* (Qur'anic commentary). By the time of the abrupt end to his education, he had almost memorized the entire *Qur'an* in Arabic.

At around age 14 or 15, Abu Bakr was taken captive by the army of Sultan Adinkra, the ruler of Bonduku, when the latter conquered the city of Bouna. Abu Bakr was enslaved, stripped naked, tied with a cord, given a heavy load to carry, and then marched to Bonduku, which was about 50 or so miles south of Bouna. From Bonduku, he was taken on an around about, 11-day or 12-day journey of over 200 miles to Kumasi, which is actually only about 50 some miles to the southeast of Bonduku. From Kumasi, he was marched another 120 miles in a meandering, multi-day journey to the port of Lago, which is actually only about 50 or 60 miles to the southeast of Kumasi. In Lago, he was sold to an English ship in either 1805 or 1807, and from there he began his three-month Middle Passage voyage to Jamaica.

Arriving in Jamaica, he was initially sold to a stonemason named Donellan. He was later resold to a Mr. Haynes, an absentee landowner who had him forcibly baptized under the Christian slave name of Edward Donlan (Donellan or Doulan). Like many other African Muslims who had been forcibly baptized, Abu Bakr discovered that his life as a slave was made easier by publicly going along with the charade that he was a Christian. In 1823, he was resold to Alexander Anderson, who assigned him work as his bookkeeper and recorder of all his accounts. In this labor, Abu Bakr kept the accounts in English words using the Arabic alphabet and script. He was so valuable to Anderson in this capacity that Anderson once refused to sell him to the Duke of Montebello, who had planned to free Abu Bakr. Finally in 1834, through the efforts of the Richard Robert Madden, a British magistrate in Jamaica, Anderson emancipated Abu Bakr in exchange for 20 pounds. (Anderson's emancipation of Abu Bakr was not all that altruistic, as an already passed British law was going to give all the slaves in the British colonies their freedom in just four more years.)

Abu Bakr was one of the four signatories to the October 2, 1834, letter to Richard Robert Madden (see entry on William Rainesford). About the same time, upon hearing of Abu Bakr's emancipation, Muhammad Kaba (see prior entry) began a correspondence in Arabic with him about the faith of Islam and directly addressed him as *Sherif*, suggesting that Abu Bakr's status as a descendant of Prophet Muhammad was well known and a cause of some celebrity among the enslaved Muslims of Jamaica.

In 1835, Abu Bakr was taken to England by a Captain Oldrey, a British magistrate serving in Jamaica. In September of 1835, he left England for Morocco as part of John Davidson's private expedition. Arriving in Morocco, he was received as a *Mulay* (prince or descendant of Prophet Muhammad) by the sultan, afforded all the status of his titles and lineage, and discovered that one of his relatives had become the ruler of Timbuktu.

After over a year spent in Morocco, Abu Bakr and the Davidson expedition left Wadi Nun in late November of 1836 to begin an overland journey into the desert to the south and on to Timbuktu. On December 18, 1836, the expedition was attacked, and Davidson was killed. Abu Bakr was somehow spared and later found his way back to his hometown of Jenne where he was reported as living in June of 1841.

During his life in the West, Abu Bakr wrote two short autobiographies. The first was written in Jamaica in 1834. It was an Arabic manuscript that Abu Bakr wrote for his benefactor, Richard Robert Madden. The second autobiography, also written in Arabic, was penned by Abu Bakr during his short stay in England and was dated August 29, 1835. Both autobiographies were translated and published. Unfortunately, the original Arabic manuscripts have been lost in both cases.

In his autobiographies, Abu Bakr emphasized his lifelong adherence and devotion to Islam, thus rejecting his earlier forced baptism into Christianity. He stressed the need to perform the five pillars of Islamic practice, i.e., saying the *Shahadah* (the testimonial of faith), performing the *Salat* (five daily prayers of Islam), fasting (*Sawm*) during the lunar month of *Ramadan*, and completing the *Hajj* pilgrimage to Makkah. In addition, he reiterated such Qur'anic principles and dictates as: keeping Islamic dietary restrictions, including the avoidance of alcohol and of meat that has not been properly slaughtered according to Islamic law; honoring one's parents; and avoidance of idolatry, bad company, dishonesty and false witnessing, murder, stealing, coveting, and hypocrisy. He closed his autobiography with a lament that he had not been able to practice his Islam as openly and as freely as he would have liked in the face of his enslavement, and he asked Allah for forgiveness for his shortcomings.

As far as is known, Abu Bakr never married nor had any children in the Americas.

F23. IBRAHIM 'ABD AL-RAHMAN DIALLO

Ibrahim 'Abd Al-Rahman Diallo, henceforward 'Abd Al-Rahman to distinguish him from his father, was born into the distinguished Diallo clan of the Fulbe (plural = Fulbe or Fulani; singular = Fula) circa 1762 in Timbuktu. When he was five years old, the family moved to Timbo, Futa Jallon, Guinea.

His father was Ibrahim Yoro Pate Sori, the second *Almaamy* (West African corruption of the Arabic *Al-Imam*, i.e., a Muslim prayer leader, but in West Africa also implying some military authority). As one of the two main military leaders of the Fulbe tribe in Futa Jallon, Ibrahim Yoro had been primarily responsible for the successful war of liberation from and conquest of the non-Muslim population of Futa Jallon, thus ending a series of wars of liberation that had begun in the late 1720s. Having been the primary architect of Fulbe rule in Futa Jallon, Ibrahim Yoro was considered to be a prince of the Fulbe and the king of Futa Jallon. He was given the honorific of *Maudo*, i.e., "the great." During the years of 1776 through 1778, Ibrahim Yoro was able to consolidate his earlier military gains and made Futa Jallon the strongest nation in that area of West Africa.

'Abd Al-Rahman received his primary education in Qur'anic studies and Arabic in his hometown of Timbo. Successfully completing these studies, he ascended the academic ladder by attending secondary education in Jenne of Masina. Once again successful in his academic pursuits, he then obtained an advanced education in Timbuktu. By the time he had completed his formal education, he was completely literate in Arabic and fluent in Arabic, the Pulaar language of the Fulbe, and the neighboring African languages of Bambara, Mandinka, and Jallonke.

Having completed his formal education in Timbuktu, he later received military training as a cavalry officer. By age 22, he was a captain in the cavalry and had already led victorious troops into battle. Two years later, he was promoted to colonel. By age 26, he was married and a father. He was also then in command of an army of 2,000 men, which he was leading west in a defensive war. Initially in this campaign of 1788, 'Abd Al-Rahman achieved a string of victories. However, as the army returned home to Futa Jallon, 'Abd Al-Rahman and his cavalry were ambushed in a narrow mountain pass by the Houbous (Hebos) in March of 1788. 'Abd Al-Rahman was shot in the shoulder, and he and about 50 of his soldiers were taken prisoner. He was then placed in chains and marched barefoot for over 100 miles to the distant Gambia River where he was sold to the captain of a British ship. His long life of slavery had begun.

Having entered into British captivity, he was placed in the small, dark, and filthy hold of the *Africa*. For the next week, the *Africa* sailed down the Gambia to the coast and then began its six-week, more than 3,000-mile, Middle Passage voyage across the Atlantic to Dominica Island in the Caribbean. From Dominica Island, he was transported to the mouth of the Mississippi River, another six-week journey of about 2,200 miles. Having reached the Mississippi, he was kept on board an additional week before being disembarked at New Orleans, a city that was then only about 67% the size of 'Abd Al-Rahman's native Timbo. After a month spent in New Orleans, he was loaded onto a riverboat in August of 1788 and began a 30-day, 300-mile trip up the Mississippi River to Natchez, Mississippi.

Arriving at Natchez, 'Abd Al-Rahman was weak and ill from his long ordeal. Nonetheless, he was restrained with a rope wrapped around him, had his long hair cut, and was sold to Thomas Foster. His attempts to communicate who he was through a Mandinka translator resulted in Foster giving him the slave name of Prince. Despite this slave name, which was probably given more in derision than in respect, 'Abd Al-Rahman was given the lowest and most physically demanding job in the hierarchy of slave labor, i.e., he was sent out to work in the fields. When he objected to this, he was whipped.

Learning the ways of slave life, 'Abd Al-Rahman patiently waited for his health and strength to return to him. Once he felt fit enough, he ran away to the woods. However, the woods of Mississippi offered little to a runaway slave other than temporary freedom. After several weeks spent fending for himself alone in the woods, he finally surrendered himself to his owner.

Thereafter, 'Abd Al-Rahman was a model slave, whom his owner described as avoiding alcohol, meanness, dishonesty, and laziness. He even made a public show of converting to his owner's Christianity and thus began to work his way up the slave hierarchy. His experience as a cavalry officer gave him a natural affinity for working with cattle and horses, and he distinguished himself in those pursuits. Eventually, over the course of many years, he worked his way up the ladder and became for all practical purposes the plantation overseer, a rare honor for an enslaved African. In addition, he was given a private garden plot and release time.

Circa 1794-1795, 'Abd Al-Rahman married a fellow slave, an African-American Baptist by the name of Isabella, who was the "doctor" and midwife to the plantation's slaves. The marriage produced five sons, four daughters, and at least eight grandchildren, all of whom were born into slavery. By 1828 and as a testimony to the hardships of slavery in the American South, only five of his children were still living.

There things might have remained had it not been for a most remarkable meeting that took place around 1807. 'Abd Al-Rahman had traveled into Natchez that day to peddle some of the vegetables he had grown in his private garden plot. He was thus engaged when he met John Coates Cox. It was a reunion over 30 years in the making!

Cox was a white physician who had wandered away from a ship on the African coast, gotten lost, become injured and ill, and somehow miraculously ended up in Timbo, the hometown of 'Abd Al-Rahman. Cox was the first white man ever to reach Timbo and was immediately brought to the attention of Ibrahim Yaro, who arranged for Cox to be lovingly nursed back to health by the Muslim inhabitants of Timbo. Cox remained in Timbo for six months at the urging of Ibrahim Yaro and came to know 'Abd Al-Rahman fairly well. When Cox finally decided to leave, Ibrahim Yaro gave Cox a guard of 15 soldiers to escort him safely back to the African coast and the gold to buy his passage home to Great

Britain. Cox subsequently immigrated to America and later settled in Mississippi. Piling up miracle upon miracle, not only did the two old acquaintances meet after a separation of over 30 years and at a distance of over 6,000 miles from where they had once known each other, but 'Abd Al-Rahman immediately recognized Cox by the way he rode his horse down the street, a testament to 'Abd Al-Rahman's expertise as a cavalry officer. When 'Abd Al-Rahman later engaged Cox in conversation as the latter inspected some potatoes 'Abd Al-Rahman was selling, Cox recognized his former benefactor and immediately clutched him in a public embrace on the street, an unthinkable action for a white man in the Mississippi of 1807.

Not forgetting the kindnesses bestowed upon him by 'Abd Al-Rahman and Ibrahim Yoro, Cox immediately introduced Governor Ware to this African prince living in slavery in their midst and tried to buy 'Abd Al-Rahman in order to emancipate him. Unfortunately, Foster rebuffed Cox and would not sell his most trusted and valuable slave, even though Cox offered to pay any price asked by Foster. Not deterred, Cox tried for years to purchase 'Abd Al-Rahman, and after his death Cox's son carried on the attempts to free his father's past benefactor. While 'Abd Al-Rahman did not receive his freedom through Cox's strenuous efforts, Foster was eventually impressed enough with what he had heard from Cox to relieve 'Abd Al-Rahman of all field duty and to give him additional release time.

Given the stories then circulating about him in Mississippi, 'Abd Al-Rahman came to the attention of Andrew Marschalk, a local newspaper editor, in the early 1820s. Marschalk occasionally interviewed 'Abd Al-Rahman and wrote several articles about him. Eventually, Marschalk suggested that 'Abd Al-Rahman write a letter in Arabic to be sent to his family in Africa through the U.S. Department of State.

Initially, the now elderly slave refused this suggestion. However, in 1826, 'Abd Al-Rahman took up Marschalk's suggestion and penned the letter.

Having received 'Abd Al-Rahman's letter, the U.S. State Department began a lengthy correspondence with Morocco, the only African country then enjoying diplomatic relations with the United States. Over the course of nearly two years, the government of Morocco continued to request the State Department to grant freedom to and to provide transport back to Africa for the elderly and enslaved prince of the Fulbe. Finally, Secretary of State Henry Clay, himself a southerner and a pro-slavery advocate, interceded with Thomas Foster. Clay suggested that the U.S. government would pay for 'Abd Al-Rahman's transportation to Washington, DC, if Foster would free him.

Foster grudgingly agreed to Clay's request on February 22, 1828, but 'Abd Al-Rahman did not want to leave without his wife. Foster initially refused this latter request but then asked for $200, a rather low price for that time and place, for the purchase of Isabella. Hearing of the situation, the local citizens of Natchez raised $293 within one day. Both 'Abd Al-Rahman and his wife were freed by the middle of March of 1828 and began a riverboat ride from Natchez, Mississippi, to Cincinnati, Ohio.

'Abd Al-Rahman's journey from Natchez to the ship that was to carry him back to Africa was something of a triumphal journey taking about 11 months. He arrived in Cincinnati by steamship on April 19, 1828. From Cincinnati, he traveled overland by stagecoach to Washington, DC. From Washington, he continued on through three New England states, New York City, Philadelphia, and Baltimore before arriving in Norfolk, Virginia.

Throughout his tour, 'Abd Al-Rahman met many notables, all of whom responded positively to him, including: Francis Scott Key, author of the *Star Spangled Banner*; Mayor Joseph Watson of Philadelphia; U.S. Representative Edward Everett, Jr.; U.S. Secretary of State Henry Clay; and President John Quincy Adams. However, the real reason for his prolonged tour was his ceaseless fundraising endeavors to gather the money to purchase the freedom of his children and grandchildren. At these events, he often wore a white turban topped with a crescent, a blue coat with yellow buttons, white pantaloons tucked at the ankles, yellow boots, and a scimitar. It must have made a colorful sight. To open the wallets of his listeners a little further, he pointed to his own pseudo-conversion to Christianity and managed to leave the impression that he would be a missionary bringing Christianity to his native Africa. These efforts were successful, and $3,500 was raised, which was sufficient to buy the freedom of eight of his descendants once he reached Africa.

On February 7, 1829, 'Abd Al-Rahman and Isabella left Norfolk on the *Harriet* for Liberia, Africa. He was about 67 years old and had been enslaved for 40 years. Upon arriving in Liberia, 'Abd Al-Rahman immediately abandoned all pretense of being a Christian and publicly embraced his Islamic religion. However, he was not to return to Timbo. Political upheavals in Futa Jallon and his advanced age kept him from making the 15-day journey up the mountains to his homeland. In June of 1829, he became sick. He died on July 6, 1829, in Monrovia, Liberia. In December of 1830, his freed descendants, eight in number, finally reached Liberia. They included two sons (Lee and Simon), Simon's wife, and Simon's five children. It is possible that more of his descendants were freed and reached Liberia in 1835 when Thomas Foster's descendants freed some of the slaves they inherited.

Like a few of his fellow Muslims who were enslaved in the Americas, 'Abd Al-Rahman wrote a brief autobiography in Arabic. The handwritten manuscript was penned in 1828 while he was in Washington, DC. In May of 1828, *The African Repository* published 'Abd Al-Rahman's own English translation of his Arabic autobiography. Unfortunately, the original Arabic manuscript is now lost.

Before closing the account of 'Abd Al-Rahman, it is instructive to take a second look at his pseudo-conversion to Christianity and his later Christian façade. 'Abd Al-Rahman left several samples of his Arabic writing, almost all of which were written by memory from the *Qur'an*. When asked by a Christian minister in Philadelphia on December 29, 1828, to write the Christians' Lord's Prayer in his native language, 'Abd Al-Rahman complied by writing *Al-Fatiha* (the first chapter of the *Qur'an*) in Arabic. For 'Abd Al-Rahman, this was his Lord's prayer, as it is repeated two to four times in each of the five daily prayers of Islam. Needless to say, the Christian minister could not read Arabic and was unaware of the scam that had been perpetrated upon him.

As to 'Abd Al-Rahman's comments on the Christians he encountered in Mississippi, he reportedly said that the *Bible*, which he had read while a slave, contained very good laws but that the Christians did not follow those laws. He went on to say that the Christians he had observed did not pray often enough, were too greedy, and were too enamored with money and wealth. In support of his indictment, he noted the condition in which Mississippi Christians kept their slaves, overworking them merely for the sake of growing more cotton. He poignantly asked where Christians found that sort of behavior condoned in the laws of the *Bible*.

F24. 'Umar Ibn Said

'Umar ibn Said was a Tukolar Fula who was born circa 1765 in Futa Toro, Bundu, on the Senegal River in what is today the country of Senegal. He was the son of Said and Umhan Yasnik and had two full brothers, one full sister, two paternal half-brothers, and four paternal half-sisters. He appears to have been from a wealthy family, as his father reportedly had 70 slaves.

His father died when 'Umar was only five years old, and he was then raised by an uncle. Despite being an orphan, 'Umar received a superlative education. He was thoroughly taught Arabic and Qur'anic studies by an older brother (Sheykh Muhammad ibn Said), Sheykh Suleyman Kembeh, and Sheykh Jibril Abdal in Futa Toro and possibly in Futa Jallon. By his report, 'Umar was a student for 25 years, suggesting that he was an intellectual and a scholar.

He described his life in Africa as having been devoted to the performance of the five pillars of practice of Islam, including prayer, fasting, the giving of obligatory charity, and pilgrimage. With regard to the last pillar of practice, 'Umar reported going on religious pilgrimages, one of which may well have included making the *Hajj* to Makkah. He was a scholar and a teacher for several years and then became a trader in salt, clothes, etc. He had no wife or children in Africa.

He was apparently living at Kebe in the Mandinka area of Bure by 1807, at which time he participated in a battle between rival armies in Senegal. He was captured and enslaved. His subsequent Middle Passage voyage to Charleston, South Carolina, took six weeks. He left no record of whatever horrors were inflicted upon him during this voyage.

Upon reaching America, he was initially purchased by an owner who was described as being reasonably good to him. However, this owner died and was replaced by an owner who overworked him and demanded heavy physical labor. In desperation, 'Umar ran away. He was recaptured in a church in Fayetteville, North Carolina, where he had gone to find shelter to pray. He was then imprisoned as a runaway slave. While in prison, his ability to write Arabic on the prison's wall and his mild and dignified demeanor drew the attention of his jailors and of the local populace.

In 1811, he was purchased by his third American owner, General James Owen. Owen apparently treated 'Umar as a frail and sickly individual who could not stand up to much physical work, did not demand much of him, and met some of 'Umar's religious requests. For example, upon 'Umar's request, Owen found an English translation of the *Qur'an* for 'Umar and had it read to him. However, 'Umar never really mastered the English language.

For many years, 'Umar publicly maintained his Islamic prayers, fasts, and dietary restrictions. However, he was eventually baptized into the Presbyterian Church in 1821 and was then a regular attendee. He was given a *Bible* in Arabic, which he apparently read with enough frequency that the *Bible* had to be recovered. Further, in his 1835 Arabic correspondence to Lamine Kebe, whose biographical sketch was previously presented, 'Umar reportedly exhorted the latter to convert to Christianity. Unfortunately, the Arabic originals of this correspondence are no longer available for analysis and re-translation. Finally, in his 1831 autobiography, 'Umar reportedly wrote: "Before I came to the Christian country, my religion was the religion of Muhammad, the Messenger of Allah, may Allah have mercy upon him and give him peace." The implication of 'Umar's statement is that he was no longer a Muslim, but then he ends the statement with a purely Islamic invocation for Prophet Muhammad.

Despite his public conversion, consistent *Bible* reading, regular church attendance, and alleged exhortation to Lamine Kebe, there is substantial evidence that 'Umar remained a closet Muslim while publicly professing to be a Christian.

(1) As noted previously, 'Umar read his Arabic translation of the *Bible* with such frequency that it had to be recovered. He also wrote numerous annotations into the margins of his *Bible* in Arabic. Of significance, these annotations always begin with an invocation to Allah and are often followed by mentioning Prophet Muhammad.

(2) Even Rev. Mathew B. Grier, the minister of the last church 'Umar attended, admitted to having doubts about the genuineness of 'Umar's public show of Christianity.

(3) 'Umar was reportedly seen by his fellow slaves as being a *Marabout* (West African term for a Muslim teacher, religious leader, and "holy" man).

(4) He started his 1831, 16-page, Arabic manuscript about his life by saying the *Bismillah* and then by going on to say, "May Allah grant his blessing upon our Prophet Muhammad." The autobiography immediately proceeds by quoting about 60 lines from the *Qur'an*.

(5) Throughout his life in slavery, 'Umar wrote at least 27 Arabic manuscripts, 14 of which still exist and most of which start with traditional Islamic invocations to Allah and for Prophet Muhammad.

(6) On several occasions, 'Umar reportedly wrote the *Bible*'s Lord's Prayer and the 23rd Psalm in Arabic for curious whites, but neither of

these Biblical passages contradicts Islamic teachings. An examination of the surviving copies of those Arabic writings reveals that 'Umar usually did write what he said he was writing. However, on at least some occasions in which he claimed to be writing the Lord's Prayer, he simply wrote down a list of the members of the Owen family. Further, he almost invariably prefaced his Arabic renditions of Biblical passages with the *Bismillah* (i.e., In the name of Allah, the Most Gracious, the Most Merciful) and often with mention of Prophet Muhammad. Perhaps most significantly, his last preserved Arabic writing purporting to be the Lord's Prayer, which was written in 1857, is actually *Al-Nasr*, i.e., the 110th chapter from the *Qur'an*. As can be seen in the following translation of *Al-Nasr*, this short chapter from the *Qur'an* is a celebration of the growth and success of Islam, i.e., "Allah's religion."

In the name of Allah, the Most Gracious, the Most Merciful. When comes the help of Allah, and victory. And thou doest see the people enter Allah's religion in crowds. Celebrate the praises of thy Lord, and pray for His forgiveness: for He is oft-returning (in grace and mercy).

(Qur'an 110:1-3)

'Umar died circa 1864 and apparently never had a wife or children in America.

F25. BILALI MUHAMMAD

Bilali Muhammad was a member of the Fulbe (Fulbe is the plural form, and Fula is the singular form) and was originally from Timbo in

Guinea. He was educated in Arabic and Qur'anic studies in Africa, and he may well have been in training to become an *Imam* (Muslim prayer leader).

The circumstances regarding his being taken into slavery are not generally known. We do know that he was initially shipped to the Bahamas where he was enslaved for an unknown, but apparently lengthy, period of time. From the Bahamas, he was shipped to the United States circa 1802, where he was purchased by Thomas Spalding of Sapelo Island, Georgia.

If one were forced to be an enslaved Muslim in the American South, one would have been hard pressed to find a better owner than Spalding. Unlike other slave owners, he gave each of his slaves his own individual plot of land to work, forced his slaves to work only six hours a day, employed no white overseers or slave drivers, and allowed his slaves the freedom to practice their Islamic faith openly. He even allowed the construction of a building to serve as a mosque on his plantation.

At the time of his purchase by Spalding, Bilali already had at least one wife and possibly two. There are two reasons for suggesting that Bilali had two wives. Firstly, we have two different names (Phoebe, who was said to be fluent in French, and Fatima) being given as his wife's name, although it could simply be that Fatima was her real name and Phoebe her slave name. Secondly, he had 12 sons, and seven daughters (Margaret, Hester, Charlotte, Fatima, Yoruba or Nyrubuh, Madina, and Bintou). While it is not impossible that he had 19 children out of only one wife, it is unlikely.

Reportedly, his wife or wives and at least his seven daughters accompanied Bilali from the Bahamas to the United States. This suggests that Bilali had been enslaved for many years in the Bahamas or that his wife and children had accompanied him into slavery from Africa. Of note, all of his daughters could speak English, French, Pulaar (the language of the Fulbe), and Arabic.

The Spalding plantation on Sapelo Island included 4,000 acres (6.25 square miles) of land in 1802, but it soon grew to encompass the entire island and employed between 400 and 1,000 slaves. Despite the size of the plantation and its many slaves, Bilali used his education, diligence, and outstanding personal character to rise to the very top of the slave hierarchy by about 1812, becoming the plantation manager in charge of the entire plantation and its hundreds of slaves. He reportedly kept all the plantation records in Arabic.

There are two surviving stories about Bilali as plantation manager that deserve retelling. The first story occurs during the War of 1812, which took place between the United States and Great Britain. Fearing British attack on Sapelo Island, Spalding and his family fled to safer areas and placed Bilali in charge of defending his plantation from British plunder. Bilali solemnly gave his word to Spalding to do his best to defend Spalding's property. In doing so, Bilali stated that he could not guarantee the behavior and loyalty of Spalding's Christian slaves but that he could guarantee that every Muslim slave would fight to the death to defend Sapelo Island. In response, Spalding actually went so far as to give Bilali 80 muskets to help in the island's defense. (This is the only known instance in the history of American slavery where a slave owner actually gave guns to his slaves.) True to his word, Bilali insured that those guns were not turned against the Spalding family to secure the slaves' freedom and kept the plantation slaves from deserting to the British, who had offered to give them their freedom. It is a remarkable testament to Bilali's honesty and integrity that he willingly sacrificed his own freedom and that of his family in order to fulfill his promise to Spalding.

The second story takes place in September of 1824. A severe hurricane was bearing down on Sapelo Island. During that hurricane, Bilali saved the lives of hundreds of his fellow slaves by herding them into huts made of *tabby* (an African concrete made of sand, lime, and oyster shell).

From what is known, it appears that Bilali's entire family continued practicing Islam as devout Muslims, despite being enslaved in the Americas. Among other observations supporting this proposition are the following. (1) Bilali and his wife were reported by a great grandchild as having been very particular about saying their prayers and about when they said them. (2) This same descendant also noted that Bilali and his wife used Islamic "prayer beads." (3) Phoebe reportedly made *Saraka* (honey and rice cakes) for '*Aid* (the two Islamic holidays) and at harvest time, a West African custom among Muslims. (4) Bilali regularly wore a *Kufi* (Islamic prayer cap) and a long coat, prayed towards Makkah, observed all Islamic dietary restrictions, always observed the fast of *Ramadan*, and celebrated the two '*Aid* holidays. (5) Bilali served as *Imam* or *Almaamy* (the West African form of the Arabic *Imam*) for the Muslim community on Sapelo Island, the only known pre-Civil War African Muslim community in the United States. (6) Bilali wrote a 13-page manual in Arabic script for his Muslim community on Sapelo Island. The Arabic title of the manuscript may be translated as "First Fruits of Happiness," and the difficult-to-decipher manuscript appears to be a manual on Islamic prayer, ablution, and faith. (7) When Bilali died in 1859, he was buried with his *Sajada* (prayer rug) and *Qur'an*.

Bilali's Islamic faith survived into at least his third generation of descendants. One of his great granddaughters, Harriet Hall, openly continued to practice Islam until 1866, at which time she publicly joined the First African Baptist Church of Sapelo Island. However, her descendants have suggested that she secretly continued to practice Islam until her death in 1922.

F26. SALIH BILALI[45]

Salih Bilali was from the Fulbe and was born circa 1765-1770 at Kianah, a famous Muslim intellectual center on the Niger River, in the district of Temourah, in the Kingdom of Massina (Mali). He was born into a wealthy family that had considerable property. He studied both Arabic and the *Qur'an* during his education in Africa. He reportedly could read Arabic quite well but had difficulty writing it.

When he was either 12 or 14 years old, he was riding alone on horseback on a return trip from Jenne to Kianah. Along the way, he was seized by slave traders. He was then sold from one owner to another as he was marched about 500 miles to the African coast. Along the way, he passed through the Bambara capital of Segu. After reaching the coast, he was shipped from Anomabu (in present-day Ghana) on the Gold Coast of Africa to the Bahama Islands. For the next 15 to 20 years, he was a slave in the Bahama Islands.

In 1800, Salih was purchased from the Bahama Islands by John Couper of Hopeton Plantation on St. Simon's Island, Georgia. He was then given the slave name of Tom and was to spend the rest of his life as a slave, first to John Couper and then to his son, James Hamilton Couper.

In 1815, Salih prevented over half of the slaves on the plantation from deserting to the British ships that had promised them freedom during the dying days of the War of 1812, citing how poorly he

---

45. The information on Salih Bilahi from Austin AD (1997) and Diouf SA (1998) has been supplemented with information from Curtin PD (1968).

had been treated by the British when he was enslaved in the Bahamas. Salih was later described by his owner, James Hamilton Couper, as being honest, intelligent, industrious, methodical, and of sound judgment and planning ability. Salih used those personal strengths to rise through the ranks of the slaves until he became the head of Hopeton Plantation in 1816, a position that he was to keep until 1846. In that position, he was in charge of about 450 slaves who labored to grow cotton, rice, sweet potatoes, cowpeas, corn, and sugarcane.

During his life of enslavement, Salih somehow managed to acquire a copy of the *Qur'an* and continued to practice his Islamic faith. In fact, James Couper reported that Salih was a strict Muslim who abstained from alcohol and kept the fast of *Ramadan*. Perhaps most remarkably for the Christian son of an American slaveholder, one of James Couper's sons later described Salih as the most religious man he had ever met. Salih's dying words in the late 1850s were, "Allah is God, and Muhammad His prophet."

During his life of slavery, Salih married and had children, at least one of whom, Bilali, married the daughter of a *Marabout* and continued to be a practicing Muslim throughout the remainder of his life.

F27. MUHAMMAD 'ALI IBN SAID

The biographical sketch of Muhammad 'Ali ibn Said is quite different than those previously given. While he had been enslaved in his native Africa, he had not come to America as part of the transatlantic slave trade. After having served 10 years in slavery in Africa, Asia, and Europe, he had come to the Americas as a free man in 1860.

Muhammad was born circa 1833 into a prosperous Kanuri family in Kuku, Bornu (present-day Nigeria) in the area just to the west of Lake Chad. Muhammad's autobiography lists his father's name as Barca Gana, even though Muhammad's own patronymic would suggest that his father was Said. Muhammad came from a large and wealthy family. He had 18 siblings and paternal half-siblings, 11 of whom were brothers and seven of whom were sisters. He was the ninth child from his mother. As testimony to the family's adherence to Islam, it can be pointed out that two of Muhammad's brothers had completed the *Hajj* pilgrimage to Makkah.

His father died when Muhammad was only about seven years old. Shortly thereafter, Muhammad began his formal schooling. He was educated in Arabic and Qur'anic studies and was beginning to learn Turkish.

When he was about 16 years old and hunting in the provinces of Yo and Lari in Denham, Muhammad was kidnapped by Taureg raiders. He was initially sold to an African-Arab trader and then marched northward in a three-month-long caravan across the Sahara Desert to Tripoli. When the caravan reached Murzuk, he was resold to a person who used him as a personal servant.

When the caravan at last reached Tripoli, he was once again resold and shipped to Alexandria, Egypt. From Alexandria, he was taken up the Nile to Khartoum (in modern Sudan). From Khartoum he was taken overland to the Red Sea coast and was shipped to Arabia. Arriving in Zula, he was taken north to Makkah and then back to Alexandria, Egypt, where he was shipped to Turkey. In Turkey, he was again sold, initially to a wealthy Turk who merely had Muhammad attend to his pipe and tobacco needs. Sometime later, this individual sold Muhammad to another Turk, who in turn sold Muhammad to Prince Alexander S. Menshikov, the Russian general. On May 21, 1853, Muhammad and his owner left for St. Petersburg, Russia.

Reaching St. Petersburg, Muhammad was sold once again, this time to Nicholas Trubertzkoy, an extremely wealthy Russian who owned extensive country property, including four villages. Muhammad acted as Trubertzkoy's personal servant, and the two traveled extensively for about a year, moving south to Georgia and down into Persia before returning to St. Petersburg. On November 12, 1854, Trubertzkoy had Muhammad baptized as Nicholas Said. Reflecting on this experience years later, Muhammad noted that he had not even known what was happening and thought that he should have had comprehension of the baptism event and been free to choose whether or not to be baptized.

Shortly after February of 1855, Trubertzkoy and Muhammad began a second set of extensive travels, this time moving across much of Europe. For the next four years, they were more or less always on the go, covering an itinerary that included St. Petersburg, Warsaw, Vienna, Prague, Dresden, Munich, Baden, Frankfurt, Cologne, Brussels, Bern, Zurich, Milan, Florence, Rome, Naples, Genoa, Paris, Athens, Trieste, and London. Their journey together ended in late 1859 when Muhammad expressed his desire to return to his native Africa. Trubertzkoy apparently freed Muhammad at that time.

Muhammad was all set to return to Africa when he was approached by a man from Holland who had the wanderlust. The Dutchman proposed that Muhammad accompany him as his personal servant on a journey to the Americas. Early in 1860, the two sailed for America. From New York City, they sailed again, this time for the Caribbean. In the Caribbean, they visited Inagua, Cuba, Jamaica, Haiti, Demerara (on the South American coast of Guiana), Martinique, and Guadeloupe, before returning to New York City. From New York City, they traveled overland to Niagara Falls and then crossed into Canada, where they visited Toronto, Montreal, Quebec, and Ottawa. Finally, in Elmer, Ontario, Canada, the Dutchman's funds became exhausted. He was dead broke.

Muhammad loaned the impoverished Dutchman $500 of his own money, which was never repaid, and the two went their separate ways.

Muhammad then crossed the border into the United States circa 1862 and was briefly a schoolteacher in Detroit, Michigan. In May of 1863, he joined Company I of the 55th Regiment of Massachusetts Colored Volunteers and fought for the Union in the United States Civil War at such battles as those at Ft. Mims and Honey Hill in 1864 and at James Island and Biggin Creek, South Carolina, in 1865. Muhammad must have been an exemplary soldier. By July of 1863, only two months after enlisting, he had risen to the rank of sergeant. In September of 1864, he asked to be reduced in rank to corporal, in order that he might be assigned to a hospital where he could strengthen his knowledge of medicine. He left the military in the latter half of 1865, being discharged while in South Carolina. He then married and dropped out of sight. He died in Brownsville, Tennessee, on August 6, 1882.

His autobiography was published in the *Atlantic Monthly* in October of 1867, by which time he could speak seven languages (including Arabic, Turkish, Russian, French, Italian, and English) in addition to his native African tongue. In his autobiography, he continues to refer to Allah.

F28. OLD LIZZIE GRAY[46]

A Muslim slave known only as Old Lizzie Gray was born in Africa circa 1733. She was educated, married, and the mother of four children in Africa before being enslaved. Her Middle Passage journey to the New World was apparently aboard an English ship during the Revolutionary War. In her old age in America, she joined the Methodist Church, even though her "conversion" to Christianity was at best a grafting of

---

46. Information on Lizzie Gray is from Hagy JW (1993) and Muhammad ANA (2005).

Christianity onto Islam. For example, she was known to say, "Christ built the first church in Makkah, and his grave was there." She died in Edgefield County, South Carolina, in September of 1860, reportedly having been 127 years old. Her physician and apparent owner at the time of her death was a Dr. E. J. Mims, who published her obituary (a rare acknowledgement for a slave) in the *Edgefield Advertiser* on September 12, 1860.

F.29. The "Sundrymoors" of South Carolina[47]

In January of 1790, four former slaves petitioned the South Carolina House of Representatives. All four of the petitioners were originally from Morocco, as were their wives, suggesting that all four men and their wives were Muslims. Their petition read as follows.

The humble Petition of Francis, Daniel, Hammond and Samuel, (Free Moors) in behalf of themselves and their wives Fatima, Flora, Sarah and Clarinda, Humbly Sheweth That your Petitioners some years past had the misfortune while fighting in the defence of their Country, to be captured with their wives and made prisoners of War by one of the Kings of Africa. That a certain Captain Clark had them delivered to him on a promise that they should be redeemed by the Emperor of Morocco's Ambassador then residing in England, in order to have them returned to their own Country: Instead of which he brought them to this State, and sold them for slaves. Since that period they have by the greatest industry been enabled to purchase their freedom from their respective Masters: And now prayeth your Honorable House, That as free born subjects of a

---

47. Information on the Moors is from Stevens ME, Allen CM (---).

Prince now in Alliance with these United States; that they may not be considered as subject to a Law of this State (now in force) called the negro law: but if they should be guilty of any crime or misdemeanor against the Laws of the Land, that they may have a just trial by a Lawful Jury. And your Petitioners as in duty bound will ever pray.

The South Carolina House of Representatives sent the petition to a committee consisting of Mr. Justice Grimke, General Pinckney, and Mr. Edward Rutledge. Mr. Rutledge reported back to the House that the committee:

Report That they have Considered the same and are of opinion that no Law of this State can in its Construction or Operation apply to them (the petitioners), and that persons who were Subjects of the Emperor of Morocco being Free in this State are not triable by the Law for the better Ordering and Governing of Negroes and other Slaves.

The committee report was approved by the House, but there is no record of the South Carolina Senate ever acting on the petition. Nothing else is presently known about these formerly enslaved Muslims in South Carolina.

F30. SUMMARY AND CONCULSIONS

Biographical sketches have been presented for 35 enslaved Muslims, 34 of whom were actively enslaved in the Americas and one of whom came to America after obtaining his freedom from slavery. Many more enslaved Muslims can be readily identified. For example, Tamerlan was a *Marabout*, teacher, and author of books who was enslaved on Saint-

Domingue in the Caribbean in the late 18th century. Muhammad Sisei from the Gambia was a teacher who was enslaved on Trinidad and who served for many years in H.M. West Indian Regiments.

Many runaway slave notices appearing in newspapers clearly identify Muslims. According to a notice in the *Charleston Courier* on February 9, 1805, Sambo was a 30-year-old, five-foot-five-inch, slender-made, runaway slave of "grave countenance." He had escaped from a plantation on the Ashley River, could write Arabic, and had a five-dollar reward on his head. The May 24, 1775, edition of Savannah's *Georgia Gazette* ran an advertisement for a missing 22-year-old slave, Sambo "of the Moorish country." The August 20, 1789, issue of the same Savannah newspaper ran a notice about a runaway slave named Hagar (a traditional Muslim name) who wore a handkerchief on her head. *The South-Carolina Gazette* of October 19, 1738, ran a notice about two runaway slaves from the Gambia named Walley (Wali) and Bocarrey (Abu Bakr). The March 1, 1773, edition of the *South-Carolina Gazette* advertised for a missing Homady (a West African form of Ahmad). Other 18th-century runaway notices in the *South-Carolina Gazette* refer to Mahomet (Muhammad) and Mousa (Musa) and to two runaways of the "Moorish breed." In 1808, *Edenton's Gazette and North Carolina Advertiser* ran a notice for an escaped Mustapha on June 23rd and for an escaped Fatima on June 19th. The June 7, 1792, edition of Savannah's *Gazette of the State of Georgia* advertised for a runaway slave named Mahomet (Muhammad) who was also known as Homady and who was said to be a 25-year-old Moor. The *Columbian Museum and Savannah Advertiser* ran a runaway notice on a slave named Abdalli ('Abd Allah) on May 11, 1802.

About 500 former slaves who fought for the British during the War of 1812 were relocated to Trinidad, where they were living in the forests and said to have "relapsed" back to Islam. An elderly slave known only as "old man Israel" kept a hidden copy of the *Qur'an* and continued to perform the five daily prayers of Islam while enslaved in Georgia. Sanim was a Nupe *Marabout* enslaved in Bahia. Djibirilu of Bahia was the son of a Yoruba *Marabout* and kept a copy of the *Qur'an* that he had imported from Nigeria. Sanim, Belchior da Silva Cunha, Dassalu, Mama, Sulayman, and Ibrahima were Muslims who were operating secret Qur'anic schools and classrooms in Bahia during the early 1830s. To these enslaved Muslims can be added the names of John Muhammad Bath (Bah) and Muhammad Maguina of Trinidad, Dandara of Bahia, and many others.[48]

In reviewing the 35 biographical sketches, a theme that is common to many of them is a sham conversion to Christianity. In some cases, this sham conversion may have eased the work burden of the enslaved Muslim. In a few cases, it may even have contributed to later freedom. In a very few instances, it probably helped the person return to Africa by allowing him to pretend to be going to serve as a Christian missionary. Based upon these 35 Muslims, it is likely that thousands, if not hundreds of thousands, of enslaved Muslims in the Americas participated in a charade of converting to Christianity. For desperate slaves working in brutal and intolerable conditions, a sham conversion to their owner's Christianity may have been seen as the only avenue open to a better life. As such, these so-called conversions must by and large be seen as a simple act of survival in an extremely hostile and dangerous world. In the vast majority of cases, these pseudo-conversions did not mean that the enslaved Muslim was actually abandoning his Islamic faith.

---

48. Diouf SA (1998); Muhammad ANA (2001); Rashad A (1995).

However, it was not just the case that enslaved Muslims in the Americas did not genuinely convert to Christianity. In at least some instances, they appear to have actively converted their fellow, non-Muslim slaves to Islam. For example, Muhammad Sisei of Trinidad, the former teacher from the Gambia, reported that an entire regiment of non-Muslim Africans serving in the British West Indian Regiments converted to Islam. Further, a group of free Mandinka Muslims in Trinidad was successful in converting about 240 out of 1,000 non-Muslim Africans who were resettled from the United States to Trinidad in the aftermath of the War of 1812.

G. MUSLIMS HELPING MUSLIMS

It has already been noted that 'Abd Al-Rahman worked diligently to free his wife and eight of his descendants after his own manumission. Likewise, Ayuba ibn Suleyman used his influence with English aristocrats to free his one-time translator, Lamine Ndiaye. While it can be argued that these were merely examples of Muslims helping close family members and friends, that argument falls apart when considering Samba Makumba, John Muhammad Bath, and the Free Mandinka Society of Trinidad.

Samba Makumba was an enslaved Muslim in Trinidad who managed to secure his freedom through his skills and frugality. Working alongside of Samba, John Muhammad Bath was an *Imam* (prayer leader) and *Qadi* (judge trained in *Shariah*, i.e., Islamic law) to the Muslim community in Trinidad. Samba, John, Muhammad Maguina, Muhammad Sisei, and others like them formed the Free Mandinka Society in Port of Spain, a city in the northwestern corner of Trinidad. Although they had once been enslaved, these freed Mandinka Muslims had been able to earn their emancipation, established themselves as free men in Trinidad, secured housing, and started businesses or gained employment. Once those immediate objectives had been accomplished, they then begin pooling their resources to buy the freedom of other enslaved Mandinka Muslims.

As each previously enslaved Muslim was purchased and emancipated by the Free Mandinka Society, he was expected to work for profit and contribute to the fund to free other Mandinka Muslims held in slavery. This enterprise was so successful that early in the 19th century every enslaved Mandinka Muslim in Trinidad had been freed. The Free Mandinka Society was then able to begin meeting the slaving ships as they arrived in Trinidad harbors and purchase and free any Mandinka Muslims even before they set foot on land. After having freed over 500 enslaved Muslims on Trinidad, the Free Mandinka Society was able to expand its efforts to free enslaved Muslims on other islands in the Caribbean.

Other commendable examples of Muslims helping Muslims can be found among the freed Muslims of Brazil in the wake of the Bahia revolts. Antonio da Costa and Joao Monteiro, both of whom were wealthy former slaves, chartered a ship to take themselves, their families, and 150 other formerly enslaved Africans back to Africa. They arrived in Africa in April of 1836. About the same time, 200-300 formerly enslaved Africans were taken back to Lagos, Nigeria, on a British ship that had been paid for by one of them who had gained his freedom, become wealthy, and then sold all that he had to finance the expedition. Of note, the man behind this philanthropic endeavor had made his own Middle Passage voyage into Brazilian slavery in 1821. Of those who sailed with him back to Africa, 60 had been fellow slaves on the very same ship that had taken him to Brazil in the first place.

These stories of Muslims helping Muslims to escape the bondage of slavery or to travel back home to Africa are inspirational testimonies to the brotherhood that exists within the Islamic faith. In each of these examples, we find Muslims willingly giving away all that they could to help their brothers and sisters in Islam escape from slavery or return home to Africa. They had sacrificed their own financial success for their fellow Muslims.

H. THE CONCEPT OF SLAVERY IN ISLAM

H1. INTRODUCTION

As reported in the section of this chapter that dealt with the biographical sketches of Muslims enslaved in the Americas, some of these enslaved Muslims or their families were themselves slave owners back in Africa. However, the concept of slavery in Islam is very different than the concept of slavery practiced in the New World by adherents to the Judaeo-Christian tradition.

As noted previously in this chapter, *Genesis* 9:18-27 not only condoned slavery, but it actually prescribed slavery for those of a particular ethnic descent, i.e., the descendants of Canaan, the son of Ham. As Ham was reported to be the progenitor of the African people, later generations of Christians often interpreted this passage from *Genesis* as a divine commandment to enslave the black-skinned peoples of Africa. In short, this was a slavery based upon a virulent racism.

Some Christians might prefer to dismiss slavery as an aberration of *Old Testament* times. However, this protest must be dismissed, as the *New Testament* book of *Philemon* documents that Paul returned a slave, Onesimus, to his owner, Philemon. Other *New Testament* passages also explicitly condone and sanction slavery.

Slaves, obey your earthly masters with fear and trembling, in single-ness of heart, as you obey Christ; not only while being watched, and in order to please them, but as slaves of Christ, doing the will of God from the heart. Render service with enthusiasm, as to the Lord and not to men and women, knowing that whatever good we do, we will receive the same again from the Lord, whether we are slaves or free. (*Ephesians* 6:5-8)

Slaves, obey your earthly masters in everything, not only while being watched and in order to please them, but wholeheartedly, fearing the Lord. Whatever your task, put yourselves into it, as done for the Lord and not for your masters, since you know that from the Lord you will receive the inheritance as your reward; you serve the Lord Christ. (*Colossians* 3:22-24)

In all fairness, it must be pointed out that the passages referred to from *Philemon*, *Ephesians*, and *Colossians* go on to dictate a far more humane treatment of slaves than that practiced by adherents to the Judaeo-Christian tradition in the Americas. Nonetheless, there remain significant differences between the Biblical and Islamic concepts of slavery.

One of those differences can be illustrated by once again turning to *Genesis* 9:18-27, which sanctioned and prescribed slavery based upon ethnicity and race. In marked contrast, Islam rejects any association between slavery and one's ethnicity or race. According to the teachings of Islam, race and ethnicity confer neither superiority nor inferiority.

O mankind! We created you from a single (pair) of a male and a female, and made you into nations and tribes that ye may know each other (not that ye may despise each other). Verily, the most honored of you in the sight of God is (he who is) the most righteous of you. (*Qur'an* 49:13)

As the above Qur'anic verse indicates, racism and ethnic bigotry are prohibited within Islam. One's particular ethnicity or race can never be the basis by which one is enslaved and must never be the basis for any bigotry and prejudice. This Islamic prohibition against ethnic and racial prejudice is made even more strongly in Prophet Muhammad's sermons during his farewell pilgrimage to Makkah, during which he instructed Muslims to obey a black-skinned slave if the slave followed the dictates of the *Qur'an* and during which he referred to the above-quoted Qur'anic verse.

O people! Listen and obey, even though a mangled Abyssinian slave is your commander, if he executes (the commands of) the Book of God (i.e., the *Qur'an*) among you...O people! Verily your Lord is One, and your father (i.e., Adam) is one. All of you belong to one ancestry from Adam, and Adam was created out of clay. There is no superiority for an Arab over a non-Arab and for a non-Arab over an Arab; nor for the white over the black, nor for the black over the white, except in piety. "Verily, the most honored of you in the sight of God is (he who is) the most righteous of you."

As one final example of Islam's prohibition against racist ideology and ethnic prejudice, it is worth noting Prophet Muhammad's injunction against pride in one's ancestry.

Abu Huraira reported the Messenger of God as saying: "God, Most High, has removed from you the pride of the pre-Islamic period and its boasting in ancestors. One is only a pious believer or a miserable sinner. You are sons of Adam, and Adam came from dust. Let the people cease to boast about their ancestors. They are merely fuel in hell; or they will certainly be of less account with God than the beetle which rolls dung with its nose." (*Abu Dawud, Hadith* #5097)

H2. STATUS OF SLAVES

As the above saying of Prophet Muhammad makes clear, a Muslim is to listen to and obey a black-skinned, Abyssinian slave if that slave judges and commands according to the teachings of the *Qur'an*. What is important is not whether one is black or white or even slave or free. What is important is one's faith and belief in God. This point is made in the following Qur'anic verses, in which Muslims are instructed that slaves who believe in God are better than unbelievers who are free. The former are suitable for marriage partners, but the latter are not.

Do not marry unbelieving women until they believe: a slave woman who believes is better than an unbelieving woman, even though she allure you. Nor marry (your girls) to unbelievers until they believe: a man slave who believes is better than an unbeliever even though he allure you. (*Qur'an* 2:221)

If any of you have not the means wherewith to wed free believing women, they may wed believing girls from among those whom your right hands possess (i.e., slaves): and God hath full knowledge about your faith. Ye are one from another: wed them with the leave of their owners, and give them their dowers, according to what is reasonable: they should be chaste, not lustful, nor taking paramours: when they are taken in wedlock, if they fall into shame, their punishment is half that for free women. (*Qur'an* 4:25)

The above Qur'anic passages speak quite eloquently to the issue of the status of slaves in Islam. They are to be evaluated according to their religious belief and faith, not according to their enslaved status. Further, Prophet Muhammad gave explicit instructions that slaves were to be seen as one's brothers (*Al-Bukhari*, Volume 1, *Hadith* #1, which is quoted below) and as one's children (*Al-Tirmidhi*, *Hadith* #984, which is also quoted below). This is clearly a very different concept of slavery than that practiced by American slave owners from within the Judaeo-Christian tradition.

H3. EMANCIPATION OF SLAVES

Like the *Bible*, the foundational sources of Islam, i.e., the *Qur'an* and the sayings of Prophet Muhammad, occasionally provide some technical allowance for slavery. However, it is also the case that both the *Qur'an* and Prophet Muhammad actively discouraged slavery in a number of different ways. That the *Qur'an* and Prophet Muhammad discouraged slavery can be seen from the following quotations, in which the freeing of a slave is dictated as expiation for the commission of sins and mistakes.

> Never should a believer kill a believer; but (if it so happens) by mistake, (compensation is due); if one (so) kills a believer, it is ordained that he should free a believing slave, and pay compensation to the deceased's family, unless they remit it freely. If the deceased belonged to a people at war with you, and he was a believer, the freeing of a believing slave (is enough). If he belonged to a people with whom ye have a treaty of mutual alliance, compensation should be paid to his family and a believing slave be freed. For those who find this beyond their means, (is prescribed) a fast for two

months running: by way of repentance to God; for God hath all knowledge and all wisdom.

(*Qur'an* 4:92)

God will not call you to account for what is futile in your oaths, but He will call you to account for your deliberate oaths: for expiation, feed ten indigent persons, on a scale of the average for the food of your families; or clothe them; or give a slave his freedom. If that is beyond your means, fast for three days. That is the expiation for the oaths ye have sworn. But keep to your oaths. Thus doth God make clear to you His signs, that ye may be grateful.

(*Qur'an* 5:89)

But those who divorce their wives by Zihar, then wish to go back on the words they uttered—(it is ordained that such a one) should free a slave before they touch each other: this are ye admonished to perform: and God is well acquainted with (all) that ye do.

(*Qur'an* 58:3)

Wathilah ibn Al-Asqa said: "We went to the Prophet about a friend of ours who deserved hell for murder. He said: 'Emancipate a slave on his behalf; God will set free from hell a member of the body (of the offender) for every member of his (the slave that is freed).'"

(*Abu Dawud, Hadith* #3953; see also
Al-Bukhari, Volume 3, *Hadith* #693)

As the above quotations from the *Qur'an* demonstrate, the expiation for accidentally killing a fellow Muslim is the freeing of a slave. Likewise, the freeing of a slave is prescribed as expiation for having deliberately made inappropriate oaths and for attempting to divorce one's wife by the process of *Zihar*. (*Zihar* was a pre-Islamic process of divorce among the Arabs. In the practice of *Zihar*, a husband would state that his wife was like his mother to him. This statement deprived the wife of all her conjugal rights but kept her in bondage to her (ex)husband and unable to remarry. Islam prohibits the practice of *Zihar* (e.g., *Qur'an* 33:4 and 58:1-5). Still further, Prophet Muhammad specifically taught that the freeing of slaves was one way to help avoid the punishment of hellfire in the afterlife.

The emancipation of slaves as expiation for a variety of misdeeds was only one of the many ways that Islam actively discouraged human slavery. For example, Prophet Muhammad also ordered the freeing of slaves during periods of solar eclipse and urged slaveholders to educate and free their female slaves.

> Asma bint Abu Bakr narrated: "The Prophet ordered us to free slaves at the time of solar eclipses."
>
> (*Al-Bukhari*, Volume 3, *Hadith* #695; see also *Al-Bukhari*, Volume 2, *Hadith* #163, and Volume 3, *Hadith* #696)

> Abu Musa narrated that God's Messenger said, "He who has a slave girl and educates and treats her nicely and then manumits and marries her, will get a double reward."
>
> (*Al-Bukhari*, Volume 3, *Hadith* #720; see also *Al-Bukhari*, Volume 3, *Hadith* #723)

Still another way in which the *Qur'an* discouraged slavery was by mandating that a Muslim's payment of his obligatory charity could be spent on ransoming slaves from their owners. Going still further, the *Qur'an* explicitly stated that "the path that is steep," i.e., the path of righteousness, in part consists of "freeing the bondman."

It is not righteousness that ye turn your faces towards east or west; but it is righteousness to believe in God and the Last Day, and the angels, and the book, and the messengers; to spend of your substance, out of love for Him, for your kind, for orphans, for the needy, for the wayfarer, for those who ask, and for the ransom of slaves; to be steadfast in prayer, and practice regular charity, to fulfill the contracts which ye have made; and to be firm and patient, in pain (or suffering) and adversity, and throughout all periods of panic. Such are the people of truth, the God-fearing.

(*Qur'an* 2:177)

Alms are for the poor and the needy, and those employed to administer the (funds); for those whose hearts have been (recently) reconciled (to the truth); for those in bondage and in debt; in the cause of God; and for the wayfarer: (thus is it) ordained by God and God is full of knowledge and wisdom.

(*Qur'an* 9:60)

And what will explain to thee the path that is steep? (It is) freeing the bondman; or the giving of food in a day of privation to the orphan with claims of relationship, or to the indigent (down) in the dust.

(*Qur'an* 90:12-16)

The freeing of slaves as expiation for one's personal misconduct, at the times of a solar eclipse, as a part of a Muslim's prescribed charity, and as a means of adhering to "the path that is steep" do not yet exhaust the ways in which Islam actively discourages slavery. Going still further, the *Qur'an* commands that if any slave asks his owner for a legal contract by which the slave may earn his freedom, the slaveholder must comply with this request.

> ...if any of your slaves ask for a deed in writing (to enable them to earn their freedom for a certain sum), give them such a deed if ye know any good in them; yea, give them something yourselves out of the means which God has given to you.
>
> *(Qur'an* 24:33)

In practice, the above Qur'anic injunction has been interpreted to mean that: (1) as soon as a slave requests a contract whereby he can earn his freedom, his owner must comply; (2) thereafter, the slave is free from his owner's work demands and is free to work in his own behalf to earn the money to purchase his freedom; and (3) once the slave has earned his purchase price and paid it, he is both practically and technically free. Furthermore, as witnessed by *Qur'an* 24:33, the slave owner is expected to contribute to the slave's fund to purchase his freedom, i.e., "give something yourselves out of the means which God has given to you."

However, it is not just through expiation for misconduct, solar eclipses, prescribed charity, and a slave asking for a contract to earn his freedom that Islam discouraged human slavery and urged the emancipation of slaves. Prophet Muhammad directly ordered Muslims to emancipate slaves, i.e., "set free the captives," and noted that "God has created nothing on the face of the earth dearer to Him than emancipation."

Abu Muisa Al-Ashari narrated that the Prophet said, "Feed the hungry, visit the sick, and set free the captives."

(*Al-Bukhari*, Volume 7, *Hadith* #552; see also *Al-Bukhari*, Volume 4, *Hadith* #282, Volume 7, *Hadith* #103, & Volume 9, *Hadith* #285)

Mu'adh ibn Jabal narrated that God's Messenger said to him, "Mu'adh, God has created nothing on the face of the earth dearer to Him than emancipation, and God has created nothing on the face of the earth more hateful to Him than divorce.

(*Al-Tirmidhi*, *Hadith* #969)

H4. TREATMENT OF SLAVES

Despite the very active discouragement of slavery to be found within the teachings of Islam, traditional Islamic thought has held that slavery per se was still technically permissible in certain situations. However, where such slavery was permitted, the slave was to be treated far differently than how he was treated in the Americas by followers of the Judaeo-Christian tradition. The following quotations represent a brief sampling of Prophet Muhammad's injunctions on how slaves were to be treated.

Serve God, and join not any partners with Him; and do good to parents, kinsfolk, orphans, those in need, neighbors who are near, neighbors who are strangers, the companion by your side, the way-farer (ye meet), and what your right hands possess (i.e., your slaves): for God loveth not the arrogant, the vainglorious—

(*Qur'an* 4:36)

Jabir ibn 'Abd Allah narrated that the Prophet said, "If anyone possesses these three characteristics, God will give him an easy death and bring him into His paradise: gentleness towards the weak, affection towards parents, and kindness to slaves."

(Al-Tirmidhi, Hadith #981)

According to the teachings of Prophet Muhammad, slaveholders were to "do good" to slaves and to treat them with "kindness." Further, in stark contrast to the institution of slavery in the Americas, Prophet Muhammad demonstrated that enslaved families were not to be broken up with different members of the family being placed with different owners, and he cursed those who did so.

'Abd Allah ibn Mas'ud narrated that when captives were brought to the Prophet, he gave away families together through dislike of separating them.

(Al-Tirmidhi, Hadith #983; see also Al-Tirmidhi, Hadith #980)

Abu Musa narrated that God's Messenger cursed those who separated a parent from his child and a brother from his brother.

(Al-Tirmidhi, Hadith #982)

Abu Ayyub told of hearing God's Messenger say, "If anyone separates a mother from her child, God will separate him from his friends on the Day of Resurrection."

(Al-Tirmidhi, Hadith #979)

Still further, Prophet Muhammad prescribed that the slaveholder must feed his slaves just as he was fed and clothe them just as he was clothed. In addition, the slave owner must actively and personally help his slaves in the performance of any arduous labor that would otherwise be too taxing for them.

Khaythamah reported: "While we were sitting in the company of 'Abd Allah ibn 'Umar, there came in his steward. He (ibn 'Umar) said, 'Have you supplied the provision to the slaves?' He (the steward) said, 'No.' Upon (hearing) this, he (ibn 'Umar) said, 'Go and give (the provision) to them, for the Messenger of God has said, 'This sin is enough for a man that he withholds the subsistence from one whose master he is.'"

(*Muslim, Hadith* #2182)

Al-Marur (ibn Suwaid) narrated: "At Ar-Rabadha I met Abu Dhar Al-Ghifari) who was wearing a cloak, and his slave, too, was wearing a similar one. I asked about the reason for it. He replied, 'I abused a person by calling his mother with bad names.' The Prophet said to me, 'O Abu Dhar! Did you abuse him by calling his mother with bad names? You still have some characteristics of ignorance. Your slaves are your brothers, and God has put them under your command. So whoever has a brother under his command should feed him of what he eats and dress him of what he wears. Do not ask them (i.e., your slaves) to do things beyond their capacity, and if you do so, then help them.'"

(*Al-Bukhari*, Volume 1, *Hadith* #1;
see also *Al-Bukhari*, Volume 3, *Ahadith* #721 & 723, &
Volume 8, *Hadith* #76; and *Abu Dawud, Ahadith* #5138-5139)

During Prophet Muhammad's final sermons on his farewell pilgrimage to Makkah, he reiterated the above themes about the proper treatment of slaves, again noting that a slaveholder should feed and clothe his slaves as he himself is fed and clothed. However, Prophet Muhammad went even further and prohibited the chastisement of slaves.

> And your slaves! See that you feed them with such food as you yourselves eat, and clothe them with the clothes that you yourselves wear. And if they commit a fault that you are not inclined to forgive, then part with them (i.e., sell them to another or set them free) for they are the servants of God and are not to be chastised.

Finally, it should be noted that Prophet Muhammad even gave instructions about how a slave was to be called by his owner. He admonished slaveholders not to refer to their slaves as slaves, but as "my lad, my lass, and my boy." In doing so, Prophet Muhammad subtly emphasized that each slave owner should treat his slaves "as generously as you treat your children."

> Abu Huraira narrated that the Prophet said, "You should not say, 'Feed your lord, help your lord in performing ablution, or give water to your lord,' but should say, 'My master or my guardian,' and one should not say, 'My slave or my girl-slave,' but should say, "My lad, my lass, and my boy.'"
>
> (*Al-Bukhari*, Volume 3, *Hadith* #728)

> Abu Bakr Al-Siddiq narrated: "God's Messenger said, 'One who treats badly those under his authority will not enter paradise.' He was asked

whether he had not told them that these people had more slaves and orphans than any other, and (he) replied, 'Yes, so treat them as generously as you treat your children, and give them food from what you eat.'..."

(*Al-Tirmidhi, Hadith* #984; see also
Al-Tirmidhi, Hadith #977)

H5. Conclusions

As can be seen, the practice of slavery within Islam was a radically different concept than the institution of slavery in the Americas. While Islam did not totally prohibit slavery, it obviously discouraged slavery and prescribed the emancipation of slaves as expiation for misconduct, during times of solar eclipse, as a form of charity, as a means of adhering to "the path that is steep," and whenever a slave asked for a contract by which he could earn his freedom. Taken together, the *Qur'an* and the teachings of Prophet Muhammad created a situation in which human slavery was bound to be eliminated over time.

Just as importantly, Islam mandated a treatment of slaves that was a far cry from the brutality and violence of the American system of slavery. A slaveholder was not to separate enslaved family members from each other, had an obligation to feed and clothe his slaves in a manner no different from his own food and clothing, and was instructed to share the burden with his slaves when it came to performing particularly arduous labor. Further, the slave owner was never to refer to his slaves as slaves, but as "my lad, my lass, and my boy." He was to treat his slaves with goodness and kindness and was to refrain from chastising his slaves. In short, he was always to remember that his slaves were to be treated as his brothers and his children.

I. Summary and Conclusions

The institution of human slavery was one of the saddest chapters in the history of the Americas. It was a brutal, vicious, and degrading institution that was based squarely upon a virulent racism. As many as 15 to 20 million black-skinned Africans were subjected to this perversion. Of these enslaved Africans in the Americas, approximately 20-30% were practicing Muslims, most of whom were highly educated professionals and military personnel. Not only were these enslaved Muslims subjected to the same indignities and horrors as other slaves, they also had to bear the extra burden of trying to maintain their Islamic faith and practices within the confines of American slavery. Their stories should serve as an inspirational lesson to contemporary Muslims around the world.

5 Muslims and Native Americans

A. INTRODUCTION

There is a wealth of circumstantial evidence that early Muslims in the Americas frequently intermarried with and were gradually absorbed by several different tribes of American Indians. In particular, this absorption of Muslims into Native American Indian tribes can be posited with regard to the Algonquin (e.g., the Chickahominy, Chippewa, Creek, Mattaponi, Pamunkey, Powhatan, and Seminole tribes), Iroquois (e.g., Cherokee and Tuscarora tribes), Siouan (e.g., Catawba, Cheraw, Keyauwee, and Yuchi tribes), and Carib.

As would be expected in such a scenario, the descendants of these Muslims eventually abandoned the Islam of their ancestors. Whether the practice of Islam died out with the original Muslims, whether it survived for a couple of generations, or whether it lasted for many generations is not currently knowable. At present, all that can be stated with certainty is that early Muslims in the Americas were incorporated into a variety of Indian tribes.

B. A BRIEF REVIEW

Much of the circumstantial evidence suggesting an early Muslim contribution to the bloodlines of American Indian tribes was previously presented in chapters II and III. However, it is worth briefly reviewing that information at this time.

(1) As early as the 12th century, Al-Idrisi reported in *Nuzhat Al-Mushtaq Fi Ikhtiraq Al-Afaq* (Excursion of the Longing One in Crossing Horizons) that a group of eight Muslim sailors from North Africa sailed west from Lisbon (Portugal). After sailing west for more than 31 days, they landed on what must have been an island in the Caribbean. The intrepid explorers were initially imprisoned by Indians but were later released when a translator appeared who spoke Arabic. The presence of this Arabic-speaking Indian suggests prolonged contact between Muslims and American Indians in the Caribbean by no later than the 12th century. Such contact would probably have resulted in inter-marriage between Muslims and Indians, followed by later absorption of the Muslim population by the Indians.[49]

(2) Circa 1310, Sultan Abu Bakari of the Mandinka kingdom of Mali sent two different fleets of ships, totaling 2,400 ships, sailing west from Africa. Quite obviously, the manning of 2,400 ships would have required thousands of Mandinka sailors. These fleets never returned to Africa and at least one of them appears to have reached Brazil. From Brazil, it appears that the Mandinka explored parts of South America, Central America, and what would later become Mexico and the United States.

No doubt some of these Mandinka would have intermarried with South American and North American Indian tribes, resulting in descendants who were later described by European explorers of the New World. For example, Columbus encountered black-skinned Indians in what is now Honduras, and Balboa was told of a black-skinned tribe of Indians living in what is now Panama. Giles Cauvet's *Les Berberes de l'Amerique* reported that a pre-Columbian tribe in

---

49. Quick AH (1998); Mroue Y (1996); Irving TB (---).

Honduras was known as the *Almamys*, a corruption of the Mandinka word for the Arabic *Imam* (the Muslim prayer leader). Additionally, a black-skinned tribe that lived at Tegulcigalpa near the Nicaraguan border was known as the Jaras, which appears to be a slight corruption of the Mandinka "Jarra," a clan designation of the Mandinka tribe living in Gambia. As late as the 19th century, the Garifuna clan of the Carib tribe of Indians was reported to be black-skinned and to have a language that was distinct from other clans of the Carib and that appeared to be of African derivation. Further, the Garifuna avoided pork (pork is prohibited in Islam) and prized crescent-shaped medallions and jewelry (the crescent is often used as a symbol for Islam). In 1861, L'Abbe Brasseur de Bourboug wrote in his *Popul-Vuh: le Livre Sacre et les Mythes de l-Antiquite Americaine* that the native people of Darien (Panama) can be grouped under two names according to their distinct origin: Mandingas (Mandinka) and Tule. In North America, J. C. Pyrlaeus's 1750 dictionary of the Nanticoke Indians of eastern Maryland later proved to be a compilation of the Mandinka language, suggesting a pre-Columbian infusion of the Mandinka into this North American Indian tribe. It is also possible that the Mandinka intermarried with and were absorbed by the Iroquois and Algonquin Indians.[50]

(3) As extensively documented in chapter II, numerous Turkish words and related meanings found their way into the languages of the Cherokee, Creek, Seminole, Algonquin, Powhatan, and Chippewa languages at least as early as the beginning of the 17th century. These words run the gamut from Chicago to Kentucky, tepee, moccasins, and tomahawk. Further, the Delaware Indians referred to themselves

---

50. Katz WL (1997); Smallwood AD (1999); Quick AH (1998); Mroueh Y (1996); Muhammad ANA (2001); Numan FH (---); Shelton SM (---).

as *Lenni-Lanape* and to their tribal records as the *Wallam Olum*. The former term conforms to the Turkish *La-ani la-nabi* (meaning "the people of the Prophet"), and the latter is almost identical with the Turkish *Vallah olum* (meaning "Allah's records"). Taken as a whole, this linguistic evidence provides strong documentation of an early Othmanic presence in the Americas that predates Columbus and that was probably reinforced throughout the 16th century. Further, the linguistic evidence suggests that people of Turkish descent and language were assimilated into many of the above tribes during the 15th and 16th centuries.[51]

At the present time, there is no way to document precisely when and where a 15th-century, Othmanic presence began to be incorporated into the Indian tribes of the American East and Southeast. However, there appears to be at least one known source of 16th-century absorption of people of Turkish descent into Indian tribes of the American Southeast.

As noted previously in chapter III, Sir Francis Drake offloaded about 200 liberated slaves of Moorish and Turkish descent on Roanoke Island, a colony that the British were temporarily abandoning, in 1586. Two weeks later, when Sir Walter Raleigh arrived at Roanoke Island, these Turkish Muslims were nowhere to be seen. They had apparently crossed over to the mainland of North Carolina where they were probably assimilated into the Powhatan, Pamunkey, Nansemond, Croatan, and Hatters tribes.

Additionally, it has been suggested that there were Morisco and Turkish men and women who were part of the Santa Elena colony established by Spain in 1566. The Santa Elena colony and its satellite forts ceased to exist in 1587. Some of the colonists sailed to the Spanish colony

---

51. Kennedy NB (1997); Kennedy NB, Kennedy RV (1997).

at St. Augustine, Florida. However, many others appear to have remained behind in what are today South Carolina, Georgia, North Carolina, and Tennessee. Once again, these colonists probably joined up with friendly Indian tribes (e.g., the Cherokee, Creek, and Catawba), intermarried, and over time became completely absorbed by the tribes, leaving no record of their presence aside from the Turkish loan words incorporated into the languages of the various Indian tribes that befriended them.

To which tribe did the Santa Elena colonists flee? It has been suggested that the Cheraw (sometimes spelled Saura or Sara) tribe likely took them in. The Cheraw tribe later merged with the Keyauwee about 1700, which is when a surveyor, John Lawson, reported that the Keyauwee Indian men wore beards and mustaches, a most unusual occurrence for Native American Indians but typical grooming for Muslim men. At about the same time, Maurice Mathews, a colonist in South Carolina, wrote that the Keyauwee were "Spanish," offering further evidence of a Muslim/Morisco infusion into American Indian tribes. [52]

C. SOME FURTHER SUGGESTIONS[53]

The above review provides an appropriate starting point for positing that early Muslims in the Americas were incorporated into Native American Indian tribes and thereby eventually lost their individual histories and heritages. However, there is also additional information suggesting a link between Muslims and the Indians of the American East and Southeast. Examples include the dress and forts of some Southeast Indians, names of some individual Indians, Cherokee art, and escaped Muslim slaves being taken in and sheltered by Indian tribes.

52. Douglas K (2002a); Douglas K (2002b).

53. Information in this section is from El Mar (1996), Abdullah AA (1996), Kennedy NB (1997), Douglas K (2002a), Kennedy NB (2002), Kennedy NB (2003a), Kennedy NB (2003b), and Kennedy NB, Kennedy RV (1997).

With regard to the dress of some Southeast Indians, one does well to consider the traditional garments of the Cherokee, Seminole, and Creek Indians. Prior to 1832, Cherokee men typically wore a turban and a shirt-like garment that descended to the knees or lower, and Cherokee women generally wore a long head covering. Likewise, 19th-century photographs of Seminole men reveal that they often wore turbans or what can best be described as a Turkish *fez*, while Creek men also wore a *fez*. Further, both Cherokee and Creek Indians wore their turban or *fez* with a single feather, which is exactly the typical 16th-century Othmanic style. While the above attire of the 19th-century Cherokee, Seminole, and Creek Indians does not constitute absolute proof of the incorporation of Muslims into those tribes, it is highly suggestive.

Another intriguing coincidence suggesting an infusion of Muslims into Native American Indian tribes concerns the Tuscarora Indians. Located in southwestern Virginia in 1751, the Tuscarora constructed and utilized forts during the Tuscarora Wars. These forts were similar to West African forts and appear to have been introduced to the Tuscarora by an escaped African slave known as Harry. However, a much earlier date can be hypothesized for an initial infusion of Muslims into the Tuscarora tribe. In 1653, an Englishman reported that he found about 30 wealthy "Spaniards" (probably Muslims or Moriscos) and their seven African slaves living with the Tuscarora.

Additionally, two different shipments of Turkish and Armenian men and women from the Othmanic Empire, almost all of whom would have been Muslims, were sent as indentured servants to the British colony at Jamestown, where they comprised a substantial percentage of the indentured-servant class. As recorded in *The Virginia Carolorum*, among these indentured servants were such individuals as: "Mehmet the Turk, Ahmad the Turk, Joseph the Armenian, Sayyan Turk," etc. These shipments took place during the mid-1600s, and the earliest written documentation of a Turkish presence at Jamestown is from 1631. These Turks became so numerous at Jamestown that 17th-century Virginia ended up passing a law prohibiting the importation of any more "Turks" and so-called "infidels" (Muslims) into the colony. Some of these Turks most likely fled their servitude and were taken in by Indian tribes.

Further considerations include the pronounced similarities of designs and motifs between Cherokee and Othmanic art and the fact that the son of the famous 19th-century Cherokee chief, Stand Watie, was given the Muslim name of Saladin (an Occidental corruption of Salah Al-Din). Still further, many Indian tribes of the American Southeast, including the Cherokee, maintained in their myths of origin that they originated from the east (i.e., from across the ocean), not from the west. Finally, one notes the similarity between the Powhatan view of the afterlife and the Qur'anic description of heaven. Both concepts offer a heaven of earthly and physical pleasures, as opposed to the strictly spiritual pleasures typically described in the Christian tradition. To illustrate this in what follows, a Powhatan description is presented first, followed by two descriptions of heaven from the *Qur'an*.

> Stor'd with the highest perfection of all their Earthly Pleasures; namely, with plenty of all sorts of Game, for Hunting, Fishing, and Fowling; that it is blest with the most charming Women, which enjoy an eternal bloom, and have an universal desire to please.[54]

---

54. Robert Beverley's *The History and Present State of Virginia* (1705) as quoted in Kennedy NB, Kennedy RV (1997).

(Here is) a parable of the garden which the righteous are promised: in it are rivers of water incorruptible; rivers of milk of which the taste never changes; rivers of wine, a joy to those who drink; and rivers of honey pure and clear. In it there are for them all kinds of fruits; and grace from their Lord.

(Qur'an 47:15)

But the sincere (and devoted) servants of Allah—for them is a sustenance determined, fruits (delights); and they (shall enjoy) honor and dignity, in gardens of felicity, facing each other on thrones (of dignity): round will be passed to them a cup from a clear-flowing fountain, crystal-white, of a taste delicious to those who drink (thereof), free from headiness; nor will they suffer intoxication there from. And besides them will be chaste women; restraining their glances, with big eyes (of wonder and beauty).

(Qur'an 37:40-48)

D. The Black Indians

D1. Introduction

Pre-Columbian Mandinka and post Columbian Turks and Moriscos were far from being the only Muslim infusion into American Indian tribes. Escaped African slaves, many of whom would have been Muslims, often found shelter and acceptance among various Indian tribes. With time, they married into the tribes and produced offspring. In addition, tribes such as the Cherokee sometimes had their own African slaves who were later absorbed into the tribes. Further evidence of the incorporation of African Muslims and of African Americans of Muslim descent into American Indian tribes can be found by noting that between the American Revolutionary War and the Civil War so-called "black" Indian tribes were reported to exist in Connecticut, Delaware, Maryland, Massachusetts, New Jersey, New York, North Carolina, South Carolina, Tennessee, and Virginia. [55]

While it cannot be definitively shown that specific Africans and African Americans who escaped to and joined up with American Indians were Muslims or of Muslim descent, it must be remembered that Muslims represented 20-30% of all Africans brought to the Americas as slaves (see chapter IV). As such, it appears reasonable to conclude that Muslims or Muslim descendants were part and parcel of the post Columbian phenomenon of so-called Black Indians.

D2. BLACK INDIANS IN LATIN AMERICA[56]

Shortly after the first African slaves arrived in Hispaniola, they began escaping from their Spanish owners. The first of the runaway slaves in the Americas, these Africans sought shelter and refuge with Hispaniola's population of native Indians, who gladly incorporated the Africans into their tribes. This prompted the Spanish governor of Hispaniola, Nicolas de Ovando, to write to King Ferdinand in 1502 that no more Africans should be sent as slaves, since: "They fled amongst the Indians and taught them bad customs and never could be captured."

Around 1685, a number of enslaved Africans and Indians escaped from their Dutch owners in Surinam, South America. These runaway slaves established their own community, intermarried, and formed a new people, the Saramaka. The Saramaka began a war of liberation that lasted until 1761, at which time the Europeans finally abandoned their attempts to recapture and enslave the Saramaka. Surviving across more

---

55. Douglas K (2002a); Katz WL (1997).
56. The information in this section is from Katz WL (1997).

than three centuries, the Saramaka continue to exist to this very day. Contemporary descendants of the original African and Indian runaways now number about 20,000 members of mixed African and Indian descent.

As early as 1650, Mexico already had a population of about 100,000 people of mixed African and Indian descent. In addition, two Black Indian communities in colonial Brazil were led by African women.

D3. BLACK INDIANS IN THE UNITED STATES & ITS PREDECESSORS[57]

The phenomenon of Black Indians was not just confined to the areas south of the border of the current United States. Black Indians also flourished in what would later comprise the United States, especially in the areas east of the Mississippi River.

One of the earliest examples of African slaves escaping from European colonists and being absorbed by American Indians occurred as far back as 1526. In June of that year, Lucas Vasquez de Ayllon established a Spanish colony near the mouth of the Pee Dee River in what is now eastern South Carolina. The Spanish settlement was named San Miguel de Gualdape, and de Ayllon peopled the colony with 500 free Spanish and 100 enslaved African settlers from Santo Domingo. Disease, lack of food, internal disputes, and lack of adequate shelter from an approaching winter greatly weakened the colony and lead to the death of about 350 of the 500 Spanish settlers. Finally, in November of 1526, the African slaves fled the colony and were taken in by the local Indians. Almost immediately thereafter, the remaining Spanish settlers returned to Santo Domingo.

The year 1622 witnessed the first major battle between American Indians and European colonists in North America. The Indians won

---

57. Information in this section is from Katz WL (1997) and --- (2003e).

a decisive victory, killing off the Europeans of the Jamestown, Virginia, colony. In marked contrast to the fate of their European owners, the Africans enslaved at Jamestown were incorporated into the Indian community.

Colonial advertisements for escaped African slaves frequently told of runaways who had Indian wives and who spoke Indian languages. Occasionally, these runaways were noted to be of mixed African and Indian descent. Examples of the key phrases from these advertisements include the following.

> ...ran off with his Indian wife...had kin among the Indians...part-Indian and speaks their language good.[58]

In South Carolina, colonists became so concerned about the possible threat posed by the mixed African and Indian population that was arising as runaway African slaves escaped to the Indians that they passed a new law in 1725. This law stipulated a fine of 200 pounds on anyone who even brought a slave to the frontier regions of the colony, the area where slaves were most likely to find a way to merge with the Indians. In 1751, the colony of South Carolina found it necessary to issue another law, warning that having Africans in proximity to Indians was deemed detrimental to the security of the colony.

In 1726, the British governor of colonial New York exacted a promise from the Iroquois Indians to return all runaway slaves who had joined up with them. This same promise was exacted from the Huron Indians in 1764 and from the Delaware Indians in 1765. Despite their promises, no escaped slaves were ever returned by the Iroquois, Huron, and Delaware Indians, who continued to provide a safe and secure home for escaped

---

58. Katz WL (1997), p. 103.

slaves. Likewise, Chief Joseph Brant of the Mohawk Indians near Ontario welcomed escaped slaves into his tribe and allowed them, perhaps even encouraged them, to intermarry with his people.

Black Indians were also found among the Natick Indians. In fact, one of America's great martyrs, Crispus Attucks, was a Black Natick Indian. Crispus Attucks was born circa 1723. Little is known about his early life, but he probably was the same Crispus who was the runaway slave who was mentioned in a 1750 advertisement by a resident of Framingham, Massachusetts. On March 5, 1770, a skirmish between British troops and a crowd of protestors in Boston erupted into British gunfire. Crispus Attucks was the first American to be killed in what would become known as the Boston Massacre. Four others were also killed. Memorialized in Samuel Adams's writings and in Paul Revere's engraving of the incident, the Boston Massacre quickly became a rallying cry for American independence. As such, Crispus Attucks became one of the very first people to lose his life in the cause of American independence. His body was carried to Faneuil Hall in Boston, where it laid in state for three days, before being buried alongside of the other four martyrs of the Boston Massacre. In 1888, a monument to Crispus Attucks was erected in Boston Common.

By the late 18th century, the inclusion of Africans and those of African descent by American Indians was also taking place in California. As an example, one can turn to the founding of the city of Los Angeles in 1781. The city was founded by 44 people. Of these 44 founders of Los Angeles, only two were Europeans, the rest being of African, Indian, or mixed descent.

As early as 1783, residents of Virginia began to petition the state legislature regarding the Gingaskin Indians. They complained that people of African descent were living among the Gingaskin. Not deterred when their petition failed, the residents petitioned a second time in 1786. Finally, in 1812, a third petition succeeded. The state legislature removed the tax exemption the Gingaskins had previously enjoyed, claiming that the Gingaskin Indians were no longer Indians, because so many of them were of at least partial African descent.

Shortly after the Revolutionary War, slaves of African descent were known to have been incorporated into the Chippewa Indians. The parents of Pierre Bonga were slaves who were brought to what is now Minnesota by a British officer. Their son, Pierre, became a trapper and interpreter of Indian languages for the North West Company and later married into the Chippewa tribe. The marriage produced two sons, George and Stephen. George, who was born when Thomas Jefferson was president and who was educated in Montreal, also married a Chippewa Indian. Both George and Stephen Bonga later worked as trappers and interpreters. In 1837, George Bonga negotiated a treaty between the Chippewa Indians and the United States at Fort Snelling.

Thomas Jefferson, the third president of the United States, once wrote about the Mattaponies of Virginia that they had come to have more African blood than Indian blood.

In an 1843 petition to the state legislature, the white population of King William County, Virginia, requested help in protecting themselves from the threat supposedly posed by the Pamunkey Indians. In making their request regarding the Pamunkey, the petitioners stated that every living Pamunkey Indian had at least one grandfather or grandmother who was "of Negro blood." The petitioners went on to state that the Pamunkeys had made their land a haven for both free African Americans and runaway slaves.

Even more detailed information exists regarding Black Indians among certain Indian tribes. In what follows, this information is reviewed for the Cherokee, Chickasaw, Choctaw, Creek, and Seminole Indians.

D4. THE BLACK CHEROKEES[59]

The Cherokee Indians were one of the larger tribes of the American Southeast to incorporate Africans and those of African descent into their tribe. There were two basic paths by which these individuals became members of the Cherokee. The first way occurred when runaway slaves were given freedom by and sanctuary with the Cherokee. The second way resulted from the fact that the Cherokee Indians had their own slaves of African descent.

The extent to which people of African descent were incorporated into the Cherokees can be appreciated by looking initially at the results of the 1835 Cherokee census. At that time, slaves of African descent comprised fully 10% of the Cherokee population. Just a few years later during the infamous Trail of Tears of 1838-1839, 14,000 Cherokee Indians were marched westward by 7,000 U.S. Army troops in the fall and winter. Of these 14,000 Cherokee Indians, only 10,000 of which survived the journey, fully 1,600 were Black Cherokees, i.e., just over 11% of the Cherokee Nation were of African descent. By 1860, 18% of the Cherokee Indians were slaves, i.e., 2,511 individuals.

The 1866 treaty between the United States government and the Cherokee nation specifically references Africans and African Americans living with the Cherokee, either as slaves of the Cherokee or as members of the tribe. The treaty refers to former African and African-American slaves of the Cherokee as "freed persons" or as "freedmen."

---

59. Information in this section is taken primary from Katz WL (1997) and Douglas K (2002a).

The following quotation from the July 19, 1866, treaty (ratified on July 27, 1866, and proclaimed on August 11, 1866) is illustrative.

All the Cherokees and freed persons who were formerly slaves to any Cherokee, and all free negroes not having been such slaves, who resided in the Cherokee Nation prior to June first, eighteen hundred and sixty-one...The Cherokee Nation having, voluntarily, in February, eighteen hundred and sixty-three, by an act of the national council, forever abolished slavery, hereby covenant and agree that never hereafter shall either slavery or involuntary servitude exist in their nation otherwise than in the punishment of crime, whereof the party shall have been duly convicted, in accordance with laws applicable to all the members of said tribe alike. They further agree that all freedmen who have been liberated by voluntary act of their former owners or by law, as well as all free colored persons who were in the country at the commencement of the rebellion, and are now residents therein, or who may return within six months, and their descendants, shall have all the rights of native Cherokees: Provided, That owners of slaves so emancipated in the Cherokee Nation shall never receive any compensation or pay for the slaves so emancipated...Every Cherokee and freed person resident in the Cherokee Nation shall have the right to sell any products of his farm, including his or her live stock, or any merchandise or manufactured products, and to ship and drive the same to market without restraint, paying any tax thereon which is now or may be levied by the United States on the quantity sold outside of the Indian Territory.[60]

Between 1898 and 1916, the Dawes Commission enrolled former slaves and freedmen of African descent into the Cherokee tribe. A

---

60. Kappler CJ (1904).

review of the Dawes Commission records indicates a total of 430 surnames enrolled into the tribe, indicating a minimum of 430 different families of African descent who were recognized as being Cherokee Indians.

D5. THE BLACK CHICKASWS AND CHOCTAWS[61]

Both the Chickasaw and Choctaw Indians also had slaves of African descent who were enrolled into their tribes. By 1860, 18% of the Chickasaws and 14% of the Choctaws were slaves, i.e., 975 Chickasaws and 2,344 Choctaws. The following quotation from the 1866 treaty between the United States and the Choctaw and Chickasaw Indians refers to these individuals of African descent.

> ...the Choctaw and Chickasaw Nations respectively shall have made such laws, rules, and regulations as may be necessary to give all persons of African descent, resident in the said nation at the date of the treaty of Fort Smith, and their descendants, heretofore held in slavery among said nations, all the rights, privileges, and immunities, including the right of suffrage, of citizens of said nations, except in the annuities, moneys, and public domain claimed by, or belonging to, said nations respectively; and also to give to such persons who were residents as aforesaid, and their descendants, forty acres each of the land of said nations on the same terms as the Choctaws and Chickasaws...on the enactment of such laws, rules, and regulations, the said sum of three hundred thousand dollars shall be paid to the said Choctaw and Chickasaw Nations in the proportion of three-fourths to the former and one-fourth to the latter, less such

---

61. Information in this section is taken primarily from Douglas K (2002a) and Katz WL (1997).

sum, at the rate of one hundred dollars per capita, as shall be sufficient to pay such persons of African descent before referred to…and be held for the use and benefit of such of said persons of African descent as the United States shall remove from the said Territory…to remove from said nations all such persons of African descent as may be willing to remove; those remaining or returning after having been removed from said nations to have no benefit of said sum of three hundred thousand dollars, or any part thereof, but shall be upon the same footing as other citizens of the United States in the said nations…And they agree, on the part of their respective nations, that all laws shall be equal in their operation upon Choctaws, Chickasaws, and negroes, and that no distinction affecting the latter shall at any time be made, and that they shall be treated with kindness and be protected against injury; and they further agree, that while the said freedmen, now in the Choctaw and Chickasaw Nations, remain in said nations, respectively, they shall be entitled to as much land as they may cultivate for the support of themselves and families…[62]

In 1885, the Choctaw admitted over 350 Choctaw and Chickasaw "freedmen" of African descent into their tribe.

D6. The Black Creeks[63]

The Creek Indians, the parent tribe of the Seminole Indians, also incorporated many individuals of African descent into their tribe, either as slaves or as freedmen.

---

62. Kappler CJ (1904).
63. Information in this section is taken primarily from Douglas K (2002a) and Katz WL (1997).

One of the earliest references to Black Creek Indians can be found in a serious of events occurring in 1750. During that year, a five-man posse set off to recapture an escaped slave living with the Creek Indians. All set to return with the runaway slave, a Creek chief intervened, placing himself squarely between the posse and the escaped slave, cutting the posse's rope into pieces, and throwing it into the fire. He thereupon announced that the Creeks would defend the slave and that the Creeks had as many guns at hand as did the posse. The posse returned without the fugitive slave, who was incorporated into the Creek tribe.

Based upon his 1770 visit with the Creek Indians, John Bartram, a botanist to the king of England, reported that slaves of African descent among the Creek Indians were treated very little differently than their Indian owners. He noted that the slaves were as well off as their masters, that they automatically acquired full freedom upon marrying, and that they and their descendants were given full equality with full-blooded Creek Indians. In short, they had totally been absorbed into the Creek tribe.

By 1860, 10% of the Creek Indians were slaves, i.e., 1,532 Creek

The following quotation from the 1866 treaty between the U.S. government and the Creek Indians specifically refers to the Black Creek Indians.

...inasmuch as there are among the Creeks many persons of African descent...and their descendants and such others of the same race as may be permitted by the laws of the said nation to settle within the limits of the jurisdiction of the Creek Nation as citizens [thereof,] shall have and enjoy all the rights and privileges of native citizens, including an equal interest in the soil and national funds, and the laws of the said nation shall be equally binding upon and give equal protection to all such persons, and all others, of whatsoever race or color, who may be adopted as citizens of members of said tribe...One hundred thousand dollars shall be paid in money and divided to soldiers that enlisted in the Federal Army and the loyal refugee Indians and freedmen who were driven from their homes by the rebel forces...Immediately after the ratification of this treaty the United States agree to ascertain the amount due the respective soldiers who enlisted in the Federal Army, loyal refugee Indians and freedmen...a roll of the names of all soldiers that enlisted in the Federal Army, loyal refugee Indians, and freedmen, be made by him.[64]

D7. THE BLACK SEMINOLES[65]

Slaves of African descent were especially likely to have merged with the Seminole Indians, and they fought alongside the Seminoles against the Americans in the First and Second Seminole Wars. The history and evolution of these so-called Black Seminoles is worth noting in some detail.

The history of African slaves running away to Spanish Florida traces back to at least 1687. In that year, the first runaway slaves from Charleston arrived in St. Augustine. By the time the British took Florida from Spain in 1763, numerous African slaves had already found freedom, or at least a milder form of slavery, in Florida. These escaped slaves frequently found welcome, shelter, and acceptance from the Seminole Indians with whom they soon settled.

---

64. Kappler CJ (1904).
65. Information on the Black Seminoles is derived from a variety of sources, including Jenkins BL (1998), Etienne-Gray T (---), Peck D (2000), Douglas K (2002a), and Katz WL (1997).

Escaped slaves and their descendants were an integral part of Seminole life ever since the Seminoles split off from the Creek tribe and moved to Florida in the 18th century. The Africans taught the Seminoles the art of rice cultivation as practiced in Senegambia and Sierre Leone, West Africa, providing a source of sustenance that the Seminoles had not previously known. Further, the Africans became some of the fiercest warriors within the Seminole Nation, adding greatly to the Seminole Indians' ability to defend themselves.

Over time, the Africans and African Americans intermarried with the Seminole Indians, were accepted by the latter as kin and allies, and became known as the Black Seminoles. By the 1800s, Black Seminoles were living in as many as 15 Seminole villages.

The number of escaped slaves living with the Seminole finally became a bone of contention for the United States government. As a result, the government authorized General Andrew Jackson (later the seventh president of the United States) to invade the Spanish-held parts of Florida and recapture African and African-American slaves living among the Seminoles. This action resulted in the First Seminole War (1817-1818), a war in which Black Seminoles and Seminoles fought side by side against the invading U.S. army.

The extent of Black Seminole participation in the First Seminole War can be seen by examining the U.S. Army's campaign against what was known as Fort Negro. When this Seminole outpost fell to army forces, there were approximately 300 Seminole Indians manning the fort. Of these 300, all but 34 were of at least partial African descent.

Despite General Jackson's burning of towns and villages in the First Seminole War and despite Spain's ceding of its last possessions in Florida to the United States, the attempt to recapture runaway slaves was largely unsuccessful and the Black Seminoles continued to exist along side their Seminole brothers. There the matter remained until the mid-1830s.

The Second Seminole War (1835-1842) was fought over the U.S. government's attempt to relocate all of the Seminole Indians from Florida to the Oklahoma Territory. The Black Seminoles initially fought this attempt, but eventually most of them surrendered. However, one indication of their contribution to the Seminole tribe during the Second Seminole War can be seen in an 1838 report of Major General Thomas Jessup upon capturing a group of Seminole Indians. General Jessup noted that he had taken 678 prisoners, of whom 165 (24%) were "negroes." Earlier, General Jessup had reported capturing 103 Black Seminoles between 1836 and 1837.

Further, evidence of the Black Seminole contribution during the Second Seminole War can be seen by examining the retinue of one of the greatest of the Seminole chiefs at that time. When Chief Osceola of the Seminoles was held captive at Fort Multrie in 1837, fully 52 members of his 55-man bodyguard were Black Seminoles. It is hard to imagine a more telling incident attesting to the high regard with which the Black Seminoles were held by their fellow Seminole Indians.

The history of the Black Seminoles becomes somewhat diverse following the Second Seminole War. Some Black Seminoles fled to the Bahamas, some removed themselves deeper into the swamps of Florida, and about 500 Black Seminoles surrendered to the U.S. Army and were relocated to the Oklahoma Territory along with most other members of the Seminole tribe. In 1850, a group of 300 Seminoles and Black Seminoles from Oklahoma migrated to Mexico, where the Mexican government gave them land at El Moral at the junction of the Rio

San Rodrigo and Rio San Antonio. Subsequently, the Black Seminoles of Mexico, who had become known as the Indios Mascogos, were moved by the Mexican government to the Hacienda de Naciniento on the Rio San Juan Sabinas.

After the abolishment of slavery in the United States at the end of Civil War, some of these Indios Mascogos believed it was safe to return to the United States. On July 4, 1870, a group of Indios Mascogos crossed the Rio Grande and entered Texas, where they were subsequently enlisted by the U.S. Army as Indian scouts and were known as the "Detachment of Seminole Negro Indian Scouts." A second group of Indios Mascogos entered Texas in late 1875, and many of them also joined the Black Seminole army scouts. Under the command of Lieutenant John Bullis, these Black Seminole scouts went on 26 expeditions and saw combat in 12 different battles against the Indians of the American Southwest without ever suffering a casualty. Their gallantry and heroism were exemplified by the four Black Seminole scouts (John Ward, Isaac Payne, Pompey Factor, and Adam Payne) who were awarded the Congressional Medal of Honor, this nation's highest military decoration.

The Black Seminoles were specifically referenced in the 1866 treaty between the Seminole Indians and the United States government, and two "freedmen" (Robert Johnson and Harry Island) were signatories to that treaty.

And inasmuch as there are among the Seminoles many persons of African descent and blood, who have no interest or property in the soil, and no recognized civil rights it is stipulated that hereafter these persons and their descendants, and such other of the same race as shall be permitted by said nation to settle there, shall have and enjoy all the rights of native citizens, and the laws of said nation shall be equally binding upon all persons of whatever race or color, who may be adopted as citizens of members of said tribe.[66]

D8. The Case of Abraham[67]

Abraham was born about 1787 in either Florida or Georgia. During the early 1800s, he had been the slave of Dr. Eugenio Antonio Sierra, a Spanish physician living in Pensacola, Florida.

During the War of 1812, Major Edward Nichols of the British army offered freedom for any slave who enlisted under the British flag. Abraham quickly did so, fought as a member of the British Colonial Marines, and helped build the British fort at Prospect Bluff. Following the end of the War of 1812, Abraham joined up with the Seminole Indians and fought alongside of them during the First Seminole War. He barely escaped death when the fort at Prospect Bluff was destroyed by the army of General Andrew Jackson during the First Seminole War. Abraham was one of the few defenders of the fort to survive. He quickly made his way to town on the Suwannee River, continued to fight the Americans alongside his fellow Seminole Indians, and earned the accolade of being referred to as *Sauanaffe Tustunnagee* (Suwannee Warrior).

Being fluent in several different languages, Abraham worked for a time as a translator following the First Seminole War. He also went into independent commerce and established a successful trade business with the Seminole Indians and the Maroons. He eventually married a woman with the name of Hagar (a typically Muslim name) or Hagan and had two sons, Renty and Washington.

---

66. Kappler CJ (1904).
67. Information on Abraham is taken from Muhammad ANA (2001) and other sources.

Accepted by both Maroons and Seminole Indians, he became the military leader of the Maroons and was appointed the "sense-bearer" of the Seminole Indians by Chief Micanopy. He was a signatory to the May 9, 1832, treaty between the United States government and the Seminole and was a member of the Indian delegation that was sent to examine the land being offered to relocate Indians by the United States in the Oklahoma Territory. Arriving in Oklahoma, the delegation was not allowed to return home until they signed the treaty of March 28, 1833, which accepted the relocation of the Seminole Indians to Oklahoma. Nonetheless, Abraham rejected the terms of the treaty, for which he was incarcerated at Fort Gibson for eight months.

Eventually returning to Florida, Abraham again fought as a Seminole in the early stages of the Second Seminole War (1835-1842), which was waged in opposition to the proposed relocation of the Seminole to the Oklahoma Territory. In February of 1838, Abraham and his family finally moved to the Oklahoma Territory and became cattle ranchers. However, Abraham's days as a Seminole leader were not yet over. In 1852, he was hired by the government of the United States to travel to Florida and then led a delegation of Seminole chiefs to Washington, DC. Not withstanding Abraham's presence, the Washington negotiations were unsuccessful in convincing the remaining Seminole Indians of Florida to move to the Oklahoma Territory. Following the negotiations' conclusion, the Seminole chiefs returned to the Everglades of Florida, and Abraham returned to Oklahoma. He died in 1870.

E. SUMMARY AND CONCLUSIONS

As noted at the outset of this chapter, much of the evidence of an interrelationship between Muslims and American Indians is circumstantial. However, the amount of such circumstantial evidence is so overwhelming as to demand recognition that early Muslims in America were absorbed into several Indian nations, including parts of the Algonquin, Siouan, and Iroquois. To what extent and for how long their Indian descendants continued to practice Islam is unknown.

6   The Melungeons

A. INTRODUCTION

For several centuries, mystery and controversy have surrounded a semi-reclusive group of people living in parts of the southeastern United States. Their hypothesized origins, ethnicity, and physical description have all been the object of debate and conjecture. Even the etymology of their name, Melungeons, has generated discussion and disagreement.

The Melungeons had already established isolated communities in the Virginia-Tennessee border region east of the Cumberland Gap by the time the first English settlers began their inroads into these mountainous recesses. Over time, the Melungeons spread into middle Tennessee and eastern Kentucky. Eventually, concentrations of Melungeons were to be found in: Hancock County, Tennessee; the Virginia counties of Lee, Scott, and Wise, where the Melungeons were sometimes known as Ramps; the Kentucky counties of Magoffin and Letcher; and Highland County, Ohio.

Throughout the history of the British colonies in America and the later United States, the Melungeons were often the object of discrimination and persecution. There were two basic reasons for this antipathy. (1) The Melungeons tended to keep to themselves in isolated or semi-isolated communities. As such, they were seen as being somewhat strange and different from their northern European peers. In fact, non-Melungeon parents in Melungeon areas often reprimanded their children by warning them that, "If you don't behave the Melungeons will get you." (2) The

Melungeons were frequently a darker skinned people than the English settlers and their descendants. Prior to the abolition of slavery in America, dark skin was seen as a legitimate reason for the enslavement of those individuals who had it. Following the end of the Civil War, dark skin continued to be a basis for the denial of basic human and civil rights to those whose skin was a darker shade than the typical person of Anglo-Saxon descent. This was especially true in the southeastern United States, which was the home of the Melungeon people.

Early records of encounters with Melungeon people recounted that they almost invariably claimed to be of Indian, Portuguese (a term frequently applied to Moriscos, whether they came from Portugal or Spain), or Turkish origin. With regard to the claim of Portuguese origin, the story was sometimes told of shipwrecked Portuguese sailors who were marooned on the Carolina coast, moved inland, and intermarried with Indian women.

Because of their typically darker skin and the racial prejudice prevalent in the 19th and 20th centuries in the American Southeast, the Melungeons were variously categorized in government records and census forms. Depending upon the time and place, they were classified as being "free persons of color," African Americans, mulattos (African-American origin mixed with Indian or Caucasian descent), Indians, and Caucasians. In the racially bigoted American Southeast of the 17th through mid 20th centuries, the first three classifications were an automatic denial of full legal standing in the region.

Compounding the confusion, controversy, and mystery even further, the physical description of Melungeons seemed to differ upon occasion. While dark skin, eyes, and hair were frequent and typical descriptors, there were exceptions to the rule. The following descriptions of

Melungeons illustrate this diversity, and the last of them is of special interest for its reference to Melungeons looking like individuals from India and Egypt.

> …of a dark copper color with Circassian features, but wooly heads and other similar appendages of our negro…Their complexion is reddish-brown, totally unlike the mulatto…high cheek bones, and straight black hair…of swarthy complexion, with prominent cheek bones, jet black hair, generally straight but at times having a slight tendency to curl, and the men have heavy black beards…swarthy complexion, straight black hair, black or gray eyes…oily skin and kinky hair…some of them are swarthy and have high Indian cheekbones…many of the Melungeons have light hair, blue eyes, and fair skin…The color of the skin of a full-blooded, pure Melungeon is a much richer brown than an Indian's skin. It is not the color of a part Indian and part white, for their skin is lighter. The full-blooded, pure Melungeon had more the color of skin of a person from India and Egypt.[68]

However, it was not just the origins, ethnicity, and description of the Melungeon people that were cloaked in uncertainty. Even their very name, i.e., Melungeon, was something of a linguistic mystery. Various linguistic theories claim to identify the etymological origins of Melungeon. One theory posits that the word comes from the French *mélange*, meaning "mixed." With regard to the Melungeons, the inferred reference is to their being of mixed ethnic and racial heritage. Another theory maintains a derivation from the West African word *mulango*, meaning "white person" or "shipmate." A third theory posits that

---

68. Winkler W (2004b).

Melungeon comes from the Greek *melan*, meaning "black." A fourth theory maintains that the origin is from the Old English *malengin*, meaning "guile or deceit." Still a fifth theory suggests a derivation from the Turkish *melun can* (from the Arabic *Melun Jinn*), meaning "damned soul" and pronounced in an identical way as Melungeon. Finally, it is hypothesized that the word comes from the Arabic *Mudajjan*, which means "one who is dark, gloomy, tamed, servile, or domesticated." Of special interest, *Mudajjan* was widely used in 14th-century Spain to identify those Muslims who lived in Spain but outside of the Muslim kingdom of Granada.[69]

Three of the six primary theories regarding the etymology of the name by which these people are known focus on languages suggesting a Muslim origin for the Melungeon people. Whether the etymological origin of the word "Melungeon" is from a West African, Arabic, or Turkish source, all three language groups were languages prominently used by Muslims.

The above introduction to the Melungeon people provides some suggestive and circumstantial evidence that the Melungeons were of Muslim origin. However, an examination of the historical and scientific records provides for a far more definitive statement and helps cement the perception that the Melungeons, at least in part, descend from early Muslims in the Americas. In what follows, the historical record of Melungeons in America is briefly described in chronological sequence. Next, the scientific evidence bearing on the Muslim roots of the Melungeon people is presented. Finally, some summary conclusions are offered about the Muslim origins of the Melungeon people.

---

69. Kennedy NB (1994b); Zahoor A (1998); Winkler W (2004b).

B. THE HISTORICAL RECORD

The following review of the historical record of the Melungeons is hardly exhaustive. However, it does provide a step-by-step, chronological sequence that helps to frame the Melungeon presence in the southeastern United States and in the prior British colonies in that area.

Between 1566 and 1575, Spain sent dozens of expeditions to Florida and other parts of the American Southeast. What was common to many of these expeditions was the shipment of Portuguese sailors and/or settlers to the area and embarkation from the Canary Islands and the Azores. In some cases, the number of Portuguese was quite small, but some expeditions numbered as many as 50 to 100 Portuguese. Might some of these Portuguese have been the original American ancestors of those Melungeons who claimed Portuguese descent?

Another 16th-century source for the origins of the Melungeons can possibly be found in South America. Many Muslims were enslaved by the Portuguese and sent to Brazil during the 16th century. These Muslims were usually sailors who had been captured in combat on the Mediterranean. In Brazil, most of these Muslims entered a life of slavery under Portuguese slave owners. However, some of them were freed on uninviting and unexplored shores, perhaps as far north as the American Southeast, where they were expected to start Portuguese colonies. These freed Muslims were called *emancipados* by the Portuguese, but they referred to themselves as *mulango* (pronounced muh-lun-zhawn in Portuguese, which was a language that was spoken by most of these Muslims).

Archival records reveal that the 17th-century French in America were referring to the Melungeons as "Moors," implying that 17th-century Melungeons descended from North African Muslims.

As early as 1654, English explorers in the American Southeast were told by Indians about a colony of bearded people who were fully clothed, wore European-style clothing, lived in cabins, smelted silver, dropped to their knees in prayer many times each day, and claimed to be "Portyghee" (Portuguese). At about the same time, there was a dark-skinned group of people living with the Powhatan Indians of eastern Virginia and North Carolina who claimed to be "Portugals."

These early reports of the people who came to be known as Melungeons have several features that are suggestive of Muslims. Firstly, the people were described as being fully clothed, a report suggestive of the modesty of dress of Muslims. Secondly, the men were reported to have beards, which is consistent with the instructions given by Prophet Muhammad regarding male grooming. Thirdly, the people dropped to their knees several times each day in prayer, a finding consistent with the five obligatory prayers of worship offered by Muslims each day. Fourthly, these people were reported to have dark skins, suggestive of a Middle Eastern, North African, or West African origin, all of which were geographic areas with a predominant Muslim presence. Fifthly, these people variously described themselves as being "Portyghee" or "Portugals," terms that had come to be almost synonymous with Moriscos following the Christian reconquest of the Iberian Peninsula.

In 1671, a group of English explorers (including Thomas Batts, Thomas Wood, and Robert Fallen) left Petersburg, Virginia, with the intention of finding a quicker route to the so-called South Sea. They were accompanied on their journey by others, including Perachute, a leader among the Appomattox Indians. About four days into their journey, Thomas Woods sent a tired or injured horse back to Petersburg with a man identified only as a "Portugal." While the identity of this "Portugal" is clearly far from complete, it is quite probable that he was an early Melungeon and that the Portugese label used to identify him was an indication that he was a Muslim or Morisco.

In April of 1673, James Needham and Gabriel Arthur reportedly explored the Tennessee Valley and the area leading up to it. Traveling in the company of eight Indians, Needham was told that another eight days of travel along the river would bring them to a community of fully clothed, Caucasian-like people with long beards and whiskers. In the midst of the community, there was a six-foot bell that was rung in the morning and evening. The community would congregate when the bell was rung, bow in the direction of the bell, and spoke in a language not known to the Indians. The Indians further reported that there were communities of "hairy people" along other rivers in the area.

Like the 1654 incident, we once again have a report by Indians of a non-Indian group of people inhabiting the hitherto unexplored recesses of the American Southeast. These people were also described in a way that is suggestive of Muslims. For example, the communities were described as being inhabited by "hairy people" with long beards and whiskers. Consistent with Muslim practice, these people reportedly dressed quite modestly, covering almost all of their bodies. Finally, it was reported that the people congregated at least twice a day and that they apparently bowed in unison, the latter report suggesting one of the postures taken in the five obligatory prayers of worship recited by Muslims every day.

However, the use of a bell to call congregants together for daily prayers is not a Muslim tradition. The use of a bell to congregate the people suggests some Christianizing influence on these presumably Muslim or Muslim-descended people. This hypothesis is consistent with a later report from the 1690s, in which French explorers discovered

"Christianized Moors" in the mountains of the Carolinas. This latter report suggests that certain Christian traditions were already beginning to make inroads among some Melungeon groups by the dawn of the 18th century.

Another tidbit of information relevant to documenting the historical presence of Melungeons in American history emerges from a 1745 advertisement in a North Carolina newspaper. The advertisement was about Emanuel, a runaway slave. Emanuel was described as being about 6.5 feet tall, "yellow" instead of black, 20 years old, and able to speak fairly good English. Of most importance for our present inquiry, Emanuel reportedly called himself a Portuguese.

The case of Emanuel is interesting in a couple of respects. Firstly, his being described as having so-called "yellow" skin suggests that he and his immediate ancestors were not from northern Europe. Secondly, his self-description of being Portuguese is consistent with his having been a Melungeon and is once again suggestive of a Morisco whose ancestors probably came originally from the Iberian Peninsula. Thirdly, we have here what appears to be a documented case of a person who was not from sub-Saharan Africa and who had been enslaved in the British colonies, suggesting that at least some Melungeons were at risk for being enslaved.

Prior to 1756, a pair of brothers with the name of Eckerlin was reported to be wandering around in the woods and mountains of West Virginia. They had reportedly been expelled from the Ephrata Cloisters for their "Ishmaelite" faith. As Prophet Muhammad and the northern or 'Adnani Arabs claimed descent from Ishmael, the first son of Abraham, the Islamic religion has often been known as the Ishmaelite faith. Here again, one appears to have the presence of Muslims in the American Southeast well before the formulation of the United States of America.

Reports from circa the 1750s noted that the Melungeons were speaking Elizabethan English in a broken and non-fluent manner, had adopted Anglicized family names, and still claimed to be Portuguese or Turkish in origin. The fact that their English was not fluent suggests that it was not their native tongue as of the mid 18th century. Further, the fact that it was Elizabethan English, i.e., the English spoken in the 16th century, suggests that their first and primary contact with the English language occurred in the 1500s. Together, these considerations suggest that the Melungeons originally entered America in the 1500s, at which time they had some initial and limited contact with English-speaking colonists.

Between 1772 and 1773, a band of what appears to have been early Melungeons moved to the area around Big Moccasin Gap, Virginia. Among that group were Captain John Blackmore, Joseph Blackmore, John Blackmore, Jr, and Samuel Alley and his daughter. Shortly thereafter, these early settlers in the area built Fort Blackmore on the Clinch River. What is intriguing about the settlers named above is the original form of their family names. For example, Blackmore was originally spelled Black-a-moor or Blackmoor, and Alley was originally spelled Allee or Ally. As Black-a-moor was a term used to describe Moorish Muslims, it appears most likely that the Blackmores were of Moorish Muslim descent. Likewise, it takes little imagination to turn Alley into 'Ali, a common Muslim name.[70]

In 1784, Governor John Sevier of Tennessee reported meeting a dark-skinned people of Moorish descent who lived in western North Carolina, who called themselves Melungeons, and who claimed to be Portuguese. It should be noted that this report not only identified the Melungeons as claiming to be Portuguese, a word that was often used for Moriscos, but

70. Hirschman EC (2005).

further identified them as being of Moorish descent, i.e., as descending from Muslims from North Africa. As such, this report provides perhaps the strongest linkage of the Portuguese label with Muslim descent. (What makes the report even more intriguing is that Governor John Sevier was himself of Moorish descent. His original family name was Xavier, and his Moorish Muslim ancestors had fled to southern France during the Spanish Inquisition.)[71]

Jonathan Swift, an Englishman who was married to a Melungeon and was living in eastern Tennessee, employed Melungeon men in his mining operation during the late 1700s. These men were dark-skinned and were known as "Mecca Indians." Not only were these Melungeons identified as having darker skin than northern Europeans, they were specifically labeled with the city name, i.e., Mecca or Makkah, of the holiest site in Islam. (Makkah, in what is now western Saudi Arabia, was the birthplace of Prophet Muhammad, the site of the initial revelations given to Prophet Muhammad, and the home of the Ka'ba or house of worship built by Prophets Abraham and Ishmael.)

By the late 1700s, there were somewhere between 1,000 and 2,000 Melungeons living in the southeastern United States. Given the prior assumption that the original Melungeon presence in the American Southeast began in the 16th century, this suggests an original, 16th-century population of about 200 Melungeon men and women.

Around 1790, some Melungeon families began migrating from Wilkes County, North Carolina, to Fort Blackmore, Viriginia. Between 1801 and 1804, they apparently began joining the Stony Creek Baptist Church near Fort Blackmore, suggesting that they were beginning to lose or had already lost their Muslim religious heritage by this time. In fact,

---

71. Hirschman EC (2005); Winkler W (2004b).

one of the earliest written uses of the word "Melungeon" appears in the minutes of the Stony Creek Baptist Church in 1813.

The institution of censuses in the United States of the 1790s provided more than a bit of a conundrum for Melungeons and for census takers. Initially, there were only four racial categories available on the census forms, and individuals were supposed to be classified as being either white, "Negro" (the term officially used at that time), Indian, or mulatto. Unfortunately for the Melungeons, they were not easily classified using that schema. As such, a new category was developed, which was "free persons of color." (By 1795, the Tennessee census listed 973 free persons of color.) Having placed the Melungeons on the other side of this new racial divide, government authorities began to strip them of their civil and legal rights. Their land was taken from them, and they began to lose their right to vote, to have legal standing in a court of law, and to have a public education. By 1834, both Tennessee and North Carolina had taken almost all rights of citizenship away from the Melungeons.

With the state governments systematically infringing upon their civil and legal rights, the Melungeons began to retreat back into the Appalachian Mountains. Fleeing from their surrounding society, the Melungeons became entrenched along: Newman's Ridge in Hancock County, Tennessee; the Blackwater area of Lee County, Virginia; Stone Mountain in Wise County, Virginia; and Caney Ridge in Dickenson County, Virginia. In addition, at least some Melungeons had migrated westward into Arkansas by 1810. Additional migrations brought the Melungeons into Oklahoma, Texas, and even California.

However, it was not possible for the Melungeons to withdraw completely from society and from the events that were going on around them. As such, many Melungeons ended up fighting for the

United States during the War of 1812. Examples of such Melungeon soldiers would include James Collins, John Bolin, and Mike Bolin. Likewise, Melungeons ended up fighting for both sides during the Civil War. A majority of these Melungeon soldiers fought for the Union, while a minority of them enlisted in the Confederate army. One Melungeon, Corporal Harrison Collins of the 1st Tennessee Cavalry, was personally awarded our nation's highest military medal, the Congressional Medal of Honor, by President Abraham Lincoln in 1864.

The 1830 census of Hawkins County, Tennessee, listed 331 "free persons of color," most of whom had Melungeon family names. Only 10 years later, the 1840 census listed these same Melungeons as being white. This discrepancy between the 1830 census and the 1840 census illustrates the difficulty of assigning ethnic and racial criteria to the Melungeons, a difficulty that erupted into legal proceedings in 1845 when the voting rights of several Melungeons were adjudicated in a Tennessee court.

According to the 1834 Tennessee Constitution, non-whites were prohibited from voting. This did not, however, stop eight Melungeons (Vardemon Collins, Solomon Collins, Ezekial Collins, Levi Collins, Andrew Collins, Wiatt Collins, Zachariah Miner, and Lewis Minor) from voting in an election in August of 1844. Subsequently, the voting rights of these eight Melungeons were challenged in court. A jury eventually decided that the eight defendants were white, even if Melungeon.

An article in the September 6, 1848, issue of the *Knoxville Register* was devoted to the Melungeons. The article noted that legend had it that the Melungeons were descended from Portuguese men and women who had migrated from coastal Virginia to the mountains of Tennessee. The article went on to state that once the Melungeons reached Tennessee, they intermarried with local Indians. Subsequently, their descendants intermarried with whites and African Americans. The *Knoxville Register* article appears to have been republished in 1849 in *Little's Living Age*.

In 1855, the North Carolina legislature prohibited Melungeons from marrying African Americans and stated that the Melungeons were Croatans, i.e., the descendants of Sir Walter Raleigh's lost colony of Roanoke. As noted previously in chapter III, the survivors of the Roanoke colony were actually Muslims of Turkish and Moorish extraction who had been deposited at Roanoke in 1586 by Sir Francis Drake.

With continuing persecutions being inflicted upon them during the 1800s, the Melungeons began to construct false histories and a bogus ethnic provenance. It was during this time that many Melungeons began to abandon their original claims of being of Portuguese, Turkish, and Indian descent. In an effort to conceal their true roots and identity, many Melungeons began to claim an origin among the "Black Dutch," the "Black Germans," and the French.

Not withstanding the attempt of many Melungeons to conceal their ethnic identity, at least some Melungeons were still claiming a North African extraction as late as the eighth decade of the 19th century. In a famous Tennessee court case in 1872, Lewis Shepard was the attorney representing the daughter of a European-American male and a Melungeon female. The girl had been denied her rightful inheritance, secondary to the fact that her mother was a Melungeon. Under then Tennessee law, the marriage of a white to an African American or mulatto was illegal. The claim was that Melungeons were mulattos, thus the marriage was illegal, and thus the girl was not a rightful and legal heir. Shepard successfully claimed on the girl's behalf that the Melungeons were of Carthaginian (i.e., North African or Moorish) origin, that these particular Carthaginians had migrated to Portugal at some unknown time after the

Roman destruction of Carthage, and that from Portugal these Carthaginians or Moors had come to America around the time of the Revolutionary War. Shephard went so far as to maintain that Shakespeare's Othello, the Moor of Venice, was of the people from whom the Melungeons descended.

An examination of the 1880 census for Hancock County, Tennessee, reveals that several Melungeon families were originally classified on the census forms as being Portuguese. This designation was later crossed out at some unknown time.

In an 1891 article in *The Arena*, Will Allen Dromgoole wrote the following concerning the origins of the Melungeons. She (despite her name, she was a woman) wrote that the origins of the Melungeons in Tennessee traced back to a Vardy Collins and a Buck Gibson who had come to the area prior to 1797. Both men, according to Dromgoole, were of partial Cherokee descent.

As can be seen by this brief review of the historical record, the early Melungeons fairly consistently claimed to be Portuguese or even Turkish in origin, sometimes stating that their ancestors were shipwrecked sailors who had landed on the American coast. These self-statements regarding their origins and early narratives about the Melungeons consistently suggest a people with Muslim origins. That suggestion becomes far more definitive when one examines the scientific record.

C. The Scientific Record

There are several types of evidence that can be submitted from the scientific record regarding the origins of the Melungeons. The first comes from the field of linguistics, the second from the medical discipline of epidemiology, and the third from the few genetic studies that have been performed on 20th-century Americans claiming Melungeon origin.

C1. LINGUISTIC EVIDENCE

With regard to the linguistic evidence, we can begin by reiterating that the early Melungeons claimed to be Portuguese in origin and that the 16th-century use of the word "Portuguese" had become almost synonymous with Moriscos and with Muslims exiled during the Spanish Inquisition. As such, any person living in early America who claimed to be Portuguese in origin was quite possibly a Muslim or Muslim descendant of Arab or Berber extraction.

As previously noted in this chapter, at least six different etymologies have been offered for the word "Melungeon." Of these etymological explanations, three are specifically tied to languages primarily associated with Muslims. To reiterate, the word "Melungeon" may derive from the West African *mulango*, the Turkish *melon can*, or the Arabic *Melun Jinn* or *Mudajjan*. The West African *mulango* means "white person" or "shipmate" and was specifically used as a self-reference by 16th-century Muslims in Brazil. As pronounced in Portuguese, *mulango* is almost identical to the pronunciation of Melungeon. The Turkish *melon can* and the Arabic *Melun Jinn* can be translated as "damned soul" or "one who has been abandoned" and are pronounced in an identical way as Melungeon. Finally, the Arabic *Mudajjan* means "one who is dark, gloomy, tamed, servile, or domesticated" and was widely used in 14th-century Spain to identify those Muslims who lived in Spain but outside of the Muslim kingdom of Granada.

There are three additional examples of the linguistic evidence for the Muslim origins of the Melungeons that can be advanced. Firstly, despite the fact that Melungeons began to Anglicize their given and family names at an early date, some Muslim-related names have survived. For example, one can point to the family names of Tunis and Calendar. The former name is identical with the North African capital city of Tunisia, and the latter may simply be an Anglicized version of the Turkish *kalendar*, a word used to denote an order of Sufi dervishes. Other examples would include Black-a-moor and 'Ali. Secondly, such Muslim first names as Mecca, Aliyah, and Omar Ishmael show up with some frequency in Melungeon genealogies.[72] Thirdly, one notes the similarity between certain Melungeon and Turkish expressions and words. Both some Melungeons and some Turkish people use a vocal clicking sound and a slight toss of the head to indicate, "No." Some Melungeons use the word "gaumy" or "gaumed up" to describe a problem or mess. Likewise, the Turkish *gam* indicates a sad or bad feeling about something. As late as the 20th century, some Melungeons called a watch by the word "satz." The Turkish word for a watch is *saat*.

Consistent with the historical record, the linguistic evidence is suggestive of a Muslim origin for the Melungeon people. However, even more definitive proof awaits us.

C2. Epidemiological Evidence

As a group, the 20th-century descendants of Melungeons are prone to several diseases that are fairly uncommon among most non-Melungeon groups of people in America. These illnesses include Familial Mediterranean Fever (FMF—a disease inherited through the presence of two recessive genes), erythema nodosum sarcoidosis, Behcet's Syndrome (Behcet's Disease—a condition with a genetic predisposition), thalassemia (an inherited group of disorders of hemoglobin metabolism), and Machado Joseph Disease (Azorean Disease—a disease of the central nervous system that is inherited through a dominant gene). All of these conditions appear to have a genetic or hereditary component to them.

---

72. Hirschman EC (2005).

Given that these illnesses show a relatively high frequency of occurrence among Melungeons and their descendants and that they have a genetic or hereditary component, finding other populations that are unusually prone to these conditions may shed some light on the origin of the Melungeon people. Consistent with the hypothesis of Melungeons having a Muslim origin, it is instructive to note that these illnesses have high epidemiological rates among the various populations of the Mediterranean, Middle Eastern, North African, and African world. In short, Muslim populations have the same relatively high frequency of these genetic and hereditary conditions as do Melungeons, suggesting a genetic link between Old World Muslims and the Melungeons of America.

C3. GENETIC EVIDENCE

Two genetic studies have been performed on 20th-century Melungeons and their descendants. The first was based on matching analyzed blood samples to various populations around the world, and the second consisted of more sophisticated and definitive DNA analysis, both mtDNA and Y-line DNA.

In 1990, Dr. James L. Guthrie analyzed blood samples from 177 Melungeons. These samples were previously taken in 1969 in Hancock County, Tennessee, and Lee County, Virginia. Dr. Guthrie compared certain gene frequencies in the Melungeon group to close to 200 other population groups. His research indicated that there was no significant difference between the Melungeon samples and the people from Libya, the Canary Islands, Malta, Cyprus, and the Galician Mountains of Spain and Portugal. Close relationships were also found with northern Iraq and Iran, extreme southern Italy, certain South American Indians, and Turks.[73]

In 2000, the first Melungeon DNA study began under Dr. Kevin Jones. About 120 female-line mtDNA samples were collected and were matched to a data bank of 20,000 mtDNA lines. The results indicated that 83% of the people of Melungeon descent in the sample traced to European lines, 05% to American Indian lines, 05% to African-American lines, and 07% to northern India, Syria, and Turkey. (The northern Indian or Siddi lines probably represent individuals who migrated from northern India into Turkey around the start of the 11th century. Some of the descendants of these Siddi probably immigrated directly from the Othmanic Empire to America and were Muslims at the time they entered America. Other Siddi migrated north from Turkey into the Balkans, became known as the Romany people or Gypsies, and migrated from continental Europe to Great Britain by the start of the 16th century. Columbus reportedly had three Gypsies aboard his third voyage in 1498, and England and Scotland had shipped Gypsies to Virginia and the Caribbean as slaves during the 17th and 18th centuries.)[74]

Samples were also taken of Y-line (male) DNA from a smaller group of about 30 Melungeon descendants and were compared to a data bank with 4,500 lines. Results indicated matches with lines from Anatolian Turkey, an Arab line, and an African-American line. Interestingly, some of the Y-line DNA from the sample could not be matched with any of the lines in the 4,500-line databank. Others could not be definitively matched but were lines that show up in 22% of the people from Syria, 12 percent of the people from Turkey, and only one percent of the people from northern Europe.[75]

---

73. Kennedy NB (1994); Kennedy NB (1997); Hirschman EC (2005).
74. Baird R (2002); Scolnick JM, Kennedy NB (2003); Winkler W (2004b).
75. Baird R (2002); Scolnick JM, Kennedy NB (2003); Winkler W (2004b).

The genetic studies provide firm and definitive evidence of Turkish, Arab, and African-American antecedents among Melungeon descendants. It may safely be assumed that the Turkish and Arab lines represent Muslim origins, and it is probable that the African-American lines do as well. Of special note, Turkish, Arab, and African-American lines were found in both the female-line mtDNA analysis and in the male (Y-line) DNA analysis. Thus, it appears that the original Melungeons were comprised of both Muslim men and women, some of whom probably comprised intact family units.

With regard to the high frequency of European lines in the data, one posits that these lines are primarily reflective of Melungeon intermarriage with Europeans between the 17th and 20th centuries. As this intermarriage occurred, the originally higher percentage of Muslim-related lines was systematically diluted.

C4. Summary

Taken together, the linguistic, epidemiological, and genetic evidence provide clear and convincing proof that the Melungeon people are of at least partial Muslim origin. More specifically, the scientific record demonstrates a combination of Turkish, Arab, and African-American antecedents. Given the results of the blood analyses performed by Dr. Guthrie, Berber contributions from North Africa are at least highly probable. Further, given the frequency of intermarriage between Melungeons and Europeans throughout the 18th through the 20th centuries, one suspects that the original Muslim contribution to the Melungeon people was much greater than that being found in genetic studies of Melungeon descendants in the late 20th and early 21st centuries.

Additional and circumstantial evidence consists of early Melungeon architectural practices. For example, consistent with Muslim architecture but inconsistent with European architecture, early Melungeon homes often had arched doorways and windows.

D. CONCLUSIONS

Combining the historical and scientific records, one can begin to reconstruct the history of the Melungeons in America. This reconstruction is necessarily somewhat speculative, although it is based upon and does incorporate the historical and scientific evidence currently available.

While a pre-Columbian contribution of Muslim bloodlines cannot be totally ruled out, it is unlikely. The historical record suggests that the Melungeons were speaking a broken Elizabethan English as late as the 1750s. This consideration suggests that English was not their native language and that they had some contact with the English in the 16th century, the period in which Elizabethan English was commonly spoken. As such, one posits that the origins of the Melungeons trace back to the 1500s.

So, who were these 16th-century people who coalesced to form the Melungeons? As the early Melungeons almost invariably identified themselves as being Portuguese (often a synonym for Moriscos from the Iberian Peninsula who were of Arab and Berber origin), Turkish, or Indian, one assumes that these three ethnic lines were instrumental in forming Melungeon origins and in early additions to Melungeon lines. Of note, this supposition is consistent with the linguistic, epidemiological, and genetic information currently available on the Melungeons. It is also consistent with the the legends of shipwrecked Portuguese (Morisco) sailors and with the historical record of Muslims and Moriscos of Arab and Berber origin being abandoned by the Santa Elena colony in 1587, with Muslims of Turkish and Moorish origin being abandoned by Sir Francis Drake at Roanoke in the 1580s, and with Turks from Karachai and Kavkas in Transcaucasia being imported by the Spanish to Florida during the 16th century (see chapter III for further details). The abandoned Muslims and Moriscos of Santa Elena, the stranded Muslims of Roanoke, and possibly the Karachai and Kavkas Turks married within themselves. They also began intermarrying with various Indian tribes as early as the late 16th century, providing the initial Indian contribution to the Melungeon gene pool.

The mid 17th century may have seen a second infusion of Muslim bloodlines into the Melungeon people. As noted previously in chapters III and V, two different shipments of Turkish men and women, almost all of whom would have been Muslims, were sent as indentured servants to the British colony at Jamestown. These shipments took place during the early and mid 1600s, and the earliest written documentation of a Turkish presence at Jamestown is from 1631. At Jamestown, these Turkish Muslims provided a substantial percentage of the indentured-servant class. Some of these Turks most likely fled their forced servitude and were taken in by Indian tribes and by the fledgling Melungeon population.

Still a third Muslim contribution to the Melungeon people can be posited. Beginning in the 17th century and continuing into the 18th and 19th centuries, runaway African and African-American slaves, many of whom would have been Muslims of West African origin, began to seek safety and freedom among the Indians of the American Southeast. Some of these escaping slaves may well have found security and marriage with the Melungeons. This suggestion is consistent with the genetic studies that have been done to date.

It is unclear how long the Melungeon people continued to practice the Islam of their ancestors. There are reports from 1654 and from 1673 that suggest at least some Islamic residuals, if not Islam per se, continuing to be prevalent among the Melungeons as of those dates. Further, the Eckerline brothers of the mid 1700s were clearly labeled to be members of the "Ishmaelite" faith. Nonetheless, it is likely that there was a steady erosion of the Melungeon's Islam over the centuries, in part due to inter-marriage with non-Muslim Indians and with Christians of European descent. By the late 1700s and early 1800s, the Melungeons were most likely "Christianized," the Islam of their ancestors was basically lost and forgotten, and most Melungeons were claiming to be Christians of the "Primitive Baptist" or "Old Regular Baptist" denomination.

Of interest, several of the practices of these "Primitive Baptist" churches demonstrate what appears to be some Muslim residual. For example, men and women were separated from each other in church, with the women being placed behind the men and sometimes even entering the church through a women's-only entrance. Consistent with the Islamic and Jewish calendars, each new day was said to start at sundown. Consistent with the practice in mosques, the churches were kept free of any religious art, crosses, other religious icons, and musical instruments. Consistent with Islamic practice, the Melungeons buried their deceased within one day of death. Furthermore, in one 20th-century photograph of "Primitive Baptists" at a riverside baptism, some males are shown praying in the *Sajood* position of Muslim prayer, i.e., toes, knees, hands, and forehead on the ground.[76]

Throughout the 19th and 20th centuries, the Muslim gene pool among the Melungeons continued to be diluted through intermarriage with Americans of European descent. By the mid 20th century, the Muslim origins of the Melungeon people had been thoroughly hidden by

---

76. Hirschman EC (2005).

the passage of time. There the matter may have remained if it were not for the research into Melungeon history that was undertaken by Melungeon descendants in the late 20th century. As these intrepid men and women began to dig through the layers of history to discover their family origins, their genealogical, historical, linguistic, epidemiological, and genetic research began to reveal the substantial Muslim contribution to the origins of the Melungeon people.

Of note, the Melungeons are probably not the only small, insulated group of Americans with Muslim origins. Others may well include the Redbones (Houmas or Sabines) of Louisiana, the Carmel Indians of Ohio, the Guineas of West Virginia and Maryland, the Lumbees (Croatans) of North Carolina, South Carolina, and Virginia, the Brass Ankles of South Carolina, the Ramps of Stone Mountain and Coeburn Mountain, and the Brown People of Kentucky. To these, one can add the Free Moors of the Carolinas, the Delaware Moors (claiming descent from Spanish Moors who settled on the Delmarva Peninsula sometime prior to the American Revolution and then intermarried with local Indians), and the Viriginia Maroons.[77]

All of the above is not to discount the possibility that many non-Muslim lines have contributed to the Melungeon people. For example, there is also convincing evidence of a Sephardic Jewish contribution to the Melungeon people. However, the present review is specific to the Muslim contribution to the Melungeon people.

---

77. Austin AD (1997), Winkler W (2004b), and Kennedy NB (1997).

7 Islamic Residuals in African-American Life

A. INTRODUCTION

As noted previously in chapter IV, between 15 and 20 million Africans were brought to the Americas as part of the transatlantic slave trade. Over the years, scholars have offered varying estimates of how many of these enslaved Africans were Muslims. Estimates have ranged from a low of 10% to a high of 30%, with the most recent estimates running in the 20% to 30% range. Combining the numbers of how many Africans were brought to the Americas as slaves with the percentage of these slaves that were Muslims yields an estimate of between 1,500,000 to 6,000,000 Muslims having been brought to the New World as slaves, with 3,000,000 to 6,000,000 being the most current estimates.

Whether the actual number was 1,500,000 or 6,000,000, it is hard to imagine that a Muslim population that large did not leave at least some legacy that was passed on through the generations to the current time. One would expect to find some residual of their Islamic beliefs among their African-American descendants. Indeed, that is exactly what one finds if one knows where to look. However, that does not mean that the Islamic residual is always recognized as being Islamic, even by the African Americans who continue to keep that residual alive.

In what follows, this chapter explores Islamic residuals in 20th-century and contemporary African-American life. We begin with some general considerations about the frequency of Muslim ancestry and then move on to review some of the Islamic residuals documented by the Savannah Writers Project, including certain religious practices with Islamic roots that are unique to African-American Christianity. Next, we explore some Islamic residuals not documented in the Savannah Writers Project. Finally, we finish by looking at a number of more or less Islamicly-based religious movements that sprang up in the 20th-century, African-American community.

B. MUSLIM ANCESTORS

For any given African American in the contemporary United States, what is the probability that he or she has Muslim ancestors that were brought to America as slaves? For almost all African Americans, the simple answer is that it is almost impossible that there were not Muslims among his or her ancestors. That this is so can be readily demonstrated by simple probability theory.

If one rolls a pair of dice, what is the probability that neither of the dice will be a six? Each of the dice has six sides, with each side having a number from one to six. Thus, if one rolls only one of the dice, the probability that it will not be a six is 5/6. What happens to the second of the two dice is independent of what happens to the first, so for each of the six possibilities for the first of the dice (i.e., one, two, three, four, five, or six), there are six possibilities for the second (i.e., one, two, three, four, five, or six). Thus, there are 36 possible outcomes, of which 25 are that there is no six. This is graphically illustrated by examining Table 1 below.

Table 1: Possible Outcomes in Rolling a Pair of Dice

	--1		--1		--1		--1		--1		--1
	--2		--2		--2		--2		--2		--2
1--	--3	2--	--3	3--	--3	4--	--3	5--	--3	6--	--3
	--4		--4		--4		--4		--4		--4
	--5		--5		--5		--5		--5		--5
	--6		--6		--6		--6		--6		--6

By examining Table 1, one can readily see that there are 36 (6 x 6) possible outcomes, that in 25 (5 x 5) of those outcomes there will be no six showing, that in one (1 x 1) of those outcomes there are two sixes showing, and that in 10 of those outcomes there is just one six [(6 x 6) – (5 x 5) – (1 x 1)]. In short, the probability of not rolling a six when one rolls a pair of dice is (5/6 x 5/6) or $(5/6)^2$.

Using the same basic procedure, we can now ask what the probability is that a given African American has no Muslim ancestors. To answer this question, we need to provide just two pieces of information. (1) For any given enslaved African brought to the Americas, what was the probability that he or she was a Muslim? (2) Within the ancestry of the contemporary African American, how many different Africans are there who were brought to the New World as slaves?

The answer to the first question has been answered variously by different scholars. Older estimates tended to suggest that 10% of all the enslaved Africans brought to the Americas were Muslims. Using this estimate and without knowing anything else about a particular enslaved African, the probability would be 90% that he or she was not a Muslim. More recent estimates that are based on newer or more complete information have suggested that anywhere from 20% to 30% of the enslaved Africans were Muslims. Using these estimates, the probability that the enslaved African was not a Muslim would range from 70% to 80%. If we choose to answer our first question by saying that 90% or 80% or 70% of the enslaved Africans were not Muslims, then the answer to our question as to the probability that a contemporary African American does not have any Muslims in his ancestry would be $(.9)^x$ or $(.8)^x$ or $(.7)^x$, where x is the number of different enslaved Africans in his ancestry.

Using the most conservative estimate of the Muslim presence among enslaved Africans in the New World, i.e., the 10% figure, one can quickly see that one only has to have seven different enslaved Africans in one's ancestry before the probability becomes less than 50% that all seven of them were non-Muslims, i.e., $(.9)^7 = .48$. Using the estimate that 30% of the enslaved Africans were Muslims, it takes only two different enslaved Africans in one's ancestry before the probability becomes less than 50% that both of them were non-Muslims, i.e., $(.7)^2 = .49$.

Using probability theory as explained above, Table #2 provides the probabilities that there were no Muslims in the ancestry of a contemporary African American. To use this chart, all one has to do is decide what estimate (10%, 20%, or 30%) one wants to use for the presence of Muslims among the enslaved Africans brought to the Americas and then determine or estimate the number of different enslaved Africans that contribute to the African American's ancestry.

Table 2: Probability of there being no Muslims in an African American's Ancestry

#*	10%**	20%**	30%**
2	.81	.64	.49
3	.729	.512	.343
4	.6561	.4096	.2401
5	.59049	.32768	.16807
6	.531441	.262144	.117649
7	.478297	.209715	.082354
8	.430467	.167772	.057648
9	.387420.	.134218	.040354
10	348678	.107374	.028248
11	.313811	.085899	.019773
12	.282430	.068719	.013841
13	.254187	.054976	.009689

#*	10%**	20%**	30%**
14	.228768	.043980	.006782
15	.205891	.035184	.004748
16	.184302	.028147	.003323
17	.166772	.022518	.002326
18	.150095	.018014	.001628
19	.135085	.014412	.001140
20	.121577	.011529	.000798
21	.109419	.009223	.000559
22	.098477	.007379	.000391
23	.088629	.005903	.000274
24	.079766	.004722	.000192
25	.071790	.003778	.000134
26	.064611	.003022	.000094
27	.058150	002418	.000066
28	.052335	.001934	.000046
29	.047101	.001547	.000032
30	.042391	.001238	.000023
31	.038152	.000990	.000016
32	.034337	.000792	.000011
33	.030903	.000634	.000008
34	.027813	.000507	.000005
35	.025032	.000406	.000004
36	.022528	.000325	.000003
37	.020276	.000260	.000002
38	.018248	.000208	.000001
39	.016423	.000166	.000001
40	.014781	.000133	.000001

#*	10%**	20%**	30%**
41	.013303	.000106	***
42	.011973	.000085	***
43	.010775	.000068	***
44	.009698	.000054	***
45	.008728	.000044	***
46	.007855	.000035	***
47	.007070	.000028	***
48	.006363	.000022	***
49	.005726	.000018	***
50	.005154	.000014	***
51	.004638	.000011	***
52	.004175	.000009	***
53	.003757	.000007	***
54	.003381	.000006	***
55	.003043	.000005	***
56	.002739	.000004	***
57	.002465	.000003	***
58	.002219	.000002	***
59	.001997	.000002	***
60	.001797	.000002	***
61	.001617	.000001	***
62	.001456	.000001	***
63	.001310	.000001	***
64	.001179	.000001	***
65	.001061	.000001	***
66	.000955	***	***
67	.000860	***	***

#*	10%**	20%**	30%**
68	.000774	***	***
69	.000696	***	***
70	.000627	***	***
71	.000564	***	***
72	.000508	***	***
73	.000457	***	***
74	.000411	***	***
75	.000370	***	***

* = number of different enslaved Africans in a person's ancestry
** = estimated percentage of enslaved Africans who were Muslims
*** = probability of not having a Muslim ancestor is less than one in one million

It is standard archaeological methodology to assume that a generation occurs about every 21 years. Taking a more conservative timeframe of 25 years and assuming an average of 250 years have lapsed since a person's African ancestors were brought to this country as slaves, one's African ancestors would typically be in the tenth generation. As there are two ancestors (one male and one female) in each line of ancestry at each generation, there are 1,024 (i.e., 2^{10}) ancestors in the tenth generation. However, given the realities of slave life, not all of these tenth-generation ancestors were likely to be Africans or people of purely African descent. Some may have been American Indians, and some may have been of Caucasian descent. Furthermore, some of these tenth-generation ancestors may appear more than once in a person's lineage. Thus, there may have been only 800 or even 600 ancestors from Africa in the lineage. Nonetheless, as seen in Table #2 and assuming that 30% of the imported Africans were Muslims, it takes only 41 different African ancestors before the probability of not having a Muslim ancestor becomes less than one in a million. Assuming that 20% of the imported Africans were Muslims, it still takes only 66 different African ancestors to reach the same probability level. Even if one assumes that only 10% of the imported Africans were Muslims, having only 75 different African ancestors results in a probability of 37 in 100,000 that there were no Muslims in one's ancestry. As one can quickly see from these figures, it is relatively safe to conclude that almost all contemporary African Americans have at least one Muslim ancestor.[78]

C. THE SAVANNAH WRITERS PROJECT

C1. INTRODUCTION

Given the above findings regarding the probability of African Americans having at least one Muslim ancestor, it should come as no surprise to learn that the residuals of their ancestors' Islam frequently surfaced in African-American life. The Savannah Writers Project of the 1930s offered numerous examples of this phenomenon in their *Drums and Shadows: Survival Studies among the Georgia Coastal Negroes.*

The Savannah Writers Project was part of the Federal Writers Project of the Work Projects Administration (WPA), a federally funded program to put over 6,000 people back to work during the dog days of the depression. Many of the people employed by the Federal Writers Project were professional writers—novelists, poets, journalists, free-lance writers, and doctoral-level academicians. The Savannah

---

78. The conclusions reached in this paragraph and in Table #2 are based on a couple of unstated assumptions. (1) It is assumed that enslaved Muslims were just as likely to have children and to have as many children as enslaved non-Muslims. (2) It is assumed that marital selection patterns were independent of the religious affiliation of each person in the marriage. Each of these assumptions could be challenged.

branch of the Federal Writers Project focused on collecting and recording the oral histories of elderly African Americans living in the coastal areas of Georgia. About 140 elderly African Americans, many of whom had formerly been slaves, were interviewed.

Despite the fact that the interviewers were primarily focused on collecting stories involving conjuring, magic, "root doctors," spells, potions, charms, etc., a surprising amount of information documenting Islamic residuals was obtained. This is even more surprising when one considers that the interviewers were white Georgians of the 1930s and that the interviewees were African Americans who were not that many years removed from slavery and who were still being subjected to the indignities of Jim Crow laws. One cannot but wonder how many more examples of Islamic residuals would have been uncovered if: the interviewers had known enough to ask about, and had been motivated to query about, Islamic residuals; the interviewers had been African Americans; and the interviewees had not been suspicious of and somewhat intimated by their interviewers.

C2. PRAYER

Many of the older African Americans interviewed by the Savannah Writers Project recalled residuals of Islamic prayer practices being maintained during their youth. Ed Thorpe of Harris Neck, Georgia, told about how his African grandmother, Patience Spaulding, would pray. She would kneel down on the floor, bow her head down three times, and say, "*Ameen, Ameen, Ameen.*"

Sophie Davis of White Bluff, Georgia, remembered that during her youth many of the old people on St. Catherine's Island used to pray at dawn and at the setting of the sun. At the end of the prayers, they would say, "*Meena, Mina, Mo.*"

Rachel Anderson of Possum Point recalled that her great-grand-mother Peggy used to pray every day at dawn, at noon, and at sunset. Consistent with Islamic prayer practice, Peggy would bow and kneel down during every prayer.

Rosa Grant of Possum Point reported that her grandmother was an African named Ryna. As a youth, Rosa observed Ryna praying every morning at sunrise. Rosa's memory was that Ryna would bow, kneel on the floor, and then would bend over and touch the floor three times with her forehead. At the end of each prayer, Ryna would say, "*Ameen, Ameen, Ameen.*" Rosa also recalled that Ryna had said that Friday was her "prayer day."

Lawrence Baker lived on Ridge Road near the town of Darien. He remembered that his grandmother, Rachel Grant, used to pray facing the sun every day at sunrise, during the middle of the day, and at sunset. At the end of each prayer, Rachel reportedly would bow.

Katie Brown of Sapelo Island recalled her grandmother Margaret talking about her parents, Bilali Muhammad and Phoebe (see chapter IV for a biographical sketch of Bilali). Margaret reportedly said that Bilali and Phoebe used to pray on a bed (prayer rug?) and were: "…very particular about the time they prayed, and they (were) very regular about the hour. When the sun came up, when it (was) straight over head, and when it set, that (was) the time they prayed. They bowed to the sun and had (a) little mat to kneel on. The beads (prayer beads) was on a long string. Bilali, he pulled a bead, and he said, '*Belambi, Hakabara, Mahamadu.*' Phoebe, she said, '*Ameen, Ameen.*'"

Phoebe Gilbert, also of Sapelo Island, reported that her grandfa-ther was Bilali Smith (the son of Hester, the daughter of Bilali Muhammad) and that her uncle Calina and aunt Hannah were:

"...mighty particular about praying. They prayed on the bed. The old man, he say, '*Ameela*,' and Aunt Hannah, she say, '*Hakabara*.'"

Shad Hall of Sapelo Island was the son of Sally, the daughter of Hester, the daughter of Bilali Muhammad. Shad recalled that his grandmother Hester and her family: "...sure prayed on the bed. They wore the string of beads on their waists—sometimes the string on their necks. They prayed at sun-up and faced the sun on their knees and bowed to it three times, kneeling on a little mat."

Ben Sullivan, whose father had the typical Muslim name of Bilali, recalled an old man from his youth on St. Simons Island. Old Israel, as Ben referred to him, used to pray on a mat (prayer rug) every dawn and sunset. In the performance of his prayers, Old Israel used a book (*Qur'an*), which he kept hidden away from public gaze. Ben also reported that Old Israel followed two other typically Muslim customs—he wore a long beard and covered his head with a type of white cloth (a *Kufi*, i.e., a skull cap often worn by Muslim men). Ben also recalled several other unnamed people from his youth who used to sneak off by themselves, hide, and then "make a great prayer." According to Ben, if these slaves didn't hide to do their prayers, they would be severely punished by their owner. Since one can hardly imagine a Christian slave owner of the mid 19th century punishing his slaves for the performance of Christian prayers, it stands to reason that these were Muslim slaves who found it necessary each day to perform their obligatory prayers in secret.

In reviewing the above examples of Muslim prayer practices, several points should be made. (1) The interviewees were all elderly and were recalling events from their youth. Thus, it is quite likely that their memories were somewhat faded, resulting in some of the distortions of Muslim prayer practices being reported, e.g., always facing the sun during prayers.

(2) Several of the interviewees reported that prayers were said only three times a day, i.e., at dawn, at noon, and at sunset. Most Muslims believe that there are five obligatory prayers each day, although there is at least one Muslim sect that follows a three-times-per-day prayer schedule. While it is not impossible that these enslaved Muslims were conforming to that sect's prayer schedule, the more likely explanation is that they were combining the noon (*Dhur*) and afternoon (*'Asr*) prayers during the noon prayer time and combining the sunset (*Maghrib*) and night (*'Isha*) prayers during the sunset prayer time. Allowance is made in Islam for combining prayers in this fashion during travel and during times of special hardship. Certainly, being enslaved would constitute a special hardship, and it appears that this hardship provision for combining prayers was routinely used by enslaved Muslims in America. (3) There are numerous indicators that the reported prayers were examples of *Salat*, i.e., Islamic prayers of worship. For example, consistent with Islamic prayer practice, the people prayed on prayer mats and at set times. They followed the Islamic positions of prayer, both bowing (*Ruku*) and kneeling with foreheads to the ground (*Sajood*). They reportedly said "*Ameen*." This pronunciation is important because, unlike the Christians' use of "Amen," Muslims say "Ameen" at the end of reciting the first chapter (*Al-Fatihah*) of the *Qur'an* in every unit (*Raka*) of every prayer. Finally, we have reports concerning the use of Muslim prayer beads and the statement by one slave that Friday was her special day of prayer, as it is for all Muslims.

C3. The Shout dance

The shout dance is a uniquely African-American phenomenon, which is confined to the American Southeast and to the Caribbean Islands. The word "shout" in shout dance derives from the Muslim use of the West African *Saut*, which in turn is derived from the Arabic

Sha'wut. In the performance of the *Hajj* pilgrimage to Makkah, Muslims circumambulate the *Ka'ba* seven times in a counterclockwise movement. This seven-fold movement around the *Ka'ba* is called *Tawaf*. One counterclockwise circumambulation is called *Sha'wut*.[79]

Enslaved Muslims in the Americas knew that their enslaved status was forever going to deny them the opportunity to perform the *Hajj* pilgrimage to Makkah. As such, they developed a procedure for symbolically performing one of the main rites of *Hajj*, i.e., they would circumambulate around some object in a counterclockwise direction. Over time, this evolved into the shout dance, which is also sometimes referred to as the ring dance, and became part of the Christian rituals of some African-American churches in the American Southeast. As practiced by these churches, the congregants would form a ring around either a central pillar or pulpit in the church or around the church itself. They would then dance in a counterclockwise circumambulation. Ironically, a decidedly Islamic practice, symbolic of one of the primary rites of the *Hajj* pilgrimage, became a cornerstone ritual in certain segments of African-American Christianity.

Many of the African-American communities of 19th-century, coastal Georgia had shout dances as part of their yearly harvest festivals (see below). Over and above the shout dances recalled as being part of these harvest festivals, F. J. Jackson of Grimball's Point recalled that the African-American community of his childhood had regular Saturday night "shouts." Catherine Wing of St. Simons Island recalled that when she was a youth, "We used to shout in a ring." Likewise, Hettie Campbell of St. Marys remembered the frequent shout dances of her youth.

---

79. Diouf S (1998), Raboteau AJ (1980), Turner LD (1969), and Parrish L (1992).

C4. Harvest Festivals

Harvest festivals were a significant part of Muslim life in West Africa. These festivals consisted of prayers to and praise of Allah for the harvest being enjoyed by the participants. This West African aspect of Muslim life was carried over into the New World by enslaved Muslims and left a strong residual among their African-American descendants.

Many of the elderly African Americans of the Georgia of the 1930s remembered the harvest festivals of their youth. Mary Stevens of Sunbury, Georgia, reported that the people would gather from across the area, dance, and have a communal supper. Josephine Stephens of Harris Neck, Georgia, added further details about these harvest festivals, noting that there was feasting, dancing, singing, and the giving of thanks for the harvested crops. Rosa Sallins of Harris Neck confirmed Stephens's account of the harvest festivals and noted that these festivals were held at the local African-American church and included much praying for the success of the next year's crops. Rachel Anderson of Possum Point recalled what she termed harvest suppers. These harvest suppers extended throughout the night, included the performance of a shout dance, and ended with saying sunrise prayers. Catherine Wing of St. Simons Island also remembered the harvest festivals of her youth. She reported that everybody would bring something from the first of the harvest to the local church, a feast would be prepared, and the people would pray and perform a shout dance. Hettie Campbell of St. Marys recalled that harvest resulted in a special festival. The people would gather, have a communal meal, pray and give thanks for their harvest throughout the night, and then perform a shout dance at sunrise. Henry Williams of St. Marys confirmed Hettie's account.

Harvest festivals were also a prominent part of 19th-century life on Sapelo Island. As noted earlier, Katie Brown of Sapelo Island was the great-granddaughter of Bilali Muhammad (see chapter IV). She remembered that the harvest festivals of her youth included the performance of the shout dance, in which the participants would move around the circumference of a large circle or ring. Phoebe Gilbert of Sapelo Island also recalled the harvest festivals of her youth, noting that they lasted throughout the entire night and that they ended with a dance (shout dance?) at sunrise. Shad Hall added to Phoebe's account of the harvest festivals on Sapelo Island. According to Shad: "(At) harvest time they had (a) big time. It came once a year and they prayed and they sang all night long, until the first cock crow. Then they started to dance and to bow to the sun as it rose in the sky. They danced round in a circle and sang and shouted."

C5. MUSLIM CLOTHING

As previously noted, Ben Sullivan of St. Simons Island reported how Old Israel used to cover his head with a white cloth (*Kufi*), a frequent article of clothing for Muslim men. Ben also reported that another man, Daphne, likewise wore a cloth over his head.

Katie Brown of Sapelo Island reported that her great-grandmother Phoebe used to wear a *Hijab* (the scarf worn by many Muslim women). While professing ignorance of the significance of Phoebe's scarf, Katie did report that Phoebe wore the scarf loosely over her head and let it hang down like a veil onto her shoulders.

C6. *SARAKA* CAKES

Yet another example of Islamic residuals among the African Americans of 19th-century, coastal Georgia concerns the making of a special rice cake known as *Saraka*.

On Sapelo Island, Katie Brown told about how Phoebe made a flat, rice cake once a year on the same day. The cake was called *Saraka*. *Saraka* appears to be a West African corruption of the Arabic *Sadaqa*, which means charity or giving in the cause of Allah. The fact that the cake was made only once a year and then on the same day each year suggests that it may have been made to be given to others during *Eid Al-Fitr*, the Islamic holiday following the end of fasting during the Islamic month of *Ramadan*. Alternatively, it is noted that Muslims in West Africa traditionally give rice balls as charity to others every Friday.[80] It may be that the impoverished status of the enslaved Muslims in Georgia resulted in this custom being reduced to once a year.

The custom of making the *Saraka* cakes was apparently passed down from Phoebe to her daughter Hester. For example, Shad Hall of Sapelo Island remembered that his grandmother Hester used to make the *Saraka* cakes. Once the cakes were made, Hester used to call the young children together, give them each a cake, and then say, "*Ameen, Ameen, Ameen.*"

C7. A CHURCH SERVICE

In a moving description of church service during the 1930s on Sapelo Island, Georgia, the Savannah Unit of the Georgia Writers Project recorded several features that are suggestive of Islamic residual having crept into the African-American Christianity of that time and place. Consistent with Islamic practice, the minister, Preacher Little, was said to have a beard and to wear a skull cap (*Kufi*). The writers even described him as "a Mohammedan looking Negro." Further, Preacher Little's sermon was separated into three sections, each of

---

80. Diouf SA (1998).

which built to its own climax. Such a segmentation of a sermon into distinct parts is atypical in traditional Christian practice. However, in Muslim practice, the Friday sermon (*Khutba*) is delivered by the *Imam* in two separate sections, with the *Imam* briefly sitting between the two parts of his sermon.

D. Some Miscellaneous Examples

D.1 Introduction

While the Savannah Writers Project provides the most comprehensive list of Islamic residuals in African-American life, several others examples can be found scattered here and there. In what follows, these are briefly reviewed.

D2. From Sapelo Island, Georgia

As a further example of Islamic residuals creeping into African-American Christianity, consider the case of Cornelia Walker Bailey, the great-great-great-great-granddaughter of Bilali Muhammad, whose biographical sketch appeared in chapter IV. Bailey was raised as a Christian as were her parents before her, the Islam of her illustrious ancestor having been lost through the generations of her family. However, residuals from her ancestor's Islam did filter down through the generations, although it was not always recognized for what it was. For example, as a small child in the Georgia of the late 1940s, Bailey was taught that she was always to face the east when praying. At the time, Bailey had no explanation for why she was to face to the east when offering her Christian prayers. It was simply part of the Christian practice and instruction of her home. However, as Muslims always pray facing Makkah and as Makkah is east from Georgia, we can see that Bailey was being taught a residual Muslim practice within her own Christianity, a Muslim residual that was no longer recognized as having Muslim origins by the very people engaged in the act. Even more significantly, all of the Christian churches on Bailey's Sapelo Island community faced east, i.e., in the direction of Makkah, thus insuring that all congregational prayers would be said in the direction of Makkah.[81]

Islamic residuals in 20th-century, African-American Christianity on Sapelo Island were not merely confined to prayer. For example, burial practices dictated that the deceased were to be laid in the grave in a manner that had them facing east in the direction of Makkah.[82]

D3. FROM BRAZIL AND THE CARIBBEAN

Diouf has noted the presence of several Islamic residuals among the cult religions that developed in the Caribbean and in South America. For example, among the Candomble in Bahia, Brazil, one of the gods in their pantheon of deities is called Allah. As late as the 1930s, the following songs were still being heard in some places of Candomble worship in Bahia: (1) *"Allah! Allah! de Deus! Allah!;"* and (2) *"Allah! Olo Allah! Baba quara da!"* In a Candomble religious cult located as late as the early 1900s in Alagoas, Brazil, the principal god was known as orixa-Allah, the priest was called *alufa* (from *Alfa*, a West African term for the Arabic *Al-Faqih*, i.e., a scholar of Islamic jurisprudence, but in West Africa it can also refer more generally to a Muslim religious leader), the walls of the religious sanctuaries were decorated with what have been described as "arabesques," and a popular religious chant included the following words: *"Edure, edure,*

---

81. Curiel J (2004).
82. Gomez MA (1994).

alilala," the latter word apparently deriving from the Arabic *La Ilaha Ill Allah*, i.e., there is no god but Allah.

Within the Santeria cult in Cuba, adherents greet one another with the Arabic phrase *Salam 'Alaykum*, i.e., the typical Muslim greeting that means peace be upon you. In the Haitian cult of voodoo, some prayers include the name of Allah, and manifestations of certain minor deities are greeted with the Arabic *Salam*, i.e., peace. In Trinidad, there is a cult that supposedly represents a branch of the Spiritual Baptist movement of revivalist Christianity and whose members are known as Shouters. However, a number of Islamic residuals can be seen within the religious practices of the Shouters. For example, Shouters are barefoot in their churches, kneel on a piece of fabric just as Muslims do on prayer rugs, and practice the shout dance around a central altar in the center of the church.

In Toco, Carriacou, and Grenada, people of African origin give *Saraka* during festivals and celebrations.

D4. IN MUSIC

Over and above her contributions in documenting Islamic residuals in South American and Caribbean religious cults, Diouf has also contributed to identifying Islamic residuals in music. For example, several songs found among African descendants contain Arabic words. As late as the 1960s, African descendants in Trinidad were familiar with Arabic songs. A decade later, an 82-year-old woman of Hausa descent in Gasparillo, Trinidad, provided interviewers with a number of prewedding songs, all of which contained Arabic words.

However, it is not just the presence of Arabic words that demonstrate Islamic influence in traditional African-American music. The haunting sounds of the Islamic call to prayer (*Adhan*) and of Muslims reciting the *Qur'an* have been identified by many musicologists (e.g., Gerhard Kubik, John Storm Roberts, and Alan Lomax) as being the original backbone of that distinctively American music known as the blues. In particular, the blues appears to have been markedly influenced by the *Adhan*. Three particularly prominent features of the blues that appear to have been directly borrowed from the *Adhan* are wavy intonation, a nasal quality, and melisma. (Melisma is the use of many notes for one spoken syllable. So instead of simply singing "ah," one sings "ah-ahhhh-ahhh-ah-ah.") In addition, such early blues staples as *Levee Camp Holler* demonstrate several parallels with the typical style of Qur'anic recitation, including elongated sounds, pauses, nasal humming, simple melody, and ornamented notes.

Given such consistent parallels between the blues, on the one hand, and the *Adhan* and Qur'anic recitation, on the other hand, Diouf has suggested the following scenario to account for the birth of the blues.

> An incident that occurred in Sierra Leone in the eighteenth century may well describe what gave birth to the blues. In the slave yard on the coast was a Muslim man of thirty-five years, who could read and write Arabic. He was in irons, awaiting departure and "sometimes he would sing a melancholy song, then he would utter an earnest prayer."[83] The melancholy song was in all probability the recitation of the Koran. Muslims like him would sing in the same manner as a consolation, time and again, on the plantations of the South, and their lonesome "song" probably became what is known as the blues.[84]

Thus, it is not too much to presume that such greats of the blues as Bessie Smith, Willie Brown, Robert Johnson, Son House, Muddy

---

83. Wadstrom CB (1794).
84. Diouf SA (1998).

Waters, Ma Rainey, Memphis Minnie, John Lee Hooker, B. B. King, etc. were the musical heirs of West African Islam. Through their music, Islamic residuals of the *Adhan* and of Qur'anic recitation continued to exist well into the 20th century of American life.

E. THE MOORISH SCIENCE TEMPLE

E1. INTRODUCTION

The early 20th century witnessed a significant turning point in the history of African Americans. Having suffered through centuries of slavery and a half century of Jim Crow discrimination and racism, several leaders in the African-American community saw the need for a new self-identity, one that would banish the slavery-induced self-concept of being a subjugated, victimized, and inferior people.

On the secular front, leaders such as Marcus Garvey of the Universal Negro Improvement Association were advocating the self-empowerment of African Americans through development of a distinct African-American economy fueled by African-American businesses and cooperatives, political involvement, and an eventual return to Africa. Other leaders, while also promoting the concept of economic ownership among African Americans, went further and attempted to forge a new self-identity by reclaiming a real or mythical nationalistic, ethnic, and religious identity that pre-dated slavery. In attempting to recreate a religious identity that antedated slavery, some of these leaders inevitably built upon Islamic residuals within the African-American community.

The two most successful movements to create a new self-identity that was at least partially based upon Islamic residuals were the Moorish Science Temple and the Nation of Islam. Each of these groups advocated a racial mythology that was designed to instill a necessary racial pride in African Americans. In this way, they provided a counterweight to the then prevalent mythology of the dominant white society, a mythology that emphasized the bogus notion of African-American inferiority. The earlier of these two religious movements was the Moorish Science Temple of Timothy Drew, a.k.a. Noble Drew Ali, which is the focus of the present section of this chapter. The following section will review the Nation of Islam.

However, before beginning our look at the Moorish Science Temple, it must be acknowledged that there are two considerations that severely limit our ability to draw firm conclusions about this religious movement. Firstly, the Moorish Science Temple was and is a semi-secretive cult, and it is extremely hard for those who have not been initiated into the movement to have access to some of the foundational literature of the cult. Secondly, after the death of Noble Drew Ali, the Moorish Science Temple split into competing factions with somewhat variant beliefs. What is an article of faith in one faction may have little credence among members of a different group. As such, some measure of qualification and caution is necessary in drawing any firm conclusions about the Moorish Science Temple.

E2. HISTORY

Timothy Drew was born on January 8, 1886, in Sampson, North Carolina, and little concrete information is known about his life prior to 1913. However, it appears that Drew migrated to New Jersey at age 14. His early years in New Jersey were spent learning the trades of a street performer and magician. According to Moorish Science legend, he joined the merchant marines in 1905. Given this supposed occupation, Moorish Science legend further claims that Drew was able to visit Palestine, Egypt, India, Morocco, and Arabia during the course of his employment. By 1910, Drew was back in New Jersey where he worked as a railway expressman and joined the Pullman Porters Union.

Moorish Science legend also claims that in the course of his travels in the merchant marines, Drew rediscovered his own Islamic and racial heritage. During these travels, he supposedly was made a nobleman by the queen of England, was given the name of Ali by 'Abd Al-Aziz ibn Saud (later the king of Saudi Arabia), was given a charter to bring Islam to African Americans by the king of Morocco, and underwent a religious test by having to find his way out of an Egyptian pyramid in which he had been entombed. Whatever the veracity of these legendary claims, Timothy Drew was basically a self-educated man who somewhere along the way picked up some bits and pieces of Islamic and Eastern religious practices and beliefs, which he successfully molded into a unique religious movement that continues to exist to the present time.

Despite the legendary claims about Noble Drew Ali and his travels, there is no record with the United States Department of State that he was ever issued a passport for international travel. Further, it appears that in 1907 Ali tried to establish a Christian sect in the Baptist tradition. This attempt was unsuccessful and soon ended in oblivion. Given these findings, it is highly debatable whether or not Ali ever traveled abroad.

In 1913, Ali founded the Canaanite Temple in New Jersey, reportedly with a Dr. Suliman, an Egyptian whom Ali had allegedly met in 1905 during his travels in the merchant marines. At this time, Ali was known as "Professor Drew, the Egyptian Adept," although he would later be known as Noble Drew Ali. Within three years, an internal struggle for leadership led to the movement splitting into two groups.

One faction was renamed the Holy Moabite Temple of the World and remained in Newark. The other faction, under the leadership of Ali, became known as the Moorish Holy Temple of Science and eventually relocated to Chicago, Illinois, in 1919. At this time, Ali began to write the foundational texts of the Moorish Science Temple, including a pseudo *Qur'an* (i.e., the *Holy Koran*) that is discussed subsequently, and to develop a variety of Moorish Science businesses (e.g., restaurants, grocery stores, variety stores, and shoe repair shops) and products (e.g., tea, mineral oil, bath compounds, and tonics) to further the economic independence of his followers. In 1928, the name of his movement was changed to the Moorish Science Temple of America. At that time, membership in Chicago was said to number 1,200 individuals.

Preaching in empty lots, basements, street corners, and private homes, Ali's message of self-reliance, family values, sobriety, ethical behavior, and the need to rediscover a positive national and religious identity as Moorish Americans (see below under the topic of racial beliefs) found acceptance in many quarters of the African-American community. As such, by 1928 Moorish Science temples could be found in Arkansas (Pine Bluff), Illinois (Chicago), Maryland (Baltimore), Michigan (Lansing and Detroit), New Jersey (Newark), Ohio (Cleveland and Youngstown), Pennsylvania (Philadelphia and Pittsburgh), Virginia (Richmond and Petersburg), West Virginia (Charleston), and Wisconsin (Milwaukee). With the movement growing and spreading from state to state, the need for some formal, centralized governance and organization became apparent, and in response Ali created the Moorish Divine and National Movement of North America.

An unfortunate byproduct of the growth of the Moorish Science temples and businesses was that the organization outstripped Ali's ability to provide firm and effective leadership. Recognizing his limitations, Ali began to enlist the help of African Americans who were better educated than he was and who had a better business background. Tragically, some of these businessmen took advantage of their positions and began to use their offices within the Moorish Science movement to enrich themselves as individuals by authorizing the sale of various herbs, magical charms and potions, etc. Not only did these unscrupulous efforts undermine the economic self-sufficiency that Ali was striving to achieve for his followers, they resulted in the introduction of religious practices and beliefs that were in opposition to Ali's pseudo-Islamic message.

As corruption grew within the business practices of the movement, a struggle developed for control of the organization. This internal warfare reached its zenith in early 1929 when Sheykh Claude D. Greene, Ali's business manager, declared himself the new leader of the Moorish Science movement and removed all of Ali's furniture from his office. On May 15, 1929, Greene was stabbed to death. Even though Ali was not in Chicago at the time of Greene's murder, he was quickly arrested by the Chicago police, although he was later released on bail.

Only a few weeks after being released on bail, Ali died under rather mysterious circumstances. Some have maintained that he died secondary to complications from beatings administered while undergoing police interrogation. Others have claimed that he died from a beating given by dissident members of the Moorish Science movement.

Whatever the cause of Ali's death, his passing resulted in an increased leadership struggle within the movement. Four individuals quickly emerged as the primary candidates to assume the mantle of leadership: Ira Johnson Bey, Mealy El, C. Kirkman Bey, and John Givens El. These four competing candidates were soon whittled down to C. Kirkman Bey, Ali's former secretary, and John Givens El, Ali's former chauffeur. At a unity meeting held later in 1929, C. Kirkman Bey was elected leader. However, John Givens El proclaimed that he was the reincarnation of Noble Drew Ali, and this claim led to a large minority of the Moorish Science temples deciding to follow the leadership of Ali's former chauffeur.

Between 1929 and 1959, the leadership of the majority of Moorish Science temples resided in the person of C. Kirkman Bey. Following C. Kirkman Bey, F. Nelson Bey assumed leadership from 1959 to 1967. In turn, he was followed by J. Blakely Bey from 1967-1971. Since 1971, Robert Love El has been the leader of the larger branch of the Moorish Science movement.

By the time of Noble Drew Ali's death in 1929, there were over 1,200 Moorish Science members just in Chicago, and the total number of adherents may have reached as high as 20,000 to 30,000. Further, it has been estimated that there were as many as 10,000 Moorish Science members or former members by the year 1950. The number of Moorish Science adherents today is not specifically known, but it has been estimated that there are about 10,000 scattered across 15 different cities in the United States.

E3. RACIAL MYTHOLOGY

It is actually rather spurious to make a distinction between the racial mythology and the religious beliefs of the Moorish Science Temple. In reality, its racial mythology is part and parcel of its religious beliefs. In fact, Noble Drew Ali reportedly maintained that it was first necessary for a people to have a nationality before it could have a religion. However, this distinction, even if somewhat bogus, allows for some measure of ease of presentation.

Central to the message of Noble Drew Ali was the belief that advancement for African Americans from their second-class citizenship in America could only be achieved through a rediscovery of their national and racial origins. To accomplish this goal, Ali proposed that African Americans were Moorish, i.e., from Morocco, in their origins and that their natural and original religion was Islam, not the Christianity of European Americans.

However, Ali's myth of racial origin did not stop with transforming all sub-Saharan Africans into Moors from Morocco. He further posited that the Moors originated in Asia from the ancient Moabite (mentioned in *Genesis* as having descended from Lot, the nephew of Abraham) and Canaanite (the inhabitants of Palestine at the time Joshua reportedly led the Israelites into Palestine) peoples. Thus, in a general sense, the ancient ancestors of African Americans were in reality "Asiatics." Ali then claimed that these Asiatic ancestors of African Americans migrated at some time in the distant past to northwestern Africa, where they became known as Moors. Thus, in a more specific sense, the ancestors of African Americans were Moors.

Given this racial mythology, Ali proposed that the proper term for African Americans was Moorish Americans, and he specifically rejected several terms then in use for identifying African Americans. For example, he rejected the terms "Negro" and "black" because they supposedly signify death. "Colored" was rejected because it means something that is painted. "Ethiopian" was rejected because it allegedly implies a division.

As part of Ali's emphasis on establishing a new racial and national identity as Moorish Americans, Ali preached that African Americans should abandon the family names their African ancestors were given during slavery. (Often these names were nothing more than the family name of the slave owner.) In place of their former "slave names," adherents to the Moorish Science Temple were given the family name of Bey or El, which Ali taught were the most prevalent family names in Morocco. A very few Moorish Science members have taken the family name of Ali, but this is reportedly an unusual occurrence within the movement.

Membership in the Moorish Science Temple was and is only open to "Asiatics," and all those of exclusively European-American heritage were denied entry.

E4. RELIGIOUS BELIEFS

As noted in the introduction to this section, there are two considerations that make it difficult to establish with complete certainty the beliefs and practices of the Moorish Science Temple. The first is the emphasis placed upon secrecy within the movement. For example, copies of Noble Drew Ali's *Holy Koran* are seldom allowed into the hands of non-members. The second follows from the fact that the Moorish Science movement split into two competing camps following the death of Ali, resulting in some discrepancies regarding beliefs and practices. For example, some Moorish Science temples teach a belief in reincarnation, while others apparently do not. As such, some measure of caution and qualification is necessary when presenting the beliefs and practices of the Moorish Science movement.

The religious beliefs of the Moorish Science Temple are examined in this section, while religious practices are reviewed in the following section. This distinction between religious beliefs and religious practices is somewhat arbitrary but does provide some needed organizational and conceptual framework.

Noble Drew Ali claimed that he was teaching Islam or "Islamism," and the Moorish Science movement claims to be an Islamic or Muslim sect. In fact, there are many Islamic elements within Moorish Science belief. However, there are also some glaring discrepancies between Islam and the Moorish Science Temple.

Consistent with orthodox Islam, the Moorish Science Temple refers to God as Allah, although it often uses the Christian "Father" when referring to Allah. Also consistent with orthodox Islam, the Moorish Science Temple stresses the absolute unity of God. Noble Drew Ali made the unity of God a "cardinal doctrine" and "the first and foremost pillar" of the Moorish Science Temple when he wrote:

> Islam is a very simple faith...The cardinal doctrine of Islam is
> unity of the Father (Allah), We believe in One God, Allah is all
> God, all mercy, and all power, he is perfect and holy, all wisdom
> all knowledge, all truth...He neither begets nor is He begotten
> because these are traits of frail and weak humanity. This unity
> of Allah is the first and foremost pillar of Islam and every other
> belief hangs upon it.[85]

The above statement by Ali brings to mind several passages from the *Qur'an*. In particular, one is struck by the almost verbatim parallel between Ali's "He neither begets nor is He begotten" and the third verse of the 112th chapter of the *Qur'an*.

---

85. Ali ND (---).

Say: He is Allah, the One and Only; Allah, the Eternal, Absolute;
He begetteth not, nor is He begotten; and there is none like unto
Him. (*Qur'an* 112:1-4)

In a manner similar to Islam, the Moorish Science Temple
acknowledges that there have been many prophets sent to
mankind. For example, the Moorish Science nationality and identification card that is given to adherents of the movement states
that they honor Jesus, Muhammad, Buddha, Confucius, and
Noble Drew Ali as prophets. In other Moorish Science texts,
Muhammad is acknowledged as being the founder of the "reunit-
ing" Islam, and Zoroaster is also noted as being one of those who
can be listed alongside of Jesus, Buddha, Confucius, and Noble
Drew Ali. Further, chapter 48 of the *Holy Koran* of Noble Drew
Ali states that Marcus Garvey was a forerunner to Noble Drew Ali
and that Marcus Garvey was to Noble Drew Ali as John the Baptist
was to Jesus.

Like the Moorish Science Temple, Islam and the *Qur'an* specifically identify John the Baptist, Jesus Christ, and Muhammad as being
prophets of Allah. Further, the *Qur'an* identifies many of the *Old
Testament* notables as being prophets and states that there have many
other prophets of Allah who are not directly mentioned in the *Qur'an*.
However, the *Qur'an* and orthodox Islamic belief do not directly identify Buddha, Confucius, and Zoroaster as being prophets, although
Qur'an 22:17 has been interpreted as including the followers of
Zoroaster as being "People of the Book," i.e., people who have received
a book of revelation from Allah through a prophet of Allah. Further,
Qur'an 33:40 states that Muhammad was the "seal of the prophets,"
resulting in orthodox Islam maintaining that Muhammad was the last

of Allah's messengers and prophets to be sent to mankind. As such, orthodox Islam specifically rejects the concept of Marcus Garvey and Noble Drew Ali as being prophets of Allah.

In 1927, Noble Drew Ali published his *Holy Koran*, which is the basic scripture of the Moorish Science Temple and a decidedly different book from the *Qur'an* as revealed to Prophet Muhammad. The *Holy Koran* of Noble Drew Ali consists of only 64 pages of compactly printed text and is organized into 48 chapters. These 48 chapters can be separated into three basic units, although no such demarcation is actually made in the *Holy Koran*. The first unit consists of the first 19 chapters and focuses on an apocryphal rendition of the life of Jesus. For example, included in this section is a story about Jesus studying in India with Ravanna at age 12. This first unit of the *Holy Koran* is in fact plagiarized from *The Aquarian Gospel of Jesus the Christ*, a book authored by Levi Dowling, a spiritualist from Ohio. The second unit consists of chapters 20-44 and includes a variety of ethical instructions covering such topics as social responsibility, marriage, family duties, justice, charity, sincerity, etc. Within this second unit, chapters 20-25 appear to have been plagiarized from the 1923 publication known as *Infinite Wisdom*. *Infinite Wisdom* purports to be an ancient Tibetan text that was subsequently translated into Chinese and then into English. The third unit, i.e., chapters 45-48, consists primarily of Ali's racial mythology, as well as some of Ali's thoughts on the need for racial purity, Christian history, eschatology, etc.[86]

Despite the fact that Noble Drew Ali created his own *Holy Koran*, the organization papers filed by the Moorish Science Temple with Cook County, Illinois, on July 20, 1928, specifically states that the

---

86. Haddad YY, Smith JI (1993), Fauset AH (1971), and McCloud AM (1995).

Moorish Science Temple derives its power and authority from the *Qur'an* of Muhammad. Nonetheless, the *Qur'an* was in little use among Moorish Science adherents during the lifetime of Noble Drew Ali, perhaps because it was not readily available in English translation at that time. Today, many Moorish Science members do read and study standard English translations of the *Qur'an*.

Noble Drew Ali reportedly taught that there are three components to each individual, i.e., the physical body, an individualized and personalized soul, and the spirit. Within the Moorish Science belief system, the spirit is seen as being non-personal and not individualized, as being genderless and unchanging, and as being part of the spirit of Allah. Salvation consists of the personalized soul realizing and accepting that the non-personalized spirit is one with Allah. In contrast, heaven and hell are perceived as being simply states of mind. For example, heaven is seen as being a condition of spiritual fulfillment and joy that can be actualized on earth. However, the ultimate goal is not heaven on earth, but unity of the spirit with Allah.

Some Moorish Science groups link the above theory of a physical body, a personalized soul, and a non-individualized spirit to the concept of reincarnation. For Moorish Science adherents who believe in reincarnation, death is the passing away of the physical body. The soul then enters the plain of the soul, which is sort of a bridge between the spiritual and physical dimensions. In the plain of the soul, an assessment is made of the person's life, from which one is to learn a variety of spiritual lessons. When these lessons are learned, the soul is then reincarnated into another physical body. This process of death and reincarnation continues until the individualized and personalized soul is no longer needed and the spirit achieves unity with Allah.

While there are some components of the above theory of "salvation," e.g., seeking spiritual unity with Allah, that have parallels with certain aspects of Sufi mysticism, as a whole the above schema of "salvation" smacks much more of classical Hinduism than of orthodox Islam. For example, in the *Chandragupta Upanishad* of classical Hinduism, one is instructed that *tat tvam asi*, i.e., that thou art. Classical Hinduism then maintains that it is only *maya* (illusion) that prevents one (in fact, there is no "one" because the very concept of oneself is a form of *maya* to be overcome) from recognizing that everything is oneness in mystical unity. *Atman* (the individualized spirit) is actually *Brahman* (the generalized spirit that is everything), and the goal of life is to overcome *maya*, accept *tat tvam asi*, and have the *atman* rejoined in perfect oneness with *Brahman*. Until *maya* has been overcome, the *atman* is trapped in the wheel of *samsara* (reincarnation), with the status of the new reincarnated body (whether human of one caste or another or animal of one species or another) being determined by the *karma* earned during the immediately prior reincarnation.

E5. Religious Practices

Like Muslims the world over, Moorish Science followers stand and face the east, i.e., towards Makkah, during their prayers. However, Moorish Science adherents remain standing throughout the entirety of the prayer, unlike Muslims who stand, bow, kneel, and prostrate at various times within the prayer. Further, the Moorish Science Temple does not follow standard Islamic practice in terms of the words used during prayer. In some temples, three daily prayers are mandated. These prayers are to be said at dawn, noon, and sunset. Such a prayer schedule is consistent with many of the Islamic residuals reported by elderly African Americans who were interviewed by the Savannah Writers Project and who probably observed Muslims combining their five daily prayers into three times because of the hardships of slavery. However, in other temples, frequent prayer is encouraged, but there are no obligatory prayer times.

Consistent with orthodox Islam, the Moorish Science Temple designates Friday as a special day within the week for religious services.

Religious services at some Moorish Science temples consist of gender-segregated seating, which is consistent with orthodox Islam. Further, the leader at Moorish Science religious services generally speaks in a low, quiet voice, sometimes described as being barely above a whisper. Once again, this is consistent with orthodox Islamic practice as the *Khutba* or sermon during a Friday service is usually delivered calmly. Within a Moorish Science "sermon," much of the message typically consists of reading from Noble Drew Ali's *Holy Koran* and from the special laws of the temple. Personal testimonials and a collection are also included in religious services. Services sometimes end with adherents standing, facing east in the direction of Makkah, raising their hands and arms in a manner similar to the beginning of prayer for Muslims, and then reciting: "Allah, the Father of the Universe, the Father of Love, Truth, Peace, Freedom and Justice. Allah is my Protector, my Guide, and my Salvation by night and by day, through His Holy Prophet, Drew Ali. Amen."[87]

Just as is the case in traditional Islam, there is no music at Moorish Science religious services, although quiet chants are sometimes performed, with such chants being variations on well-known Christian hymns. For example, one chant transformed "Give me that old time religion..." into "Muslim's that old time religion..."

---

87. Fauset AH (1971).

With regard to dress, men are instructed to wear a red *fez* at all times, are forbidden to shave (orthodox Muslim men typically are bearded), and in at least some cases are discouraged from wearing neckties. In some Moorish Science groups, women are instructed to wear a headscarf or turban, which is consistent with traditional Islamic practice, and are forbidden to wear makeup and short dresses. Hair straightening is prohibited for both sexes.

Adherents to the Moorish Science Temple are taught certain basic dietary restrictions. Consistent with orthodox Islam, the Moorish Science Temple prohibits the consumption of pork and alcohol. However, some Moorish Science groups, primarily those who stress a belief in reincarnation, go well beyond the boundaries of Islam and also prohibit the ingestion of meat and eggs.

The Moorish Science Temple insists that marriage must be monogamous and rarely permits divorce. Like Islam, the Moorish Science Temple also stresses family duties and responsibilities, insists on modest dress, and prohibits gambling. Moorish Science holidays include January 8th (the birthday of Noble Drew Ali), January 15th (their New Years Day), and Flag Day in August.

E6. CONCLUSIONS

As can be seen, the Moorish Science Temple represents a strange amalgamation of Islamic residuals, classical Hinduism, and a unique racial mythology. The specifically Islamic aspects of the Moorish Science Temple include: belief in the absolute oneness of God (Allah); belief in the prophethood of John the Baptist, Jesus Christ, and Muhammad; belief in the *Qur'an* as divine revelation given to Prophet Muhammad; standing and facing east towards Makkah when beginning prayers; designating Friday as a special day for religious services;

sermons delivered in a calm and quiet voice; lack of music during religious services; modest dress and grooming; dietary prohibitions against pork and alcohol; an emphasis on family values and responsibilities; and a prohibition on gambling.

F. THE NATION OF ISLAM

F1. INTRODUCTION

While slavery ended in theory with the Emancipation Proclamation and while slavery ended in fact with the end of the Civil War and the passage of the 13th Amendment to the Constitution in 1865, the formal practice of slavery was merely replaced with the indentured servitude of feudal sharecropping, the restrictions and inhumanities of Jim Crow laws, and the second-class status imposed by segregation, denial of education, restriction of voting rights, and marked constriction of opportunity in almost all walks of life. Further, there were a reported 1,831 lynchings of African Americans by European Americans between 1891 and 1911, with estimates suggesting an additional 600 lynchings that were not reported. Just within the 15 years spanning 1900 and 1914, 1,100 African Americans were lynched. Another 28 African Americans were burned alive between the years of 1918 and 1921, and uncounted others were lynched, shot, and otherwise killed.

It was within this context of racial hatred and bigotry that the Nation of Islam was born in 1930. Like the Moorish Science Temple before it, the Nation of Islam was built upon a foundation of racial mythology, Islamic elements, and some decidedly non-Islamic beliefs and practices. With Noble Drew Ali having died in 1929, with the Moorish Science Temple then being racked with internal disputes and schisms over leadership, and with the Nation of Islam arising in 1930, it is not surprising that a number of former Moorish Science adherents later joined the Nation of Islam. Over the next four decades, the Nation of Islam combined a pseudo-Islamic message with a racial mythology that was designed to uplift the African-American community and to instill a needed sense of racial pride.

Interest in the Nation of Islam by African Americans was insured by continued racial bigotry and prejudice in American society. For example, with the exception of Moses Fleetwood Walker and a handful of other African Americans in the old American Association of the 1880s, it wasn't until 1946 that African Americans were allowed to play organized baseball. It would take several more years before African Americans could walk the streets without fear of lynching. It was not until 1954 and the landmark Supreme Court decision of Brown vs. The Board of Education of Topeka that African Americans were given the legal right to attend integrated public schools throughout the entire breadth of the United States. It would be several additional years before that legal right was enforced, at times only secondary to the military intervention of the National Guard. It was not until 1964 that a comprehensive Civil Rights Act was passed into law by a reluctant congress. It was not until the 24th Amendment to the Constitution in 1964 that the restrictive poll tax was prohibited as a criterion for voting in federal elections. It would take several more years before African Americans could exercise unfettered voting rights. However, the end of legally sanctioned racial injustice did not spell the end of covert racial injustice, a situation that continues to this very moment.

F2. History

The Nation of Islam has gone through more than one name over the course of its history. It was originally founded as the Allah Temple of Islam. Later, the name was changed to the Lost-Found Nation of Islam. However, it is more popularly known as the Nation of Islam or as simply the Nation.

The history of the Nation of Islam begins in the summer of 1930 in Detroit, Michigan, with a man variously known as Wallace Fard Muhammad, Farrad Muhammad, F. Muhammad Ali, Professor Ford, Wali Farrad, and W. D. Fard. There have been as many theories regarding his origin and background as there were names used by him. Some have maintained that he was a Palestinian Arab. Others claimed that his father was a Jamaican of African descent and that his mother was a Muslim from Syria. Other theories have variously posited that he was from Turkey, that he was a member of the Quraish tribe of the Hijaz (what is now part of western Saudi Arabia), that he was from the Indian subcontinent, and that he was a native of New Zealand with a multiple imprisonment record in California for bootlegging, narcotics trafficking, fraud, and theft.

Whatever his origins and from wherever he came, Fard was plying the trade of a door-to-door peddler in the African-American community of Detroit in the summer of 1930. Initially, Fard was selling raincoats. Later, he began selling silks, which he claimed were exactly like those worn by the people of Africa, an area he claimed to have visited.

Eager to learn about the homeland of their ancestors, African Americans began inviting Fard into their homes and peppering him with questions. These informal conversations about their African homeland quickly turned into a succession of small meetings that moved from house to house. As interest continued to grow, it finally became necessary to rent a hall in order to accommodate all those who wished to hear this mysterious stranger expound about Africa and its people.

At first, Fard's message was basically confined to narratives about his travels in other lands. Gradually, his message expanded to talking about the history and religion of the African people. During this early phase of his ministry, Fard often used the *Bible* as a sort of rudimentary textbook to illustrate his points. Eventually, he began to attack the *Bible* as a corrupted book, to blame the white man for the suffering of African Americans, to recommend certain dietary restrictions, to instruct his listeners in the glorious history of black Africans, and to insist that the religion of his listeners' ancestors was Islam, which he claimed was the only true religion of the black-skinned peoples of the world. To back up his claims, he frequently referenced the *Bible*, the pamphlets and literature of the Jehovah Witnesses and Freemasonry, certain history books, and the *Qur'an*.

What had started as informal get-togethers in scattered living rooms had now become a formal religious movement with a membership examination procedure, a registry of group members, an organizational hierarchy, and an extensive educational program. Literacy classes were introduced to teach members to read and write. The University of Islam (a private elementary and secondary school) was established. The Muslim Girls Training Class was instituted to teach young women of the movement the basics of home economics and how to be an effective wife and mother. The Fruit of Islam was created for men as a paramilitary unit to insure the self-defense of the community against the prevalent racism of the times. In addition, Fard wrote two manuals for his followers: *The Secret Ritual of the Nation of Islam* and *Teaching for the Lost Found Nation of Islam in a Mathematical Way*.

As the movement continued to expand, a permanent place of

worship (Temple 1) was established. In addition, Fard appointed a more elaborate organizational hierarchy and gradually turned over the day to day running of the movement to an assistant, a Minister of Islam. By this time, Fard was being routinely referred to by his followers as a prophet, Fard had reportedly described himself to the Detroit police as "the Supreme Ruler of the Universe," and some of Fard's followers considered him to be divine.

In June of 1934, after having created a religious, self-help, and racial movement of about 8,000 members (some estimates place the number at more than 25,000), Fard disappeared as mysteriously as he had arrived. As is the case in most such sects when a charismatic leader dies or disappears, the fledgling movement was initially racked by internal schism. Arising out of this period of schism and lost membership, Elijah Muhammad assumed control as the Minister of Islam and moved the organization from Detroit to Chicago, where he established Temple 2.

Elijah Muhammad was born Elijah Poole on October 7, 1897, in Bold Springs in the vicinity of Sandersville, Georgia. His parents were sharecroppers and former slaves, and his father and grandfather had been Baptist ministers. Because of poverty, Poole was forced to quit school at an early age in order to help with the family farm work. By age 14, he was working on his own in various jobs.

On May 2, 1917, Poole married Clara Evans, and their first child, Emmanuel, was born in 1921. In 1923, the Elijah Poole family moved from the South to Detroit, Michigan. He was introduced to Fard in 1930, quickly thereafter renounced his Christian background in order to embrace Fard's teachings, abandoned his "slave name" of Poole, and was renamed Elijah Muhammad by Fard. Succeeding Fard as leader of the Nation of Islam in 1934, Elijah Muhammad patiently worked to insure a slow but steady growth of members over the next decade. As time went on, he assumed the title of prophet and messenger of Allah, and Fard became more clearly identified as being Allah or an incarnation of Allah. By 1946, there were branches of the Nation of Islam in Chicago, Milwaukee, and Washington, DC.

During the early days of World War II, Elijah Muhammad urged his followers to avoid the draft and expressed solidarity with the Japanese people, whom he saw as being part of the wider non-white community of the world. As a result, he was charged with interfering with the Selective Service Act and was imprisoned on May 8, 1942. He was not released until 1946. Many of his followers, including his brother (Willie) and his oldest son (Emmanuel) were also imprisoned for Selective Service violations.

In the 1950s and early 1960s, the Nation of Islam began to achieve growing attention in the African-American community secondary to its activist and militant role in the civil rights movement and success in rehabilitating alcoholics, drug addicts, and prison inmates. Sparked by the preaching of Malcolm X (see chapter IX), more and more African Americans flocked to the banner of the Nation of Islam and its racial mythology. In response, the national media began to look at Elijah Muhammad's movement for the first time, and CBS ran a nationwide documentary on the Nation of Islam in the summer of 1959. At the time, membership in the movement was estimated to be somewhat less than 30,000. With the increased publicity provided by CBS, membership more than doubled within the next month. By the end of 1960, there were 69 temples scattered across 27 states, and membership may have reached as high as

100,000. Two years later, some estimates placed the membership of the Nation of Islam at 250,000. At its peak, it may have had a membership as large as one million.

More publicity followed in late February of 1964 when, having just won boxing's heavyweight championship of the world as a decided underdog, 22-year-old Cassius Clay (see chapter IX) announced that he had joined the Nation of Islam. The following month, he changed his name to Muhammad Ali.

The Nation of Islam was also extremely active in promoting an African-American economy and established a number of successful businesses in the 1950s and 1960s. For example, the Nation of Islam owned grocery stores, bakeries, clothing stores, restaurants, department stores, and numerous establishments providing various services, e.g., barbershops. In addition, the Nation of Islam established a thriving agricultural sector and owned farms in Michigan, Alabama, and Georgia. According to the movement's *Muhammad Speaks* newspaper of November 12, 1971, the Nation of Islam's farms consisted of around 10,000 acres (over 15.6 square miles) and were producing 12,000 dozen eggs, 2,200 gallons of milk, thousands of pounds of fish, and tens of thousands of pounds of beef per week. Over 200 lambs were being slaughtered and sold each day. In addition, 1971 saw the production of 75,000 pounds of apples, 1,200,000 pounds of watermelon, and tens of thousands of pounds of navy beans.

Elijah Muhammad, although only having a few years of formal education, was acutely aware that a successful African-American economy and the advancement of African Americans were contingent upon education. As such, the Nation of Islam was actively involved in establishing private schools. By 1972, the Nation of Islam was operating 14 private schools, each staffed by accredited teachers and each having a 50-week school year. The regular academic curriculum (science, reading, math, history, arts, and language) was supplemented with an Arabic language course and instruction in the racial mythology and religious beliefs of the Nation of Islam. Gender separation was practiced in the schools, and a strict dress code was implemented. Boys had to wear ties and jackets, and girls had to wear ankle-length white gowns and head-wraps.

The appeal of the Nation of Islam to the African-American community can be seen in the reflections of a 1970 convert to the movement.

> I was attracted to the spirit and love of brotherhood and sisterhood that I witnessed among its members…(Its) message was strictly based on the liberation of the African-American people…I would see the young men of the Nation of Islam standing on the street corners of Philadelphia and selling the *Muhammad Speaks* newspaper, as it was called during those days. These young men all had a certain, distinguishable look and were easily recognized by their style of dress. Their apparel consisted of a suit, white shirt, and bow tie. Their grooming was typically impeccable and was characterized by a close-cut hairstyle and clean face (no facial hair). However, they would sometimes wear blue and red FOI (Fruit of Islam) uniforms. The brothers, as they were called, had an appearance of cleanliness and intelligent behavior…This was the Nation of Islam inviting all African Americans to come to the mosque and listen to the minister talk about the rise of the Black man and the fall of the White man…my attraction to the Nation of Islam was simply to find a good husband…An additional benefit was the Muslims Girls Training (MGT) classes where we were taught how to be women

and how to take care of our bodily needs, such as cleanliness of the body and hair. We were also taught how to keep our homes neat and clean, cook and sew, and take care of our children. The men were taught how to be respectful towards their wives and how to be responsible providers for the household....(There was) unity and cohesiveness among the sisters and brothers. I also witnessed love, respect, and a willingness to create businesses within the African-American community. This last issue was important, as the development of African-American businesses directly contributed to the economic advancement and uplifting of the entire African-American community.[88]

In some ways, 1963-1964 may have been the high water mark for the Nation of Islam. In December of 1963, Malcolm X was suspended from the movement following some "politically incorrect" comments he had made in the aftermath of the assassination of President John F. Kennedy. In March of 1964, Malcolm formally left the Nation of Islam, repudiated the racial mythology of the Nation of Islam, embraced orthodox Islam, and formed his own Islamic organization. Moreover, Malcolm was not the only one who had become increasingly aware of how the Nation of Islam diverged from orthodox Islam. During the 1960s and 1970s, Warith Deen Mohammed, the son of Elijah Muhammad, was suspended at least twice from the Nation of Islam for teaching concepts of orthodox Islam that deviated from those of the Nation of Islam. Following each suspension, he was later reinstated. Schism was beginning to bite at the heels of Elijah Muhammad.

---

88. Beruni KR (2003), pages 176-179.

Nonetheless, by the end of 1972, the Nation of Islam still had at least 50 temples, and Elijah Muhammad continued to claim a membership base of a few hundred thousand. At least one estimate claims there were Nation of Islam temples in more than 150 cities scattered across the United States, the United Kingdom, Jamaica, Ghana, Bermuda, and Belize at the time of Elijah Muhammad's death in 1975. The Nation of Islam's newspaper, *Muhammad Speaks*, was said to enjoy a weekly circulation that included 950,000 copies, making it the largest African-American owned weekly in the history of the United States.

F3. RACIAL MYTHOLOGY

Following in the footsteps of the Moorish Science Temple, the Nation of Islam also constructed a racial mythology. After centuries of being taught by the dominant white society that they were a mentally and morally inferior people, a subconscious residue of this instruction had become part of the African-American self-identity.

Na'im Akbar, a psychologist and African American, has posited a number of ways in which the legacy of slavery has affected the self-identity and psychological functioning of African Americans, and thus adversely affected many of their behavioral patterns. Akbar hypothesizes that this legacy of slavery has resulted in: (1) a distorted and self-detrimental attitude among African Americans regarding work, in which labor continues to be seen as something that only profits the "White master" and fails to be of direct benefit to the "Black slave;" (2) a failure to appreciate property rights, resulting in the vandalism and destruction of the "White master's" property and the failure to maintain the "Black slave's" property; (3) the disrespect of African-American leadership, as such leadership is still largely perceived as being either a puppet of the "White master" or a threat to the "White master" that will likely bring retribution down upon all African Americans; (4) a tendency to play the clown as a way of avoiding self-responsibility and punishment from the dominant "White master;" (5) a profound sense of personal inferiority; (6) self-destructive divisions within the African-American community; (7) a lack of marital and family commitment and responsibility arising out of the arbitrary manner in which the "White master" selectively bred his "Black slaves" and dissolved their families via the auction block; and (8) an in-house practice of color discrimination reflected in the once popular jingle: "yellow, your mellow; brown, stick around; black, to the back."

The Moorish Science Temple attempted to counteract this mind set among African Americans by stressing racial equality via a racial mythology for African Americans that emphasized their glorious Moorish past and that provided a genealogy tracing to the ancient Moabites and Canaanites. The Nation of Islam went much further and replaced the racial equality of the Moorish Science Temple with a doctrine that trumpeted the inherent racial superiority of African Americans.

According to the racial mythology of the Nation of Islam, the black man is and always has been divine, was co-existent with the creation of the universe, was innately and inherently Muslim, and peopled a planetary body consisting of a combined earth and moon. Approximately 66 trillion years ago, an immense explosion ripped the moon and earth into two different cosmic bodies, with the black men and women of the tribe of Shabazz being miraculously saved on what is now the earth.

After the cosmic separation of the earth and moon, black men and women increased in numbers, explored and settled the surface of the earth, and established great civilizations along the Nile River Valley and elsewhere. A golden age of black civilization ensued, major scientific advancements were the norm, lifespans were enormous, and a prolonged period of peace and prosperity was enjoyed by black mankind. It was apparently during this era that all of history was written in advance by 24 black scientists under the direction of a 25th black who served as final judge and arbiter. There things remained until approximately 6,000 years ago.

In 4,686 BCE, Yakub, a mad scientist who was rebelling against Allah, began experimenting with creating a new race of people via genetic manipulation of the two "germs" contained in each black person. The stronger of these two germs is black, the weaker is brown, and together they account for all the races and ethnicities of the earth except for whites. (According to this racial mythology, the word "negro" should be rejected in favor of black man, as "negro" is nothing more than a white neologism that was created for the purpose of separating blacks from their Asian brothers.)

For 600 years, Yakub labored in his research. Finally, in the year 4,086 BCE, Yakub was able to graft the brown germ into its final stage, which is white. With that scientific discovery, the white race came into existence.

Given its origins, the white race is genetically inferior to the black race. Deprived of color, whites are also deprived of the black man's divinity/humanity and physical and moral stamina. By their very nature, whites are a race of liars, murderers, and treacherous individuals. Unlike blacks who are divine and who are born Muslims, whites are a race of blue-eyed devils who are innately predisposed to reject Islam. Thus, while blacks are Muslims from birth, whites are not. Furthermore, only a few, truly exceptional whites are capable of becoming Muslims by a later act of faith.

(With reference to labeling all whites as blue-eyed devils, this may have been based on an idiosyncratic and literal, as opposed to idiomatic, translation of one verse from *Qur'an* 20:102. In referring to the Judgment Day, this verse is usually translated as: "The day when the trumpet will be sounded: that day, We shall gather the sinful, bleary-eyed (with terror)..." In the above verse, the Arabic word that is translated as "bleary-eyed" is *Zurqa*. A literal translation of *Zurqa* would be "blue-eyed." However, the more meaningful and idiomatically correct translation is "bleary-eyed" or "blind-eyed.")

In the divine scheme of things, the white race was given 6,000 years to rule the earth, with that rule ending in 1914 (the same year that Charles Taze Russell, the founder of the Jehovah's Witness movement, predicted would mark the beginning of a major war between capitalism and communism/socialism that would lead to the End Times). For 6,000 years, the whites were allowed to enslave blacks, destroy black civilization, and rob blacks of their nationhood (the Afro-Asiatic, black nation of the tribe of Shabazz), language (Arabic), names, and natural religion (Islam). Whites were also allowed to create their own religion (Christianity) to keep blacks confused, docile, enslaved, and ignorant of their glorious past and divine nature. In short, blacks were a lost nation. In 1914, a 70-year period of grace was extended to white rule in order to allow blacks to find themselves as a nation. Hence, the Nation of Islam was frequently referred to as the Lost-Found Nation of Islam.

Somewhat consistent with the eschatology of the Biblical book of *Revelation*, the Nation of Islam posited a final battle between the forces of good and evil which is to occur at Armageddon, also known as Har-Magedon or Megiddo (see *Revelation* 16:16). However, this apocalyptic event was interpreted through the lens of the Nation of Islam's racial mythology. As such, the Plain of Megiddo or Esdraelon becomes North America, the forces of good become blacks, and the forces of evil becomes whites. Following this Battle of Armageddon, blacks inherit the earth, and whites are banished.

Having briefly reviewed the racial mythology of the Nation of Islam, it is time to turn to its racial goals. Concisely stated, the Nation of Islam advocated a separation of the races. Typically, this separation of the races was stated as a three-step goal. The first step was social and personal separation of the races. As such, interracial socializing and marriage were prohibited, and the concept of equal but separate educational facilities was promoted. The second step was economic separation of the races and the creation of a separate African-American economy. To achieve this goal and to advance African Americans financially, members were told to shop only at African-American stores and to buy only African-American products. The third and final step was political segregation of the races. To achieve this end, the Nation of Islam sought a separate state or territory of their own within the geographic confines of the United States.

There is nothing even remotely similar in orthodox Islam to the racial mythology of the Nation of Islam. More specifically, the racial exclusivism of the Nation of Islam directly contradicts the universal brotherhood of mankind espoused by Islam. As noted previously in chapter IV, within Islam race and ethnicity confer neither superiority nor inferiority.

O mankind! We created you from a single (pair) of a male and a female, and made you into nations and tribes that ye may know each other (not that ye may despise each other). Verily, the most honored of you in the sight of God is (he who is) the most righteous of you. (*Qur'an* 49:13)

O people! Listen and obey, even though a mangled Abyssinian slave is your commander, if he executes (the commands of) the Book of God (i.e., the *Qur'an*) among you...O people! Verily your Lord is One, and your father (i.e., Adam) is one. All of you belong to one ancestry from Adam, and Adam was created out of clay. There is no superiority for an Arab over a non-Arab and for a non-Arab over an Arab; nor for the white over the black, nor for the black over the white, except in piety. "Verily, the most honored of you in the sight of God is (he who is) the most righteous of you." (Prophet Muhammad's Farewell Sermon in Makkah)

Abu Huraira reported the Messenger of God as saying: "God, Most High, has removed from you the pride of the pre-Islamic period and its boasting in ancestors. One is only a pious believer or a miserable sinner. You are sons of Adam, and Adam came from dust. Let the people cease to boast about their ancestors. They are merely fuel in hell; or they will certainly be of less account with God than the beetle which rolls dung with its nose." (*Abu Dawud, Hadith* #5097)

F4. RELIGIOUS BELIEFS

Building upon Islamic residuals within the African-American community, the Nation of Islam claimed to be Islamic and maintained that the original and inherent religion of African Americans was Islam.

However, the fundamental beliefs of the Nation of Islam were often diametrically opposed to orthodox Islam. As a first example of this discrepancy between Islam and the Nation of Islam consider the concept of God.

Like traditional Islam, the Nation of Islam claimed that Allah was God. However, there the similarities ended. For example, the Nation of Islam claimed that all Afro-Asiatics were divine and that the supreme man among them was Allah. This supreme black man or Allah was then said to be incarnated in the person of W. D. Fard. In making these claims, the Nation of Islam was in complete violation of the most cardinal tenets of Islamic theology and was maintaining that Afro-Asiatics were different from Allah only in degree.

The Nation of Islam, like orthodox Islam before it, maintained that both Jesus Christ and Muhammad were prophets of Allah. In fact, the Nation of Islam maintained that several of the parables attributed to Jesus in the *Bible* (e.g., the Lost Sheep and the Prodigal Son) were in reference to African Americans. However, the Nation of Islam stated that Jesus was much less of a prophetic figure than was Muhammad. In making this comparison in this manner, the Nation of Islam directly contradicted the teachings of the *Qur'an*.

> Say ye: "We believe in Allah, and the revelation given to us, and to Abraham, Ismail, Isaac, Jacob, and the tribes, and that given to Moses and Jesus, and that given to (all) prophets from their Lord: we make no difference between one and another of them: and we bow to Allah (in Islam). (*Qur'an* 2:136)

> The messenger believeth in what hath been revealed to him from his Lord, as do the men of faith. Each one (of them) believeth in Allah,

His angels, His books, and His messengers. "We make no distinction (they say) between one and another of His messengers." (*Qur'an* 2:285)

To those who believe in Allah and His messengers and make no distinction between any of the messengers, We shall soon give their (due) rewards: for Allah is oft-forgiving, most merciful. (*Qur'an* 4:152)

Further, the Nation of Islam violated a basic belief of Islam when it initially claimed that W. D. Fard was a prophet of Allah and then later claimed that Elijah Muhammad was a prophet and messenger of Allah. Furthermore, it was commonly believed within the Nation of Islam that Elijah Muhammad would not actually die but would simply vanish for a while. Afterwards, he would return with Allah in the incarnation of Fard. Within orthodox Islam, Prophet Muhammad is seen as being the final and universal prophet to mankind. He is the seal of the prophets, and there will be no prophets after him.

Muhammad is not the father of any of your men, but (he is) the messenger of Allah, and the seal of the prophets: and Allah has full knowledge of all things. (*Qur'an* 33:40)

One of the six basic beliefs of Islam is that there will be a Judgment Day and that there will be an afterlife for each individual in either heaven or hell. Contrary to this Islamic belief, the Nation of Islam maintained that there was no afterlife and no heaven or hell other than that which is found on earth. Hell on earth is a result of white rule, while heaven on earth follows from black rule.

In terms of scripture, the Nation of Islam nominally accepted the *Qur'an* as their divine scripture. One might well wonder how members of the Nation of Islam would not constantly trip over the contradictions between the *Qur'an* and the religious beliefs and racial mythology of the Nation of Islam. The answer lies in the fact that members were taught that they were not ready for the *Qur'an*. As such, they could have a *Qur'an* and should put it in an honored and elevated place, but they were not yet ready to read and understand the message of the *Qur'an*. As such, despite being the nominal scripture of the Nation of Islam, its members widely ignored the *Qur'an* as the basic textbook of religious instruction.

In fact, the *Bible* was probably used as much if not more so within the Nation of Islam than was the *Qur'an*. However, like orthodox Islam, the Nation of Islam was quick to point out that the *Bible* was a largely adulterated and contaminated book.

F5. RELIGIOUS PRACTICES

Initiation into the Nation of Islam was a *rites de passage* in which the initiate totally exchanged his former identity as a member of a lost nation into a new identity as a member of a newly refound nation of divine African Americans. This *rites de passage* was reinforced by having to change one's behavior, name, religion, and racial and national identity.

Upon deciding to apply for membership in the Nation of Islam, the initiate was required to copy a form letter to Elijah Muhammad. This form letter had to be copied perfectly right down to the smallest letter and punctuation mark. Any error of any kind would result in the letter being sent back and the applicant having to recopy the form letter once again.

Once the letter had been accepted, a new name was assigned to the initiate. Typically, this consisted of using the initiate's first name, discarding the family name that had been assigned to his enslaved ancestor by the white slave master, and substituting the letter "X" for the former family name. The use of the letter "X" was highly symbolic. It represented both: the unknown variable that was the family name of the initiate's pre-slavery ancestor, and the concept that the initiate was an "ex" with regard to most aspects of his former life. If the initiate's temple already had a member with the same first name as the initiate, a number was assigned prior to the X. Thus, John 3X would be the third person named John to have joined that particular temple. Occasionally, Elijah Muhammad would later assign a new family name of Arabic origin to replace the X designation.

To a certain extent, the above practice of name changing has its parallel in orthodox Islam. Some converts to Islam do change their birth names to Arabic names upon conversion. However, this change in names is not a requirement for becoming a Muslim, and many converts choose not to change their names.

There are five basic pillars of religious practice within Islam. These are the testimonial of faith (saying that there is no god but Allah and that Muhammad is His messenger), performing the five obligatory prayers of Islam during their set times each day, fasting during the Islamic month of *Ramadan*, paying the *Zakat* (usually consisting of giving 2.5% of one's economic surplus to charity), and performing the *Hajj* pilgrimage to Makkah at least once in one's lifetime. With regard to these five pillars of practice, the Nation of Islam made significant modifications to most of them.

With regard to the first pillar of Islamic practice, i.e., the testimonial of faith, the Nation of Islam did refer to God as Allah and did recognize Prophet Muhammad as a messenger of Allah. However, the

Nation of Islam went on to define Allah in a way that was totally different from that of traditional Islam and recognized prophets after Prophet Muhammad.

The second pillar of Islamic practice is *Salat* (the five obligatory prayers of Islam), which is preceded by ritual ablution (*Wudu*). The Nation of Islam did teach ritual washing before prayers, and it also taught the performance of five daily prayers at set times conforming to the Islamic prayer schedule. Further, the Nation of Islam required members to face towards Makkah while performing those prayers. However, the prayers of the Nation of Islam did not include the various body postures and movements entered into by orthodox Muslims during the performance of their prayers. There was no bowing, kneeling, or prostration. Further, the verbal content of the prayers of the Nation of Islam was totally different from that said by Muslims.

With regard to the remaining pillars of Islamic practice, the Nation of Islam instituted significant modifications in each of them. In place of the Islamic fast during the lunar month of *Ramadan*, the Nation of Islam substituted fasting during the solar month of December. While the Nation of Islam insisted on obligatory alms being given to the movement, such charity did not conform to the Islamic rules governing *Zakat*. While the performance of the *Hajj* pilgrimage was highly honored within the Nation of Islam, it was not a requirement on those who were physically and financially able to perform it.

Other practices of the Nation of Islam were in closer conformance to Islam. For example, members were forbidden to drink alcohol, eat pork, gamble, or engage in adultery or fornication. Provocative, revealing, flashy, or ostentatious clothing was prohibited, and men and women were segregated from each other during religious services. Further, the Nation of Islam prohibited several practices that are often actively discouraged in Islam, e.g., smoking, dancing, overeating, and any woman being alone in a room with a man other than her husband. Still further, the Nation of Islam strongly discouraged several practices that are forbidden in Islam, e.g., buying on credit (and thus paying interest) and marrying outside the group. (Within Islam, a Muslim male can only marry a Muslim, a Christian, or a Jew, while a Muslim female can only marry a Muslim.) Like Islam, the Nation of Islam actively discouraged divorce and stressed family values and responsibility.

Certain other practices of the Nation of Islam have no parallel within Islam. For example, members of the Nation of Islam were forbidden to eat cornbread and collard greens, most cosmetics were prohibited, and male members were to be clean-shaven and to maintain close-cropped hair.

F6. The Nation of Islam Post Elijah Muhammad

Elijah Muhammad died on February 25, 1975. Shortly thereafter, his son, Warith Deen Mohammed, whose last reinstatement into the Nation of Islam had happened only in the final year of his father's life, assumed leadership of the movement. The son quickly began to reinterpret some parts of the philosophy of the father and to reject other parts of it. In particular, the racial mythology of the Nation of Islam was rejected, as was the deification of Fard. During this period of transition, Warith Deen Mohammed changed the name of the Nation of Islam to the World Community of Islam in the West. In 1982, the name of the organization was changed yet again, this time to the American Muslim Mission. In May of 1985, the American

Muslim Mission was dissolved by W. D. Mohammed, and he then led most of the former members of the Nation of Islam into the world-wide community of traditional and orthodox Islam.

There were, however, those who rejected the move to orthodox Islam and likewise rejected the leadership being provided by W. D. Mohammed. Both Louis Farrakhan and John Muhammad, the latter being the brother of Elijah Muhammad, instituted schism within the ranks, and each led some members of the Nation of Islam off into his own splinter group. The resulting legal battles in the American court system drained off much of the former wealth and assets of the Nation of Islam. When all was said and done, Louis Farrakhan and his reconstituted Nation of Islam succeeded in acquiring the Chicago temple and the former residence of Elijah Muhammad. Many of the former schools and businesses of the Nation of Islam were sold by W. D. Mohammed to cover the legal fees incurred during litigation.

Louis Farrakhan broke with W. D. Mohammed's leadership in 1977. Two years later, he resurrected the Nation of Islam and began publishing an in-house newspaper, the *Final Call*. Ahariof has recently estimated that Farrakhan's Nation of Islam may consist of as many as 100 temples and 50,000 members.

The basic beliefs and practices of Farrakhan's Nation of Islam may be summarized as follows. (1) Members believe that there is no god but Allah, who came in the person of W. D. Fard. (2) Fard is also the messiah of the Christians and the *Mahdi* of the Muslims. (3) Elijah Muhammad is the messenger of Allah. (4) Elijah Muhammad is not physically dead but was only made to appear as such. (5) The *Qur'an* is accepted as revealed scripture, and members are taught to believe in the scriptures that preceded the *Qur'an*, e.g., the *Bible*. However, it is held that the *Bible* has been tampered with and must be reinterpreted. Nonetheless, both the *Qur'an* and the *Bible* are used in religious services. (6) Just as more than one scripture has been revealed across time, there have been many prophets. (7) Resurrection of the dead is seen to be a mental process and is not in any way a physical resurrection. (8) Members believe in a judgment. Consistent with the teachings of the original Nation of Islam, it is believed that the first judgment will occur in America. (9) Racial segregation is upheld, and much of the racial mythology of Elijah Muhammad continues to be preached. (10) The December fast is still practiced in opposition to the *Ramadan* fast, although Farrakhan has suggested that members also fast during *Ramadan*. (11) Initiates must still send an application letter requesting membership and a name change. However, members are no longer assigned "X" as a name but are given an Arabic family name. (12) Instruction in *Zakat* and the *Hajj* is generally ignored, although the giving of alms to the organization is stressed.

The reestablished Nation of Islam of John Muhammad is much smaller than that of Louis Farrakhan's group and probably consists of less than 1,000 members. The basic beliefs and practices of this group are said to be totally consistent with that previously preached by Elijah Muhammad and include the following. (1) Allah came in the person of W. D. Fard. (2) Elijah Muhammad was the last messenger of Allah, he died a physical death on February 25, 1975, and he will not return. (3) The white race is the devil. (4) The December fast continues to be substituted for the Islamic fast of *Ramadan*. (5) None of the five basic pillars of Islam are upheld and practiced.

F7. Summary

As strange and bizarre as some of the beliefs of the Nation of Islam may appear to contemporary readers, the Nation of Islam's racial mythology did provide many African Americans with a needed counterweight to combat the abhorrent theory of African-American inferiority and the racial injustices and bigotry that were once so prevalent in American society. More importantly, the Nation of Islam served hundreds of thousands of African Americans as a steppingstone leading them to the embrace of Islam under the leadership of W. D. Mohammed. Spawned in part from Islamic residuals within the African-American community, the Nation of Islam can be seen as a transitional movement back to the religious heritage of the originally enslaved ancestors of today's African Americans.

G. Conlusions

While the Islam of millions of enslaved Africans did not survive the centuries of slavery and a century of Jim Crow legislation inflicted upon their descendants—at least not in a pure form and in a fully organized manner, Islamic residuals have had their impact on African-American life. Vague and partial memories of Muslim ancestors, religious practices peculiar to certain African-American churches, the quintessential American music known as the blues, and religious movements such as the Moorish Science Temple and the Nation of Islam all testify to the presence of Islamic residuals.

8 The Immigrants

A. INTRODUCTION

While millions of African Muslims were brought to the New World as slaves, many Muslims from around the world have freely immigrated to the Americas for one reason or another. For some of these free immigrants, the lure may have been nothing more than a sense of adventure. For others, there was the promise of establishing a better life, obtaining a college or graduate school education, or avoiding the crippling hardships of economic deprivation in their countries of origin. For still others, the goal may have been to escape political or religious persecution. In other words, the goals, dreams, and aspirations of Muslim immigrants have basically been no different than those of non-Muslim immigrants.

Many Americans think of Muslim immigration to America as being a relatively recent phenomenon. However, the historical record clearly indicates that Muslims have been immigrating as free men and women to the Americas for centuries. Muslim immigrants fought to obtain American independence from Great Britain during the Revolutionary War. Muslim immigrants also helped to tame the American Wild West. Admittedly, the number of Muslim immigrants to the Americas was not great until after the Civil War. However, a series of successive waves of Muslim immigrants began entering the United States in large numbers beginning in the late 19th century and continuing throughout most of the 20th century.

The current chapter presents a brief review of the history of Muslims who freely immigrated to the Americas. Within that context, the primary focus of this chapter is on those Muslims who immigrated to what is now the continental United States.

B. The Early Immigrants

B1. Introduction

Information on the first Muslims to immigrate freely to the Americas is necessarily somewhat limited. However, a few of these early immigrants received enough notoriety that bits and pieces of their history have been preserved. Among these individuals, two in particular deserve special notice. They are Yusef Ben-en-Hali in the 18th century and *Hajji* 'Ali in the mid 19th century. Both immigrated to what is now the United States, both served their new country with honor in the United States military, and both enjoyed somewhat of a lasting fame among their contemporaries. Their stories and that of a few other early Muslim immigrants follow.

B2. The Wahab Brothers

The Wahab brothers were shipwrecked with a shipment of Arabian horses on the outer banks of North Carolina in the 1770s or slightly before then. Reportedly, they were emissaries of an Arab king, who had assigned them the task of establishing Islam in the New World. Surviving their shipwreck, they settled down, married, started a farm, and established Wahab Village, the site of an inn that is still owned by their descendants.

B3. Yusef Bin 'Ali

Yusef bin 'Ali (also variously known as Yusef Ben-en-Hali and Joseph Benenhaly or Benenhaley) appears to have originated among Arab stock in 18th-century North Africa, probably from Morocco. Although he was sometimes called a Turk, this designation was probably used only because the Othmanic Empire controlled so much of North Africa at the time and because all residents of the Othmanic Empire were often referred to as Turks. Little is known about his life before coming to America, but it has been suggested that he had either been a pirate or had been captured by pirates.

In any case, Yusef was found in the American wilderness by General Thomas Sumter, who recruited Yusef to fight with him against the British in the American Revolutionary War. Yusef was a scout for General Sumter and was one of the first to volunteer for General Sumter's brigade. After the war, Yusef moved with Sumter to near Stateburg in Sumter County, South Carolina. Although he was apparently listed in the 1790 census for Sumter County, he was not listed in later Sumter County census rolls. He later married Elizabeth Miller and had at least three children: Francis Benenhaley, a boy born circa 1802; Joseph Benenhaley, a boy born circa 1805; and Locadia, a daughter born on March 12, 1809. Francis Benenhaley married a woman named Sarah with whom he had at least five children: James S., born circa 1835; John W., born circa 1843; Henrietta, born circa 1845; Francis W., born circa 1847, and Elizabeth, born circa 1849. Joseph Benenhaley married a woman named Catherine with whom he had at least five children: William, born circa 1838; Thomas, born circa 1840; Elisabeth, born circa 1842; Randal, born circa 1845; and Mary A., born circa 1846. Locadia Benenhaley married a William Taylor with whom she had either seven or 11 children.

Descendants of Yusef bin 'Ali continue to live in Sumter County, South Carolina, where they are known as the Turks of Sumter County.

B4. *Hajji* 'Ali

Little is known about *Hajji* 'Ali before his immigration to the United States. Even his birth name is unknown, and there is some controversy about his place of birth. Turkey, Syria, and even Egypt have been variously proposed as his native land, although most sources list Syria. He was born circa 1828 to an Arab father and a Greek mother. At some point prior to 1856, he became a Muslim, took the name of 'Ali, and completed the *Hajj* pilgrimage to Makkah, thus appending the title of *Hajji* to his name. As a young adult, he reportedly served with the French army in Algiers. Those who would later know him in the United States described 'Ali as being a short, heavyset, happy-go-lucky Arab.

In 1856, he left Smyrna in western Turkey and traveled to the United States on the storeship *Supply* in the company of a load of 33 camels that had been purchased for the United States Army by Major Henry C. Wayne and Lt. D. D. Porter, the former of the U. S. Army and the latter of the U. S. Navy. Both 'Ali and the camels were part of a project promoted by Jefferson Davis, the then Secretary of War under President Franklyn Pierce and later President of the Confederate States of America. Davis was urging the army to experiment with camels as a means of transportation in the deserts of the American Southwest. The purchase of the camels and the hiring of 'Ali as their herder were in direct response to Davis's promptings. A subsequent shipment of camels from the Middle East brought the total number of camels to 74 and the total number of camel herders to six.

'Ali entered the United States at Indianola, Texas, on February 10, 1856. On November 25, 1856, 'Ali began work for the U.S. Army as a camel herder at Valverde, Texas, at a salary of $15 per month. About this time, Americans who were unfamiliar with the pronunciation of 'Ali's name began to corrupt *Hajji* 'Ali into Hi Jolly. The latter corruption of 'Ali's name was to stick with him the rest of his life.

On June 25, 1857, 'Ali left San Antonio, Texas, with Lt. Edward Fitzgerald Beale's camel expedition. The expedition marched to El Paso, Texas, and then on to Albuquerque, New Mexico Territory. From Albuquerque, the expedition traveled across the northern New Mexico desert, arriving at the Colorado River on October 18, 1857. From there, the expedition continued on to Fort Tejon, California. From November 1, 1859, to May 31, 1860, 'Ali continued his work for the army at Fort Tejon as a camel herder, and he was then being paid $30 per month. By July 29, 1861, he was again in the employ of the army as a camel herder at Los Angeles, California, his salary had been increased to $50 per month, and he was in charge of 31 camels. He was again discharged on August 5, 1861. On November 17, 1862, 'Ali was again hired as a camel herder, this time earning $35 per month at San Pedro, California. His pay was increased to $50 per month on May 1, 1863. On July 1, 1863, his salary was increased to $75 per month, and he was promoted to being an express rider whose duties included carrying the express to Fort Mojave. Exactly six months later on January 1, 1864, he was transferred to Benicia Depot, California, as an assistant wagon master earning $90 per month. In that capacity, he remained in charge of the army's camels until February 29, 1864.

The army's experiment with camels failed in large part, because the mules and horses of the American Southwest had never before seen camels and panicked at the mere sight of them. Runaway mule trains and horses soon led to civilians taking potshots at the camels whenever they appeared. Reportedly, many of the camels were killed in this manner. Finally responding to the complaints of civilians, the U. S. Army cancelled their experiment with the camels. Some of the camels were sold off or given to individuals, and some were merely set free to roam and reproduce in the wild.

Of those that were retained by individuals, 'Ali acquired several and used them to start a freight line between Yuma and Tucson in the Arizona Territory. The operation eventually failed, and 'Ali reluctantly freed his last camel near Gila Bend in 1868. From May 13, 1868, to August 7, 1869, 'Ali was once again employed by the army, serving as packmaster at Fort McDowell, Arizona Territory, at a salary of $100 per month. On October 25, 1869, he started work as an army packer at $45 per month. On January 1, 1870, his duties were changed to being a guide and scout, a position he continued to hold until June 20, 1870.

In 1880, 'Ali became a naturalized citizen of the United States under the name of Philip Tedro. Later that same year, he married Gertrudis Sema of Tucson. The marriage produced two daughters, whom 'Ali raised as Muslims. However, a settled life was not to 'Ali's liking, and by 1889 he eventually drifted off to spend the last years of his life prospecting for gold in Arizona from a small cabin at Tysons Wells (now Quartzsite, Arizona).

Hajji 'Ali died at Tysons Wells on December 16, 1902. According to local legend, 'Ali died when he went out into the desert to find a wild camel. When his body was found, he had one arm wrapped around the dead camel. In 1938, the Arizona Highway Department recognized 'Ali's contributions to settling the West by erecting a monument over his grave and by burying the ashes of the last government camel with him. The monument is by far the largest in the city and is topped with a large copper camel in recognition of 'Ali's contribution to the U.S. Army's camel experiment. The epithet on the monument reads as follows.

> The last camp of Hi Jolly, born somewhere in Syria about 1828. Died at Quartzsite December 16, 1902. Came to this country February 10, 1856. Cameldriver-packer-scout-over thirty years a faithful aid to the U. S. government.

A highly fictionalized account of *Hajji* 'Ali's role in the U. S. Army camel program was immortalized in the movie *Hawmps*.

B5. CONCLUSIONS

The Wahab brothers, Yusef Ben-en-Hali, and *Hajji* 'Ali were certainly not the only Muslims to immigrate as free men to the Americas. Others were undoubtedly present from an early age, but their historical legacy has not been recorded in any detail. For example, Muhammad (2001) notes that two unnamed Muslims, both males from Algeria, landed in Virginia in 1786 and then traveled overland to Charleston, South Carolina. Their eventual disposition remains unknown. Further, the 1820 United States census indicates that there were at least 21 Turks in the United States at that time, most of whom would have been Muslims.

Yet another example of free Muslims immigrating to the Americas comes from the post-slavery days in the British-held islands of the Caribbean. Following the abolition of slavery in 1807, there was a tremendous shortage of labor, which prompted William Burnley, a wealthy estate owner in Trinidad, to suggest that individuals from the Indian subcontinent be imported as laborers. As such, the 19th century witnessed over 500,000 Indians, many of whom were Muslims, immigrating to the islands of the Caribbean.

C. Wave after Wave

C1. Introduction

It is generally acknowledged that four successive waves of Muslim immigration to the United States began following the end of the American Civil War in 1865. During the late 19th century, immigration to the United States began to skyrocket at an ever increasing pace. Immigrants from all over the world and from all walks of life began to flock to American shores in search of their own, self-defined, American dream. According to the four-wave theory, Muslims were no exception to this phenomenon, and the late 19th century and the 20th century witnessed a first, second, third, and fourth wave of American immigration.

The problem with the four-wave theory is that it overlooks the millions of enslaved Muslims who were brought from Africa to the Americas beginning in the 16th century and extending through the early 19th century. Although not often acknowledged as being one of the successive waves of Muslim immigration to America, their rightful place as the first wave of Muslim immigration cannot realistically be denied. As such, in what follows, the four-wave theory of Muslim immigration has been recast. Instead of talking about a first through fourth wave of Muslim immigration, this chapter proposes a second through fifth wave.

C2. The Second Wave

Given the above reformulation of the four-wave theory into a five-wave theory, the second wave of Muslim immigration to America can be seen as occurring between the end of the American Civil War and the start of World War I.

Muslim immigration to the United States had been sparse prior to the second wave, in part due to existing laws governing U.S. citizenship.

The 1790 Naturalization Act had stipulated that only whites could become citizens of the United States, and this no doubt discouraged many dark-skinned Arab, Indian, and African Muslims from immigrating to the United States. While the provisions of this 1790 Naturalization Act remained in place throughout the second wave of Muslim immigration to the United States, the 14th Amendment to the Constitution was ratified in 1868 and stipulated that anyone who was born in the United States was automatically a citizen of the United States, regardless of race or color. Thus, dark-skinned, Muslim immigrants could look forward to their children becoming U. S. citizens, so long as those children were born in the United States, even if citizenship was still barred to the immigrants.

During the second wave of Muslim immigration, Muslim immigrants to the United States were primarily comprised of Arabs from the Othmanic Empire who settled along the eastern seaboard and in scattered locations in interior states east of the Mississippi River. As an example of the latter area of settlement, Mecca (Makkah), Indiana, was founded in 1873 by Arab Muslims. In terms of modern nation states, Arab Muslims of the second wave of immigration were mainly from what are now Syria, Lebanon, Jordan, and Palestine. For many of these Arab immigrants, the promise of economic opportunity was a powerful motivating force behind their immigration. As such, it is not surprising that the 1876 Centennial Exposition in Philadelphia, the 1893 World's Fair in Chicago, and the 1904 World's Fair in St. Louis prompted upsurges in Muslim immigration from the Arab world.

However, it was not just Muslims from Syria, Lebanon, and Palestine who comprised the second wave of Muslim immigration to America. Beginning in the late 19th century, the second wave was reinforced by some Muslims from the Indian subcontinent, many of whom initially immigrated to Canada before moving south into the United States. Unfortunately, the Indian component to the second wave was relatively small, in part due to the racism of U. S. citizenship laws, which stipulated that only whites could become naturalized citizens of the United States.

Nonetheless, one Indian immigrant who braved the discrimination of American immigration laws was Budruddin 'Abd Allah Kur. Budruddin was a wealthy Muslim from Bombay who apparently immigrated to the United States shortly after the Civil War. By 1873, he had established the American Propaganda Islamic Movement, the purpose of which was to spread Islam among Americans. By 1891, several large American cities had branches of this movement, and membership was said to have been in the several hundreds by 1900.

In addition to Arab and Indian immigrants, the second wave also included some Muslims from southeastern Europe, e.g., from what is now Albania, Bosnia, Kosovo, Greece, and the Ukraine. With regard to the Polish/Ukrainian immigrants who arrived late in the 19th-century and early in the 20th-century, it should be noted that about 3,000 of them settled in New York and successfully created the Muhammadan Society of America in Brooklyn, New York, established a mosque in Brooklyn in 1928, and were able to maintain their identity as a distinct community until the 1950s and 1960s. In addition, Albanian Muslims established a mosque in Biddeford, Maine, in 1915 and a second mosque in Connecticut in 1919. Other immigrant Muslim groups established mosques in Ross, North Dakota, in 1912, in Highland Park, Michigan, in 1912, in Bridgeford, Maine, in 1915, in Waterbury, Maine, in 1919, in Michigan City, Indiana, in 1924, in Dearborn, Michigan, in 1924, in Cedar Rapids, Iowa, in 1925, in Quincy, Massachusetts, in 1930, in Grand Rapids, Michigan, in 1932, and in Sacramento, California, in 1941.

Unfortunately, many of the descendants of the Muslims who comprised this second wave of immigration gradually lost the Islam of their forefathers. Either through intermarriage with non-Muslims or through gradual assimilation of the dominant, American-Christian way of life, many of them became completely absorbed into America as non-Muslims.

C3. THE THIRD WAVE

If the years between the end of the American Civil War and the start of World War I constituted the second wave of Muslim immigration, then the period between the end of World War I and the beginning of World War II represented the third wave.

During this period, a number of new immigration laws and court decisions affected the ebb and flow of Muslim immigration to the United States. For example, the U.S. courts had ruled in the 1910 case of the United States vs. Balsara that Asian Indians are Caucasian, and thus Muslim immigrants from the Indian subcontinent were eligible to be naturalized as U. S. citizens. This decision was reaffirmed in the 1913 Supreme Court decision of Ajkoy Kumar Mazumdar. However, any gains made by Muslims in these court decisions were quickly obliterated by the Immigration Act of 1917, which created an Asiatic Barred Zone that prohibited immigrants from India, Afghanistan, and Arabia. The provisions of the Immigration Act of 1917 were somewhat loosened in the National Origins Quota Act of 1921. According to the provisions of this legislation, yearly immigration from other countries was now limited to 03% of the total number of people of that nationality already living in the United States. This provided a small window of opportunity for Muslim immigrants. However, only three years later, the 1924 Immigration Exclusion Act (aka the Oriental Exclusion Act and the Johnson-Reed Act) dropped the quota from 03% to 02% and completely prohibited the immigration of anyone who was not eligible to be naturalized as a U. S. citizen, i.e., anyone who was not a Caucasian. The subsequent 1929 Immigration Act reinstated the quotas at 03%.

Prominent in the third wave were many, poor, Muslim immigrants from Yemen, who managed to get around the provisions of the Immigration Act of 1917. Many of these began work for the Ford Motor Company and established a thriving community in Dearborn, Michigan. Other Yemeni Muslims settled in Buffalo, New York, where they found work in heavy industry. Both of these communities have continued to exist to the present time. A fewer number of these Yemeni Muslims clustered together in Brooklyn, New York.

The third wave of Muslim immigration also included a trickle of Muslims from the Punjab region of the Indian subcontinent. However, the number of immigrants was small, secondary to the ever-changing standards of immigration created by United States legislation and judicial decisions. The Immigration Act of 1917 had barred immigrants from India, and this total exclusion of Muslim immigrants from the Indian subcontinent was not lifted until the Origins Quota Act of 1921. Thereafter, yearly immigration from the Indian subcontinent could not exceed 03% (1921-1924 and 1929 and thereafter) or 02% (1924-1929) of the number of Indians already living in the United States. However, this slight opening in the doorway allowing immigration from the Indian subcontinent was firmly closed by a combination of events.

As noted previously, the Naturalization Act of 1790 barred citizenship to any immigrant who was not white. This restriction appeared to have been lifted by the 1913 Supreme Court decision regarding Ajkoy Kumar Mazumdar. At that time, the Supreme Court had declared that people from the Indian subcontinent were Caucasians and were eligible to become naturalized citizens. However, in the 1923 case of the United States vs. Bhagat Singh Thind, the Supreme Court partially reversed itself. Stripped of its legalese, the Supreme Court basically maintained that if the Caucasian immigrant's skin color was a shade too dark, citizenship could still be denied. In the particular case in front if it, the Supreme Court opined that even though the plaintiff was a Caucasian according to expert and scientific testimony, he was not a Caucasian according to the perception of the typical Caucasian man in the street. As such, citizenship could be and was denied. Furthermore, Muslims from the Indian subcontinent who had previously been naturalized as U. S. citizens had their citizenship automatically revoked. Quite obviously, such sentiments and their legal ramifications actively discouraged Muslim immigrants from the Indian subcontinent.

However, the discouragement of immigration from the Indian subcontinent quickly became an actual prohibition. As noted previously, the 1924 Immigration Exclusion Act prohibited the immigration of individuals who were not eligible to become naturalized citizens. With the passage of this legislation, the trickle of Muslim immigration from the Indian subcontinent was totally curtailed. As Muslim immigrants from the Indian subcontinent who had previously entered the United States were denied citizenship or had their prior citizenship revoked, many of them eventually left for Europe or returned home to Asia.

Before leaving our discussion of the third wave of Muslim immigration to the United States, it is important to acknowledge the life of one such immigrant. Sheykh *Al-Hajji* Daoud Ahmed Faisal was born in 1891. His father and paternal grandfather were from the Bambara tribe of Morocco. His paternal grandmother was born in Mauritania, although her lineage traced to the Indian subcontinent. His mother was from the Caribbean. Faisal immigrated to the United States as a young man and married his wife, Khadijah, in 1920. Thereafter, he began an active missionary program that spread Islam among Americans, primarily among African Americans. In 1928, he founded the Islamic Propagation Center of America in Brooklyn, New York. Six years later, he established the Muslim Village Madinah Al-Salaam near Fishkill, New York. In 1965, the Islamic Propagation Center published his 280-page book, *Islam the True Faith, the Religion of Humanity.* Faisal died in February of 1980.

C4. THE FOURTH WAVE

A fourth wave of Muslim immigration to the United States began after the cessation of hostilities at the close of World War II. This wave continued unabated until the early 1960s. The fourth wave of Muslim immigration was primarily characterized by immigrants from the Indian subcontinent and from Palestine.

The Chinese Exclusion Repeat Act of 1943 repealed the provisions of the 1924 Immigration Exclusion Act, allowing Muslims from the Indian subcontinent once again to immigrate to the United States. Five years later, the Luce-Cellar Bill of 1946 opened the door for immigrants from the Indian subcontinent to become naturalized citizens of the United States. Unfortunately, the Indian subcontinent was initially allowed a quota of only 100 immigrants per year. With the Indian subcontinent gaining self-rule from Great Britain in 1947, there quickly became far more applicants for immigration than there were openings on the quota list. Fortunately, the Immigration Act of 1952 increased the quota of immigrants from the Indian subcontinent. In response, Muslim immigrants from what are now India, Pakistan, and Bangladesh began to arrive in America in large numbers for the first time.

These immigrants from the Indian subcontinent quickly became a force in Muslim affairs in America. They established the Islamic Circle of North America (ICNA) as an Urdu-speaking, Muslim organization in the 1970s. In 1980, the official language of ICNA was changed to English, and it became one of the first large-scale, national Muslim organizations in America. Immigrants from the Indian subcontinent were also instrumental in forming the Islamic Society of North America (ISNA) as an umbrella organization over a variety of local and regional Muslim groups and organizations in the United States and Canada. Since then, a majority of the ICNA and ISNA leadership have been descendants or immigrants from the Indian subcontinent.

As a result of the first Arab-Israeli war and the formation of the state of Israel in 1948, thousands upon thousands of Palestinian Muslims were displaced from their ancestral homes and forced into refugee status. Some of these Palestinians found sanctuary in Jordan, Syria, and other Arab countries, but many began immigrating to America. By and large, these Palestinian Muslims comprised a professional and highly educated class of immigrants.

Towards the very end of this fourth wave, Muslims from sub-Saharan Africa began to immigrate to America. In part, this immigration was prompted by the African journey of Malcolm X and his invitation to Sheykh Ahmed Hassoun of Sudan to come to America to teach orthodox Islam for Malcolm X's newly organized Muslim Mosque, Inc.

C5. The Fifth Wave

The fifth wave of Muslim immigration to the United States began in the wake of the 1965 Immigration and Nationality Act, which abolished the national quotas system of immigration. In place of the quotas, the Act allowed 120,000 immigrants from the Western Hemisphere and 170,000 from the Eastern Hemisphere to enter the United States each year. However, a cap of 20,000 immigrants from any one country was set for countries in the Eastern Hemisphere. Muslim immigration to the United States was further advanced by the 1978 Immigration Act, which abolished the hemisphere quota system and allowed for a total of 290,000 immigrants each year.

In addition to the provisions of the 1965 Immigration and Nationality Act and the 1978 Immigration Act, this fifth wave of Muslim immigration was fueled by geopolitical events in the Middle East. With regard to that observation, three specific events have been crucial. The 1967 Israeli military occupation of the West Bank displaced thousands upon thousands of Palestinian Muslims, many of whom sought refuge in the United States. The 1979 revolution that led to the formation of the Islamic Republic in Iran prompted a large number of Iranian Muslims to seek a less oppressive political climate in America. Finally, the 1982 Israeli invasion of Lebanon resulted in large numbers of Lebanese Muslims immigrating to the United States.

However, Muslim immigration during the fifth wave was not just the result of geopolitical oppression. As always, the quest for economic opportunity was also a contributing motive to Muslim immigration. For example, the 1965 Immigration Act gave birth to a large number of Muslim immigrants from Syria, Egypt, and Palestine. By and large, these immigrants were not nearly as well educated as their Palestinian predecessors in the fourth wave, and economic advancement was a key purpose behind their immigration.

In addition, the 1980s witnessed the first substantial immigration of Muslims from West Africa since the days of slavery. Spurred by economic motives, Muslims from Gambia, Ghana, Guinea, Mali, Nigeria, and

Senegal began to enter the United States in increasing numbers.

D. The Ahmadiyya in America

D1. Introduction

It would be remiss to close this chapter on Muslim immigration to America without some mention of the Ahmadiyya. Although the Ahmadiyya claims to be a sect of Islam, they are generally viewed by orthodox Muslims as being a heterodox sect at best and outside the boundaries of Islam at worst. Nonetheless, as Ahmadiyya missionaries had a rather profound effect in America and as many American converts have used the Ahmadiyya sect as a steppingstone to orthodox Islam, the following brief review is offered.

D2. History of the Movement

Mirza Ghulam Ahmad was born to a Muslim family in Qadian in the Punjab region of India in 1835. He was said to have devoted much of his early life to religious studies. In 1876, shortly after the death of his father, Ahmad began to experience what he interpreted to be divine revelations. Initially, he appears to have considered his role to have been that of a *Mujaddid* or renewer of the Islamic faith. However, by 1889, he was publically proclaiming himself to be both the messiah (who the *Qur'an* clearly identifies as being Jesus Christ) and the *Mahdi*, the latter being an eschatological figure who many Muslims believe was foretold by Prophet Muhammad. Still later, the claim was made that he was a prophet and the 10th *avatar* (reincarnation) of the Hindu god Vishnu. Mirza Ghulam Ahmad died in 1908, and his movement, variously referred to as the Ahmadiyya and the Qadiani, split into two groups, the Lahore group and the Qadiani group. The latter group continued to uphold Mirza Ghulam Ahmad as being a prophet, while the Lahore group did not.

With regard to the teachings of the Ahmadiyya, there are several of their beliefs that are rejected by most orthodox Muslims and that have caused many Muslim organizations to list the Ahmadiyya as being outside of Islam. Chief among these would be the belief of the Qadiani group of Ahmadiyya that Mirza Ghulam Ahmad was a prophet. As noted previously, most all Muslims maintain that the statement in *Qur'an* 33:40 that Muhammad was the "seal of the prophets" negates any possibility of there being a prophet after him. Other Ahmadiyya beliefs that typically run counter to traditional Islamic teachings include the following. (1) In contrast to the Islamic belief that Jesus was not crucified (*Qur'an* 4: 157-158), the Ahmadiyya believe that Jesus was hung on the cross but that he fainted instead of dying. (2) The Ahmadiyya believe that once the unconscious Jesus was taken down from the cross, he recovered and went to teach in Kashmir, where he later died a natural death at the age of 136. In contrast, *Qur'an* 3:55 and 4:158 say that Jesus ascended to Allah, a statement which most Muslims interpret to mean that Jesus never died a natural death.

D3. THE AHMADIYYA IN NORTH AMERICA

The first Ahmadiyya missionary to enter North America was Muhammad Sidiq in 1920. Sidiq began his mission work in New York City and then moved to Chicago in the late 1920s. He and other early Ahmadiyya missionaries were most effective in prosletyzing among African Americans, probably because of Islamic residuals that were still present in their community. However, many of these African-American converts later converted to orthodox Islam.

By 1933, Ahmadiyya centers could be found in Chicago, Cincinnati, Detroit, Indianapolis, Kansas City, New York City, and Pittsburgh.

American membership in the group was said to have reached 5,000 to 10,000 by 1940. By 1990, there were 35 Ahmadiyya centers scattered across various cities of the United States and over 20 branches of the movement in Canada.

E. CONCLUSIONS

There can be no doubt that Muslim immigration to America has been a major catalyst in shaping the present nature, direction, and growth of the Muslim community in America. However, as these Muslim immigrants came to the United States from all over the Muslim world, they have also contributed to one of the unique problems facing Islam in America, i.e., the tendency for the Muslim community to divide and fragment upon ethnic and nationalistic lines. This issue will be dealt with in more detail in chapter X.

9 The Converts

A. INTRODUCTION

How many, if any, converts to Islam resulted from the prosletyzing efforts of pre-Columbian Muslims in the Americas must remain largely a matter of speculation. However, surviving records from the 16th century do document Spanish fears that the enslaved Muslims in the Caribbean were already making progress in converting non-Muslim slaves from Africa and local Indians to Islam. Nonetheless, the history of non-Muslims converting to Islam in the Americas is murky at best until the late 19th century. Since then, there has been a steady stream of American converts to Islam from all walks of life, from every stratum of American society, and from a wide variety of ethnic backgrounds.

In what follows, brief biographical sketches of seven of the more well-known converts to Islam are presented. Of these, two (Mohammad Alexander Russel Webb and Homer Calvin Davenport) were of European extraction and six (Wali Abdul Akram, Malcolm X, Warith Deen Mohammed, Muhammad Ali, and Kareem Abdul-Jabbar) were or are African Americans.

B. SOME BRIEF BIOGRAPHIES OF CONVERTS TO ISLAM

B1. MOHAMMED ALEXANDER RUSSEL WEBB

Alexander Russel Webb, the son of Alexander Nelson Webb, was born into a reasonably wealthy family on November 9, 1846, in Hudson, New York. He was raised within the Presbyterian denomination of Christianity but rejected the religion of his youth when he was 20 years old.

Thereafter, he studied extensively in an intellectual quest to find spiritual fulfillment. In what is probably hyperbole, it has been claimed by others that he read about 13,000 books during the course of his transformation from Christian to Muslim. By his own report, he studied the philosophical writings of Mill, Locke, Kant, Hegel, Fichte, Huxley, and many more philosophers while still a young man. It appears that he also gave more than some passing thought to various Eastern religions, including Buddhism.

Webb's early life was not, however, one spent entirely in the mental contemplation of the world's religions. He also worked in the family newspaper business, for a while serving as editor and publisher of his father's newspapers in Unionville (*Missouri Republican*) and St. Joseph (*St. Joseph Gazette*), Missouri. In 1887, Webb was appointed American Consul to the Philippines by President Grover Cleveland. While stationed in the Philippines, he began an intensive study of Islam, which culminated in his conversion to Islam in 1888. (Webb's wife and children were also said to have become Muslims.) He subsequently appended the name Mohammed to his own birth name.

There are many paths to conversion. For some, conversion is the result of an intensely emotional experience. For others, such as Webb, conversion comes through intense intellectual and mental effort. He described his own path to Islam by noting that: "...my adoption of Islam was not the result of misguided sentiment, blind credulity, or sudden emotional impulse, but it was born of earnest, honest, persistent, unprejudiced study and investigation and an intense desire to know the truth."

Not one to keep quiet about his newly embraced faith, Webb immediately came to the notice of several members of the Ahmadiyya from India, one of whom, Abdulla Kur, published several of Webb's letters about Islam in his Bombay newspaper. These letters were eventually noticed by *Hajji* 'Abd Allah Arab, a wealthy Muslim from Madinah, a city in what is now Saudi Arabia. *Hajji* 'Abd Allah was deeply devoted to the propagation of Islam and had previously established an Islamic missionary society in Bombay. Inspired by Webb's letters, *Hajji* 'Abd Allah arranged to visit Webb in the Philippines in 1892, became impressed with Webb's religious sincerity, and then arranged for Webb to lecture about Islam throughout India. Webb's 1892 lecture tour of India included stops at Delhi, Bombay, Calcutta, and Hyderabad and must have been quite successful, as *Hajji* 'Abd Allah subsequently arranged for one third of his personal fortune to be diverted to Webb's future work in spreading Islam in America.

The lecture tour of India wasn't Webb's only excursion during 1892. He subsequently journeyed to Egypt and Turkey, where he continued his studies in Islam. It was while he was visiting in Istanbul that Webb finally resigned his consulate post. By 1893, Webb had returned to the United States and settled down in New York City.

Back in America, Webb may have retired from his State Department career, but he certainly did not retire from public life. Backed by the financial patronage of *Hajji* 'Abd Allah, Webb created the first Muslim periodical published in the United States in May of 1893. Webb's publication, the *Muslim World,* was a 16-page periodical, which was devoted to Islamic thought and which served as the primary vehicle for Webb's newly established American Muslim Propagation Movement (also known as Islamic Propagation in America and as the Islamic Propaganda Mission in the U.S.A.). The year 1893 also saw Webb start up the Oriental Publishing Company and a book store called Orientalis, which included a lecture room, a prayer hall, and a library. Both ventures were located in

New York City, as was the mosque that Webb established on upper Broadway. However, Webb's work in 1893 was still not over. That same year, he served as the representative for Islam at the First World Parliament of Religions in Chicago, where he delivered two lectures ("The Influence of Islam on Social Conditions" and "The Spirit of Islam"). Both lectures were subsequently printed in the official, two-volume publication on the proceedings of the Parliament.

Webb continued his efforts on behalf of Islam throughout the remainder of his life and died on October 1, 1916, at the age of 70. He left behind a literary legacy about Islam that included *The Three Lectures of Mohammed Alexander Russel Webb, Lectures in Various Locations, Islam in America,* and *A Few Facts about Turkey under the Reign of Abdul Hamid II.* Judging by his writings and the contents of his bookstore, Webb advocated an Islamic theology that was influenced by the mysticism of the Sufi branch of Islam. A strong Sufi influence was often a common denominator among 19th-century Westerners who ended up embracing Islam.

B2. HOMER CALVIN DAVENPORT

Homer Calvin Davenport was born on March 8, 1867, in the Oregon Wilderness, the son of Timothy and Florinda Davenport. In examining his childhood, one can identify two events that offer some psychological insight into Davenport's later life and to the circumstances that led to his eventual conversion to Islam.

Firstly, the young Homer Davenport developed a special closeness to his father, even before the age of three. In large part, this closeness centered on the ability of the elder Davenport to absorb his son's attention in vivid stories of the grandeur and fire of the legendary Arabian horse. The child was an eager listener to these stories, was constantly begging his father for more, and began to dream of journeying to Desert Arabia and of importing Bedouin-bred Arabians into the United States.

Secondly, when Davenport was only three years old, his mother died in a deadly small pox epidemic. His mother's dying request was that her son become a cartoonist. Spurred by his mother's deathbed request, Homer demonstrated a pronounced artistic tendency at a very young age, and many of his earliest childhood drawings were of Arabian horses, horses that he had only seen in his imagination.

Davenport's early vocational life was anything but one of marked success. He suffered through a series of short-lived jobs, including work as a jockey, a stable hand, a circus clown, a cobbler, a clerk at a grange store, a member of a haying crew, and a railroad hand. Although only a young man, he appeared to be destined to a life of repeated failures.

Despite these early setbacks, Davenport did not give up and continued to pursue the goal his mother had set for him as her dying request. His first published picture was printed in the Portland *Evening Telegram*. Significantly, it was a one-shot publication, and Davenport was not paid for his drawing. His first paid position with the art department of a newspaper was with *The Oregonian*, where he worked for a couple of months in the summer of 1890. He was apparently let go by September and was then unemployed in newspaper circles until early in 1891. At that time, he hooked up for a brief stretch with Portland's *Sunday Mercury*, a weekly sports paper. Once again, this job was short-lived, and Davenport was once again forced to return as a failure to his family in Silverton, Oregon.

Davenport's first big break came when he was hired by the San Francisco *Examiner* in 1892. He worked there for about a year, earning $10.00 per week. Nonetheless, Davenport was kept under wraps to a great extent and was not allowed to draw editorial and political cartoons.

After a year in the employ of the *Examiner*, Davenport had the temerity to ask for a raise to $12.50 per week. His request was met with his release from the newspaper.

By early in 1893, Davenport was drawing for the San Francisco *Chronicle*. He soon left this position in order to attend the Columbian Exposition (1893 World's Fair) in Chicago. In Chicago, he landed a job with the *Daily Herald*, where he was hired to draw pictures of horses at the racetrack. This job was once again short-lived, and upon the close of the Columbia Exposition Davenport was without a job. However, Davenport's attendance at the Columbia Exposition had given him what was probably his first opportunity to see real Arabian horses. These horses had been imported from the Lebanese and Syrian portions of the Othmanic Empire by the Hamidie-Hippodrome Society, and Davenport visited them on a daily basis while the Exposition was in progress.

Despite having had the joy of finally seeing pure Arabian horses in the flesh, Davenport, the aspiring cartoonist, was once again out of work. It must have seemed like just one more failure in a long sequence of failures. However, Davenport's fortunes were about to change for good.

In 1894, Davenport was once again back at the San Francisco *Chronicle*. He started at only $15.00 per week, but he was given a chance to do some political cartooning for the first time. Immediately, Davenport became a maker and breaker of California politicians, a molder of public opinion, and a man of influence in the public sector. His salary was soon more than doubled to $35.00 per week.

With Davenport's influence and popularity growing exponentially, William Randolph Hearst decided it was time to bring Davenport back to the San Francisco *Examiner*. By late 1894, the transfer to the Hearst newspaper had been made, and Davenport was earning a then princely salary of $75.00 per week. However, Davenport's second stay at the *Examiner* would be short. This time, however, his leaving was not a sign of failure but a sign of success.

In October of 1895, Hearst purchased the *Journal*, a New York City newspaper with an unprofitable circulation of just 40,000. One of Hearst's first acts was to send for Davenport, hoping that his popular San Francisco cartoonist could infuse life into the moribund *Journal*. Turned fully loose by a newspaper for the first time, Davenport more than fulfilled Hearst's expectations and quickly became the talk of the town as his cartoons promoted populist themes against graft, government corruption, and big business monopolies. Once again, Davenport could make and break politicians, but this time not just on a local level, but on a national level as well. Within six years of Davenport's arrival, the *Journal* had a circulation of over one million readers, making it the widest read newspaper in the world at that time. Davenport had reached the zenith of his profession and was earning as much money as the president of the United States.

On July 1, 1904, the New York *Evening Mail*, a Republican-leaning newspaper that was being seriously hurt by the competition from the Democratic-leaning *Journal*, pulled off one of the biggest newspaper coups of the time. It managed to hire away Davenport from the *Journal*. Davenport was to be paid $25,000 for his first six months of work, making him the highest paid cartoonist in the world. (Note: when Davenport's *Evening Mail* salary is adjusted for inflation, it becomes equivalent to about $700,000 a year in 1996 currency.) Davenport had ridden the newspaper trail from successive failure to the pinnacle of success.

Newly signed on at the *Evening Mail,* Davenport drew the most influential cartoon of his career. It was the 1904 presidential race, and Davenport threw his political influence behind Theodore Roosevelt in a cartoon that showed Uncle Sam standing behind President Roosevelt, with his left hand resting on Roosevelt's shoulder. Under the picture was the caption, "He's good enough for me." The cartoon became the greatest vote-getting cartoon in American history and helped elect Roosevelt to the Oval Office, paving the way for the fulfillment of Davenport's boyhood dream.

Davenport had now achieved a station in life where he could financially afford to actualize his boyhood dream of importing pure Arabian horses from Desert Arabia. Unfortunately, there still remained two very real and formidable obstacles. Firstly, the Bedouin tribes had historically been quite reluctant to part with pure Arabian mares. Secondly, the Othmanic government, which then ruled over much of Arabia, had officially prohibited the export of pure Arabian mares as a matter of law.

Both of the above obstacles were overcome through the personal intervention of President Theodore Roosevelt. Partly due to gratitude for the vote-getting cartoon noted previously and partly due to his own interest in establishing a United States remount based on Arabian bloodlines, President Roosevelt personally intervened with Sultan Abdul Hamid II of the Othmanic Empire. Through this presidential intercession, Davenport was able to secure a special *Irade*, which gave him dispensation to export a few Arabian mares from Syria to the United States.

On July 5, 1906, Davenport began his historic journey from America to Syria. He arrived in Aleppo on August 6th and the next day met an important benefactor in the person of Sheykh Ahmad Al-Hafez. Over the course of the next 18 days, Davenport managed to acquire a total of 28 horses, at least 24 of which were secured through the help of Al-Hafez. Of these horses, 10 were mares or fillies, and at least eight were gifts, including one stallion whose owner had previously refused to sell the horse at any price to the Italian government. One horse died in route back to America, leaving 27 horses that landed in America on October 6th at Hoboken, New Jersey. Of these 27 horses, 24 were eventually registered with the Arabian Horse Club, and 20 left registered descendants. According to a random sample of 100 registered Arabian horses from *Studbook 50* of the Arabian Horse Registry, fully 90% trace to one or more of the horses imported by Homer Davenport in 1906.

Never before in the history of the Arabian horse had so many pure Arabian horses been acquired in Desert Arabia in such a short period of time by any importer. European importers had typically spent months in Arabia in order to acquire a mere handful of horses. To be given eight gift horses was unprecedented. For Bedouins to part with 10 mares and fillies was beyond belief. Even as late as the 1990s, Arabian horse breeders in Syria referred to the Davenport importation as being the only time in recorded history in which an outsider had managed to acquire the best of the Bedouins' breeding stock. How and why had these miracles happened? Those questions were to plague Arabian horse historians and enthusiasts within the United States for the next 88 years. It was not until 1994 that the answer began to emerge in published texts.

Out of all the Westerners to go to the Syrian Desert to purchase pure Arabian horses, why was Davenport the only one to acquire so many gift horses? Why was he the only one to acquire so many pure Arabian horses in such a short period of time? Out of all the early Arabian breeders in North America, why was Davenport the only one who appeared to maintain extensive contacts with Arabs living in the United

States? The clues had always been there. Davenport's own writings had recorded the words of his "blood-brother" ceremony with Sheykh Ahmad Al-Hafez, but Westerners didn't grasp the true meaning of the ceremony.

The United States of the early 20th century had far less tolerance for religious diversity than is found today. A prominent man might find his vocational and economic worlds ruined if his religious beliefs were known to vary markedly from the majority of Americans. Thus, it is not surprising that Davenport did not publicize the true meaning of his brotherhood with Sheykh Ahmad Al-Hafez. There were few Americans in the early 20th century who had the necessary background to understand Davenport's published oath of brotherhood with Sheykh Ahmad Al-Hafez. As for others, they could read right over Davenport's transliteration of the Arabic prose and fail to understand.

Wallah! Wallahi!...Wallah! Wallahi!...Bilah! Billahi! Tillah! Tillahi!...Akhwan, Akhwan, el yom wa bookra wa l'al abad, akhwan.[89]

The above is Davenport's recording of his oath of brotherhood with Sheykh Ahmad Al-Hafez. The Arabic can be translated as: "Oh, Allah! Oh, Allah! Oh, Allah! Oh, Allah! In Allah! In Allah! I swear by Allah! I swear by Allah! Brothers, brothers, today and tomorrow and forever, brothers." The clue lies in the repeated appeal to Allah. This was not a simple "blood-brother" ceremony. Rather, Davenport and Sheykh Ahmad Al-Hafez had become brothers-in-Allah. In other words, Davenport had become a Muslim.

---

89. Davenport H: *Davenports Arabians.* Fort Collins, Caballus Publishers, 1973. Page 134. This is a reprint of Davenport's *My Quest of the Arabian Horse*, originally published in 1909.

Independent confirmation of Davenport's embrace of Islam was finally published in 1994, almost 88 years after Davenport's conversion. The
impetus was a letter received from members of the Al-Hafez family in
Aleppo, Syria, a family that had carefully preserved the oral history of their
ancestor's friendship with an American visitor in 1906. The following
quotation is a translation of the Arabic contained in a June 15, 1993, letter from Muhammad 'Ali Al-Hafez.

> When Mr. Davenport came…one of the best people who could
> accept him and meet him in the northern land of Sham was
> my grandfather (Sheykh Ahmad Al-Hafez). When he knew his
> request of purchasing horses, he gave him a gift of an Asil (pure,
> from the root) horse, and he made brotherhood with him…
> And the American, Mr. Davenport, was a truthful one, he was
> trustworthy, and he liked manhood characteristics in people, and
> he also liked the truth, and he liked the honesty. And so he asked
> from my grandfather, whom he truly loved, to be his brother. So,
> my grandfather made with him brotherhood-in-Allah…And
> my grandfather was talking about treating his American brother
> with love and with truthfulness. And he also was talking about
> Davenport's love for good and love of the religion of Islam and
> Muslims. Since he (Davenport) said, "If the Muslims are in that
> truthfulness and that straightness, then I am a Muslim also"—a
> declaration of Islam. [90]

It probably should have been understood earlier. We now know why
Davenport was the recipient of so many gift horses, horses that money
could not buy, why he was able to purchase horses that other Westerners

---

90. Al-Hafez M'A, Rabia JAA, Dirks DL, Dirks JF (1994).

could not have acquired, and why he was able to acquire so many pure Arabian horses in such a phenomenally short period of time. Not only was Davenport a Muslim dealing with fellow Muslims, he was also the only Muslim from the West who ever journeyed to the Arab world to acquire horses. Further, he was a new convert, and as such he enjoyed the benefits of a longstanding custom within the Muslim world, i.e., he was showered with gifts from his elders in Islam.

Unlike Mohammed Alexander Russel Webb, Davenport did not make his Islam public. Given his position in newspaper and political circles, he appears to have remained a "closet" Muslim whose religious beliefs were known only to fellow Muslims. One wonders, however, if Davenport and Webb didn't communicate with each other about Islam. Both were in the New York area at the same time, Davenport must have known that Webb was a fellow Muslim, and both appeared to have accepted a form of Islam influenced by Sufi mysticism. Unfortunately, the possibility that these two converts maintained a relationship must await future research.

What is known is that Davenport maintained written contact with Sheykh Ahmad Al-Hafez back in Aleppo and with President Theodore Roosevelt. He exhibited his imported Arabians across the country, and one of them even starred in Buffalo Bill Cody's Wild West Show. He became the moving force behind the creation of the Arabian Horse Club (later the Arabian Horse Registry of America). Finally, he continued to influence public opinion with his political and editorial cartoons.

By April of 1912, Davenport was seriously ill with pneumonia. Nonetheless, upon hearing the startling news of the sinking of the *Titanic* on April 14, 1912, Davenport forced himself out of his sickbed to draw two final cartoons. The last of these two cartoons was a drawing of an iceberg serving as a monument to those who perished when the Titanic went down. It was published in the April 19th edition of the New York *American* and created an immediate sensation with the public.

Davenport's condition continued to deteriorate, and William Randolph Hearst spent $12,000 on eight different doctors in just three days in a desperate effort to save Davenport's life. It was to no avail. Homer Davenport died on May 2, 1912, at the age of 45. To this date, he remains the most influential political and editorial cartoonist in the history of America.

B3. *EL-HAJJ* WALI ABDUL AKRAM

Wali Abdul Akram was born on August 4, 1904, on a farm near Bryan, Texas, and his name at birth was Walter Reice Gregg. He was raised as a Christian in the Baptist denomination, and the *Bible* was always a prominent fixture in his childhood home.

His father died when he was nine years old, and Walter and his older brother were forced to begin working to support their mother and five younger brothers. The two boys hired themselves out to neighboring farmers to repair broken farm equipment, and they soon developed a reputation as the best blacksmiths in the area. On the side, they made baseball bats and also began to tinker with various inventions, soon inventing a machine gun whose patent they sold for $50. Despite the above successes, financial times were hard, and the brothers soon had to take contract jobs with the Santa Fe Railroad to repair tracks, cars, and locomotives. Before long, they were supplying most of the contract repairs for the Santa Fe Railroad in eastern Texas.

In 1918, at only 14 years of age, Walter left home to attend Prairie View State College, a segregated land-grant college in Texas, where he studied electrical engineering. After two years of college, Walter left school to work as a roughneck for Deroloc Oil in the oil fields of eastern Texas. This work soon proved unrewarding, and Walter moved to Houston, Texas, where he worked as a mechanic for the railroad. Within only a few months of beginning work in Houston, he invented a new prototype for coupling together railroad cars. The device was patented as the Reice Coupler, and the Reice Coupler quickly became the standard coupler used on the railroad and continued to be used until after World War II. Unfortunately, Walter did not reap any financial bonanza from his invention, as he had sold his patent to the railroad for a month's wages.

Money for the sale of his patent in his pocket, Walter hoboed his way north on the Santa Fe Railroad, grabbing surreptitious rides on freight trains. Alighting at some destination, he would usually find a temporary job as a mechanic in order to replenish his funds before grabbing another freight train heading north. By 1921, Walter had settled down to living in St. Louis, Missouri, where he worked as a janitor at Principia College, a segregated white school.

It was in St. Louis that Walter met an Ahmadiyya missionary and convert by the name of Sheykh Ahmad Din, who had previously been known as Paul Nathaniel Johnson. Under Din's influence, Walter converted to the Ahmadiyya in 1923 and changed his name to Wali Abdul Akram a year later.

In 1924, Akram, as he was now known, married Kareema, an Ahmadiyya convert formerly known as Hannah Dudley. Soon thereafter, they opened a grocery store that was to prove to be a good and steady source of income for the newlyweds. Moreover, the grocery store allowed Akram the time to begin to study an English translation of the *Qur'an*, as well to learn the intricacies of operating a printing press that he had purchased and that he used to print handbills promoting the Ahmadiyya.

Unfortunately, Akram soon exhausted the knowledge of Sheykh Ahmad Din and felt that his advancement in Arabic studies and knowledge of the *Qur'an* had come to a halt. As such, in October of 1925, Akram and Kareema left St. Louis in the company of another Ahmadiyya missionary, Sheykh Ashiq Ahmad, who ministered to Ahmadiyya converts in Cincinnari and Dayton, Ohio. It was in Cincinnati and Dayton that Akram began to master the Arabic language under Sheykh Ahmad's tutelage, perfect his knowledge of the *Qur'an*, and develop a systematic crossreference between the *Qur'an* and *Bible*.

In 1927, the Akram family moved to Cleveland. Once again, the family began a grocery store business, but Akram spent most of his time proselytizing in the African-American neighborhood between East 40th and East 54th streets along Central Avenue. Within a few years, he had recruited about 150 families to the Ahmadiyya, and the Ahmadiyya had bestowed the title of "sheykh" upon him, making him one of about 50 Americans to earn this title from them. In addition, he founded the First Cleveland Mosque in 1932.

From 1932 through 1936, Akram was tireless in his efforts to build the Ahmadiyya movement in Cleveland and in the surrounding areas. He acquired a printing press on which he printed Ahmadiyya handbills and other material. In addition, he wrote and published pamphlets on the Arabic language, Qur'anic commentary, and Islamic history. Throughout all of this, he continued his study of the *Qur'an*.

Finally in late 1936 or early 1937, Akram had had enough. He was tired of Ahmadiyya officials from the Indian subcontinent bleeding off the scarce financial resources of his African-American community. In addition, his own study of the *Qur'an* had resulted in his recognizing the intrinsically non-Islamic elements in the Ahmadiyya doctrines. As such, he broke with the Ahmadiyya, led the First Cleveland Mosque into orthodox Islam, created an alliance of like-minded mosques in neighboring cities, and developed an organization known as the Muslim Ten Year Plan.

Under Akram's leadership, the First Cleveland Mosque quickly became a beacon of Islamic light throughout Ohio and the American Midwest. Besides providing regular Friday prayer services, the mosque also instituted a weekend Islamic school, where attendees could learn Qur'anic commentary and such basics of Islamic practice as how to make ritual ablution (*Wudu*) and pray (*Salat*). It was around this time that Akram began printing the first Islamic calendar that was readily available in North America. Not stopping there, Akram's printing press was also kept busy publishing workbooks, instructions in how to perform *Salat*, histories of Islam, and other Islamic texts. Further, Akram's grocery store provided meat that was slaughtered in the Islamicly prescribed manner.

The First Cleveland Mosque was soon complemented by Akram's Muslim Ten Year Plan, a not-for-profit organization whose goal was to remove African Americans from the welfare rolls via education, the development of practical skills, and cooperative buying power. Members of the plan paid 50 cents to one dollar a month into a common fund that was used to purchase a variety of educational and vocational materials, as well as such necessities of life as food and clothing. By pooling their resources, members of the Muslim Ten Year Plan were able to buy products in bulk and at discount prices. These products could then be sold back to the community at reduced prices, thus expanding the purchasing power of every member. By purchasing textbooks and other educational resources, it became possible to help members acquire a variety of marketable job skills, thus increasing the economic development of the community on this front as well.

In 1938, Akram started to develop the Uniting Islamic Society of America (UISA), an umbrella organization for such diverse Muslim groups as the Muslim Ten Year Plan, Muhammad Ezaldeen's Adenu Allahe Universal Arabic Association and several other Muslim groups. The first convention of the UISA was in Philadelphia in August of 1943. Akram was elected president and was re-elected president at the Pittsburgh convention in 1944. This convention of the UISA was significant in that Muslim women participated as delegates and were appointed to key committee assignments. It was the first time that Muslim women had been given such a prominent role in Islamic affairs in America. No convention was held in 1945. The 1946 convention was held in Cleveland in August of 1946. Once again, Akram was re-elected president of the UISA. Unfortunately, representatives from only five different Muslim groups attended, making this the last UISA convention. Throughout its history, the UISA had been constantly pulled apart by political and sectarian differences, as different groups lobbied for their turf in the power structure, hotly debated the role of women in American Islam, and argued about the proper relationship between Islamic law and the secular laws of the United States. As such, the UISA ceased to exist shortly after the 1946 convention. Nonetheless, it was the first truly national organization for all ortho- dox Muslims in America.

Akram continued his commitment to Islam throughout the remain- der of his life. His 12 children, 60 grandchildren, and more than 75 great-grandchildren were all raised and educated as Muslims. In 1957, he completed the *Hajj* pilgrimage, becoming only the second native-born

American to be legally admitted to Makkah. Thereafter, he appended *El-Hajj* to his name. *El-Hajj* Wali Abdul Akram died in August of 1994, and his funeral attracted over 1,000 mourners. At the time of his death, he had 27 electrical and mechanical patents to his name.

B4. MALCOLM X

Malcolm Little, or Malcolm X as he is usually known, was born on May 19, 1925 in Omaha, Nebraska, the son of Earl and Louise Little. He was one of seven children.

Malcolm's early life was scarred by the racial hatreds and bigotry of the times and by repeated psychological traumas. For example, Malcolm's mother was the result of his maternal grandmother having been raped by a white man. Building upon that legacy, trauma followed upon trauma.

When he was only one year old, the family's home in Omaha was burned to the ground. Three years later, the family moved to a home on four acres just south of Lansing, Michigan. The family comprised the only African Americans in the area, and within three months the surrounding white families went to court to prevent the Little family from living in the midst of the otherwise all white neighborhood. The local judge quickly ruled that the Little acreage was restricted to whites, but the Little's defied the judge's ruling and continued to reside in their house. Shortly thereafter, the house was firebombed by the Ku Klux Klan, the white supremacist group that sprang up in the American South in the aftermath of the Civil War. When fire trucks refused to come to their rescue, the house burned to the ground.

In September of 1931, when Malcolm was only six years old, his father was run over by a streetcar late one night. His body was almost completely severed into two parts by the wheels of the streetcar. The police ruled the death an accident, but popular opinion among the African-

American community was that Malcolm's father had been pushed under the wheels by members of the Ku Klux Klan. Seven years later on December 23, 1938, Malcolm's mother was psychiatrically institutionalized at Kalamazoo State Hospital with a diagnosis of being paranoid. She would remain hospitalized for the next 26 years.

After his mother's institutionalization, Malcolm was separated from his siblings and sent to a foster home. A few years later, but while still a teenager, he moved to Roxbury, Massachusetts, a predominantly African-American suburb of Boston, to live with his oldest sister. It was on the streets of Boston that Malcolm initially learned the trades of the con artist, street hustler, and petty criminal. He also obtained employment working in the kitchen on the New Haven Railroad's train from Boston to Washington, DC.

In 1942, Malcolm moved to Harlem in New York City. In Harlem, Malcolm's life of petty crime became habitual, and he was twice arrested. In 1945, he moved back to Boston, and his life of crime escalated to burglary. In late 1945, he was arrested for breaking and entering and the related crime of burglary. He was sentenced to eight to 10 years in the state prison and became prisoner #22843 at the Charleston, Massachusetts, Correctional Center.

His initial attitude and behavior in prison were bad and angry enough that the other prisoners began calling him Satan. However, Malcolm's persona began to change after his brothers and sisters began to write to him about the Nation of Islam during his second year of incarceration. Malcolm then began to read the teachings of Elijah Muhammad, and this experience was transformative for him. He began to embrace his African heritage fully for the first time, began to study to improve his education, and even joined and became a star on the prison debate team.

On August 7, 1952, Malcolm was paroled after having served six and a half years in prison. Malcolm immediately journeyed to Chicago, met with Elijah Muhammad, was accepted into the Nation of Islam within one month of arriving in Chicago, and changed his name to Malcolm X.

An effective and charismatic orator with a flair for creating memorable phrases, Malcolm was initially appointed as the assistant to the leader at Detroit's Muhammad Temple #1. However, his stay in Detroit was relatively brief, as Malcolm was made the leader of the Nation of Islam in Boston and was soon representing the Nation on speaking tours around the country. Within five months of his arriving back in Boston, he had increased membership to the point that a small storefront building could be established as a temple. Before long, he was readily acknowledged as the Nation's most effective orator and grassroots organizer and had organized Nation of Islam temples in Boston, Hartford, and Philadelphia. Under his leadership, what had been a largely stagnant membership in the Nation soon began to grow at a never before seen rate of increase. With membership mushrooming and new temples springing up around the country, Malcolm was transferred out of the Boston temple and was appointed the leader of Temple Number Seven in the Harlem area of New York City. Stationed out of New York, Malcolm was an indefatigable worker for the Nation of Islam. Besides being the minister at Temple Number Seven, he continued to speak for the Nation across the country and started the *Muhammad Speaks* newspaper as the official media organ of the Nation. His efforts in behalf of the Nation were rewarded by Elijah Muhammad giving him the last name of Shabazz to replace the "X" that he had been using.

Motivated by his own experiences as a victim of discrimination and racism and captivated by the racial mythology of the Nation of Islam,

Malcolm became a champion of racial segregation, African-American pride, and African-American self-dependence. While he initially derided the civil-rights movement as led by Dr. Martin Luther King, Jr., as being too passive in its approach and erroneously focused on racial integration, he was nevertheless a tireless advocate for the rights of African Americans throughout the 1950s and early 1960s.

In 1957, Malcolm married Betty X, a college graduate living in Harlem. The marriage eventually produced five children.

By 1963, Malcolm had begun to have some ongoing contact with immigrant Muslims from Africa, including Ahmed Osman, a Sudanese student in the United States. Prodded by their vision of Islam as a universal brotherhood that crossed all racial and ethnic lines and becoming increasingly exposed to the teachings of the *Qur'an* and orthodox Islam, Malcolm quietly began to question some of the teachings of the Nation of Islam. This questioning was only amplified as Malcolm became increasingly aware of Elijah Muhammad's sexual dalliances outside of the bonds of marriage, which had resulted in his fathering eight children out of six different teenage girls who had at one time or another been his secretaries.

In December of 1963, Malcolm was suspended from the Nation of Islam following his reference to the assassination of President John F. Kennedy as being a "case of chickens coming home to roost." On March 8, 1964, Malcolm formally left the Nation of Islam, embraced orthodox Islam, and formed his own Islamic organization (the Muslim Mosque, Inc.) with headquarters in Harlem. The next month, under the urgings of Ahmed Osman and others, Malcolm made the *Hajj* pilgrimage to Makkah and changed his name to Malik El-Shabazz. Having completed the rites of a *Hajj* pilgrim, he also appended the title of *El-Hajj* to his newly claimed name.

The *Hajj* pilgrimage was truly a transformative experience for Malcolm. As he later wrote, his *Hajj* experience convinced him that Islam did offer a universal brotherhood of all believers, regardless of race, ethnicity, and skin color. At Makkah, Malcolm had witnessed and personally experienced this Islamic brotherhood, as members of all races stood, walked, and prayed side by side in performing the rites of *Hajj*. He realized that the white Muslims who were worshipping next to him were not devils but were brothers.

While still in Saudi Arabia, Malcolm met with several members of the Saudi royal family. Leaving Saudi, Malcolm spent three weeks visiting Africa. He finally returned to New York City on May 21, 1964. He was a changed man.

Malcolm now repudiated his prior belief in racial segregation, in all aspects of the racial mythology of the Nation of Islam, and in the corruptions of Islam that were inherently built into the Nation of Islam's philosophy and theology. As an outspoken and highly visible apostate from the Nation of Islam, Malcolm's embrace of orthodox Islam resulted in numerous death threats against him from the Nation. In July of 1964, he was assaulted on the street in front of his home by several men, but he managed to escape.

Later that same month, he was invited to attend the Organization of African Unity Conference in Cairo, Egypt. Following the conference, he traveled to 14 countries and met with 11 different heads of state. He was welcomed wherever he went, as is shown by the people of Nigeria bestowing a name on him that can be best translated as "the son returns."

Returning to the United States in late November of 1964, he immediately redoubled his efforts for Islam and for civil rights for African Americans. One month later, he was at Oxford University in England.

where he debated at the Oxford Union. Unfortunately, this effective work for orthodox Islam and his high visibility in the world's media only intensified the hatred for him by some elements of the Nation of Islam.

On February 13, 1965, his home in Harlem was firebombed while the family slept within it. Malcolm quickly blamed Elijah Muhammad and the Nation for this criminal act. Thankfully, no one in Malcolm's family was seriously injured. Just over one week later, Malcolm was assassinated by members of the Nation of Islam (i.e., Thomas 15X Johnson, Norman 3X Butler, and Talmadge X Hayer) on February 21, 1965, while he was giving a speech at the Audobon Auditorium in Harlem. His bullet-ridden body fell stiffly to the floor beside the podium; he had become a martyr for Islam.

His funeral was held on February 27, 1965, in New York City. Mourners included his wife, four children, one unborn child, and thousands of followers. He was buried in Ferncliff Cemetary.

Shortly before the end of his life, his series of interviews with Alex Haley formed the basis of a book, *The Autobiography of Malcolm X,* which quickly became a literary milestone and classic following his death.

B5. WARITH DEEN MOHAMMED

Warith Deen Mohammed was born in Detroit, Michigan, on October 30, 1933, the seventh child of Elijah and Clara Muhammad. His name at birth was Wallace Delaney Muhammad, his name having been selected for him by W. D. Fard, the founder of the Nation of Islam, who predicted that the newborn would one day succeed Elijah Muhammad as the leader of the Nation.

Wallace was only about 12 years old when he first became aware of the discrepancies between the message of the *Qur'an* and the teachings of his father. In particular, the young Wallace questioned the identification of W. D. Fard with Allah. As he later recounted it in a speech in 2002:

> I had this experience, where I was home alone one night and became afraid. I began to pray and saw before me the face of Fard, and something stopped me. So I prayed, "Oh Allah, if I am not seeing you correctly, please help me see you correctly." And then I made my prayer. I didn't know how to see God. [91]

After completing high school, Wallace began working within the Nation of Islam. At age 25, he was appointed minister of Temple #11 in Philadelphia, Pennsylvania. This work for the Nation was interrupted in 1961, when he was sentenced to three years in prison for refusing to be drafted into the military. While in prison, he had time to study the *Qur'an* and orthodox Islamic doctrine in greater detail. Convinced of the large discrepancies between Islam and his father's Nation of Islam, he resigned from the Nation in 1963. At age 32, he was finally released from prison.

Following the assassination of his close friend, Malcolm X, in 1965, Wallace returned to the Nation of Islam, hoping to transform it into a truly Islamic movement. Reinstalled within the Nation's hierarchy, he began a gradual but constant push to bring the Nation's theology into line with orthodox Islam. As a result of these activities, he was twice suspended from the Nation, the first time in 1969 and again in 1971.

During the last year of his father's life, Elijah Muhammad reportedly named Wallace to succeed him as leader of the Nation of Islam and gave his son license to transform the Nation of Islam into pure Islam. However, it was stipulated that Wallace had to wait until Elijah Muhammad was dead before undertaking this momentous change.

---

91. Umar KB (2005), page 42.

Following the death of his father on February 25, 1975, Wallace became the Supreme Minister of the Nation of Islam and immediately began a process of change that would result in the largest conversion of people to Islam in the history of America. In 1976, he changed the name of the Nation of Islam to the World Community of Al-Islam in the West, changed his own name to Warith Deen Mohammed (note the different spelling of his last name at this time), and changed his title from supreme minister to the more traditional Islamic title of *Imam*. More importantly, he rejected the racial mythology and highly corrupted theology of the prior Nation of Islam, and he led a systematic and mass movement of his followers into the folds of orthodox Islam. For the first time, former members of the Nation of Islam were taught to pray five times a day according to the standard rules and practices of Islam. They were taught to fast during *Ramadan* instead of during December. They received instruction in the giving of obligatory charity (*Zakat*), and they were encouraged to make the *Hajj* pilgrimage.

(Precise estimates of the number of Nation of Islam members that Warith Deen Mohammed led into Islam are difficult to obtain, in part because Nation of Islam membership figures were always fairly secretive. Various estimates have placed the number as low as just over 100,000 to as high as a little less than 1,000,000.)

In 1977, he completed the rites of *Hajj*. One year later, the name of his organization was changed again, this time to the American Muslim Mission. In 1985, the name was changed to the Muslim American Society (also known as the Ministry of W. Deen Mohammed). Within the last few years, *Imam* Warith Deen has left the Muslim American Society and has concentrated his efforts on his The Mosque Cares organization.

Over the last quarter of a century, *Imam* Warith Deen Mohammed has been one of Islam's greatest champions of interfaith dialogue in America. In 1992, he became the first Muslim to perform the morning prayers in the United State Senate. Four years later, he was invited to meet with Pope John Paul II at the Vatican. During the presidency of Bill Clinton, he was twice invited by the president to attend the president's interfaith breakfasts.

As of this writing, Imam Warith Deen Mohammed continues to serve as a spiritual and religious guide to about 2.5 million Muslims in America. It is likely that he has been influential in converting more people to Islam than any other living Muslim in the world today.

B6. MUHAMMAD ALI

Muhammad Ali was born on January 17, 1942, in racially segregated Louisville, Kentucky. He was the son of Cassius Marcellus Clay, Sr., and Odessa Grady Clay. His name at birth was Cassius Marcellus Clay, Jr., and he had one brother. His father supported the family by working as a billboard painter, and his mother worked as a domestic servant.

Life was not easy for the young Cassius. He was an African American growing up in segregated Louisville, subject to all the discrimination and racism of the times. While his family attended a Christian church, they were required to sit in the back of the church simply because their skin was a shade too dark for their white co-religionists. Complicating matters still further, Cassius's father was said to have been prone to violence and reportedly abused Cassius's mother physically, issues that reportedly led to the police being called to the residence on at least one occasion.

When he was 12 years old, Cassius had his bicycle stolen while he was attending an event. He reported the theft to a Louisville policeman, Joe Martin, who proved to be sympathetic. However, there was little that this white policeman could do to recover the bicycle. As he turned away from

Martin, the young Cassius muttered under his breath that if he found the person who stole his bike, he would "whup" him. Martin immediately inquired if the 12-year-old Cassius knew how to fight. When Cassius replied in the negative, Martin took the boy under his wing and began to teach him the art and skills of boxing.

Guided by Martin, Cassius set off on a dazzling, six-year, amateur career as a boxer. At age 17, he won the Golden Gloves championship. At age 18, he was crowned with an Olympic gold medal in the 175-pound (light heavyweight) division at the 1960 Olympic Games in Rome. (Sometime later, he threw his Olympic gold medal into the Ohio River in protest of America's racial policies.) Almost immediately thereafter, the 18-year-old Cassius turned professional as the protégé of 11 wealthy white men known as the Louisville Sponsoring Group, who arranged for him to be trained and managed by Angelo Dundee, one of the great boxing trainers at that time.

Beginning in late 1960 and continuing through the end of 1963, Cassius won 19 consecutive fights as a professional, 14 of them by knock out. Throughout these early fights, he displayed uncanny foot and hand speed, lightning-fast reflexes, and a most unorthodox style of evading his opponent's punches, i.e., instead of bobbing up and down or slipping his head to the side to allow the punch to pass by his face, he pulled his head backwards just out of reach of his opponent's fist. Needless to say, Cassius quickly rose through the heavyweight rankings and frequently predicted with uncanny accuracy the round in which he would KO his opponent.

On February 25, 1964, the 22-year-old Cassius Clay stepped into the ring against Sonny Liston, the then reigning heavyweight champion of the world. Few gave him much of a chance against Liston, who was viewed by many boxing experts as being practically invincible. Afterall, Liston had dethroned Floyd Patterson in a first round knock out and had again KO'd Patterson in the first round of a rematch. The oddsmakers made Cassius an eight-to-one underdog against the formidable Liston.

As the championship fight progressed, Cassius demonstrated that his speed and unorthodox defense were too much for Liston to master. Despite being blinded for two rounds due to liniment getting into his eyes, Cassius danced his way out of trouble, displayed his self-proclaimed ability to "float like a butterfly and sting like a bee," and scored a totally unexpected TKO when Liston was unable to come out of his corner at the start of the seventh round. At just over 22 years of age, Muhammad had become the youngest person in history to win the heavyweight championship of the world. As he so eloquently and concisely proclaimed at the end of the fight, "I shocked the world!"

Shortly after winning the heavyweight crown, Muhammad shocked the world yet again when he announced that he had turned away from the Christianity of his youth and that he had embraced the teachings of the Nation of Islam. It was a move that alienated and estranged many Americans during the emotionally charged Civil Rights era of the mid-1960s. On March 6, 1964, he also rejected his birth name and took the name of Muhammad Ali, a name given to him by Elijah Muhammad.

Throughout the remainder of 1964, Muhammad Ali took a well-deserved vacation from the world of boxing. Upon the urging of Malcolm X, he became the first, major sports star to tour Africa, where he was greeted as a hero. He also found time to marry, taking Sonji Roi as his first wife. The marriage did not last long, as Sonji had a difficult time adjusting to the restrictions of the Nation of Islam, and soon ended in divorce.

Muhammad's return to boxing was on May 25, 1965, when he met Sonny Liston in a rematch for the heavyweight championship. Any lingering doubt that Muhammad's earlier victory had been an aberration was quickly dismissed by his first round KO of Liston with a right hand punch that traveled so fast that many ringside observers failed to see it. Having easily defeated Liston, Muhammad successfully defended his heavyweight crown eight more times between 1965 and 1967. By this time, many within boxing's inner circle were acknowledging the fact that Muhammad Ali might very well be the greatest boxer of all time.

Muhammad Ali was sitting atop of the boxing world. Wealth, fame, and athletic glory were his for the taking. Yet, he was willing to give them all away to stand on principle. On April 28, 1967, during the height of the Vietnam War, Muhammad refused induction into the United States Army and claimed a religious exemption from the draft as a minister of the Nation of Islam. The repercussions were merciless. Every state boxing commission revoked Muhammad's license to box, he was stripped of his heavyweight championship, and he was formally indicted for refusing to be inducted into the U. S. Army. His case was heard on June 20, 1967, and he was convicted and sentenced to five years in prison.

Free from prison while he appealed his case through the court system, Ali was nevertheless barred from boxing. As such, he had to struggle to pay his bills by appearing in a play, giving lectures, and accepting charity from others. He had become a pariah in American society, because he had chosen to stand on his religious principles.

As a brief digression, it should be noted that Muhammad's refusal to be inducted had nothing to do with fear or cowardice. As the reigning heavyweight champion of the world, Muhammad would never have seen combat in Vietnam. He would have spent his entire army career boxing exhibitions bouts for the army and doing public relations and morale-building work. Muhammad knew this, but he never considered compromising his principles.

The first two years of the 1970s saw Muhammad's fortunes improve. His initial conviction was unanimously overturned by the United States Supreme Court, and he was once again allowed to return to the ring. However, his absence from the ring had cost him greatly. He had missed four years of his prime as an athlete, he would never be the boxer he had once been, and he was no longer the heavyweight champion of the world. Both athletically and financially, he had made the ultimate sacrifice.

Muhammad's return to the ring occurred in October of 1970. He quickly won two fights and had positioned himself to fight the reigning heavyweight champion, Joe Frazier. The two met on March 8, 1971, in what was billed as the "Fight of the Century." It was a fight that lived up to its billing, and after 15 grueling rounds Joe Frazier won a unanimous decision. Muhammad Ali had lost his first professional fight.

For the next two years, Muhammad boxed on, winning 10 fights in a row, eight of them against ranked contenders. However, on March 31, 1973, Muhammad's career seemed to suffer an irreversible setback when he lost a 12-round decision to Ken Norton, a fighter who was little known and lightly regarded at the time. Despite this loss, Muhammad kept boxing, defeating Norton and Frazier in rematches.

On October 30, 1974, Muhammad met heavyweight champion George Foreman in the first heavyweight championship fight to be held in Africa, a fight that Muhammad promoted as the "Rumble in the Jungle." Foreman had viciously knocked out Frazier in an early round to win the championship and was a heavy favorite going into the fight. The first several rounds all appeared to be going Foreman's way. Time and time again, he pinned Muhammad against the ropes and flailed away with sledge-hammer-like punches, which Muhammad usually managed to take on his arms. While it looked like Muhammad was taking a terrible beating, it was in reality a defensive strategy that he had developed specifically for the Foreman fight. He called it the "Rope a Dope," and what he was doing was allowing Foreman to punch himself out. Finally in the eighth round, Muhammad began fighting back in earnest against the now arm-wearing Foreman. Punch after punch was finally culminated in a right hand that sent Foreman to the canvas in unconscious oblivion. Muhammad Ali had become only the second man in history to win the heavyweight championship of the world on two separate occasions.

From 1975 through 1977, Muhammad successfully defended his title 10 times, winning five times by knock out. By this time, most of the earlier antagonism against him had been replaced by the public's love and admiration. More importantly, the 1970s also saw Muhammad Ali embrace orthodox Islam and abandon the racial mythology and corrupted theology of the Nation of Islam. Boxing's heavyweight champion was now a Muslim.

In 1978, his boxing skills seriously eroded by age, Muhammad Ali lost his championship in a 15-round decision to Leon Spinks, a former Olympic champion with only seven professional fights to his credit. Later that year, Muhammad rose up once again and defeated Spinks via a 15-round decision in a rematch. Muhammad Ali had become the only person in boxing history to win the heavyweight championship of the world three times. Following his victory, he retired from the ring.

Unfortunately, Muhammad returned to the ring in 1980. He fought once that year and once the next, losing both fights. By this time, he was apparently already suffering from the early stages of Parkinson's Syndrome, a condition that was probably caused by the repeated blows to the head he had taken throughout his illustrious career. His final record stood at 56 wins (37 by knockout) and five losses.

Muhammad married Yolanda Williams in 1986. He had previously married and divorced Sonji Roi, Belinda Boyd (aka Kaleelah), and Veronica Anderson, and he had fathered nine children.

Despite declining speech and motor skills secondary to his Parkinson's, Muhammad became boxing's best-loved former champion and an ambassador to the world. During his period of physical decline, repeated honors have flowed to him. In 1996, he was chosen to light the Olympic flame in Atlanta, Georgia. *Sports Illustrated* named him "Sportsman of the Century," and the United Nations named him one of their nine "Messengers of Peace."

As of this writing, Muhammad Ali remains the world's most famous and easily recognized Muslim.

B7. KAREEM ABDUL-JABBAR

Ferdinand Lewis Alcindor, Jr., was born on April 16, 1947, in New York City. His legendary basketball prowess was already well demonstrated by the time he was in high school. As a 6-foot, 8-inch player for Power Memorial Academy, he starred on the varsity for four years, scored 2,067 points, and thereby set a New York City record for total points made by a basketball player.

In 1965, he entered UCLA on a basketball scholarship. In his first game, he tallied 56 points, which set a UCLA scoring record. He subsequently led UCLA to three successive NCAA (National Collegiate Athletic Association) national championships in basketball (1966-1968). Throughout his basketball career at UCLA, the team lost only two games, establishing a mark of collegiate excellence in basketball that has never been surpassed. It was while he was attending UCLA that he converted to Islam, and he later took the name of Kareem Abdul-Jabbar in 1971.

His National Basketball Association (NBA) career demonstrated his continued dominance of the game that he first displayed in high school and later verified in college. Playing as a 7-foot, 1 and 3/8-inch center for the Milwaukee Bucks (1969-1975) and later for the Los Angeles Lakers (1975-1989), Kareem won NBA Rookie of the Year honors in 1970 and was voted the NBA's Most Valuable Player a record six times. Throughout his professional basketball career, he led his teams to six NBA championships (1971, 1980, 1982, 1985, 1987, and 1988). He currently holds the following NBA career records: most points scored (38,387), most field goals made (15,837), and most minutes played (57,446). He entered the Basketball Hall of Fame in 1995.

C. Conclusions

American converts to Islam represent an ever-growing contribution to Islam in America, and their contribution is not just limited to their numbers. Increasingly, American converts have assumed positions of leadership within their Muslim communities and have become voices of Islamic scholarship in America. The face of Islam in America is as much that of native-born Americans as it is that of immigrants.

10 Islam in Modern North America

A. INTRODUCTION

A lot has happened in the over 1,100 years between the 889 voyage of Khashkhash ibn Saeed ibn Aswad and the present time. A perilous voyage by sea of well over a month has been replaced by air travel that takes only a few hours. Muslim Andalusia is no more, and the Mandinka kingdom of Mali has come and gone. A New World that was once seen through European lenses as being the backwater of the world has become the home of the world's sole superpower and a dominant economic force.

Throughout all these changes, Muslims have come and gone from the Americas. During the heyday of the transatlantic slave trade, the number of Muslims in the Americas probably numbered in the millions. With the passing of time and generations, the Islamic heritage of African Americans gradually faded into the hidden recesses of their communities and was often no longer recognized for what it was. The number of Muslims in the Americas was soon reduced to a relatively small handful, and at the dawn of the 20th century it appeared that Islam was destined for extinction in North America. Three factors then coalesced to reverse this trend in dramatic fashion.

The first factor was the return of African Americans to their Islamic heritage. In their search for racial equality and an acceptable self-identity, African Americans in the first half of the 20th century began to rediscover their religious roots in Islam. This search originally resulted in many highly corrupted and contaminated sets of beliefs, such as those encapsulated within the Moorish Science Temple and the Nation of Islam. Nonetheless, those beliefs, however flawed they may have been, eventually served as invaluable steppingstones that led an untold number of African Americans back to the Islam of their ancestors.

The second factor spawning the reemergence of Islam in North America was 20th-century immigration of Muslims to America from the Indian subcontinent, the Middle East, and elsewhere. Resulting from economic and political dislocation overseas and from changes in American immigration laws, wave after wave of Muslim immigrants reinforced the Islamic presence in North America.

Finally, the last quarter of the 20th century witnessed thousands upon thousands of Americans converting to Islam every year. Unlike the earlier influx of African Americans to Islam, these conversions were not mass or group conversions. These were generally individual conversions or conversions of nuclear families. Further, these conversions were not just coming from one ethnic or racial group. Americans from all walks of life, every educational level, every socio-economic strata, and diverse ethnic and racial heritages started to embrace Islam.

At present, Islam is probably the second largest religion in America. It is also the fastest growing religion in America. As one indication of the fact that Islam is now part and parcel of the fabric of America, it should be noted that in 2000 both the Democratic and Republican national conventions began with prayers by Muslims. Talat Othman delivered the Islamic convocation for the Republicans and Dr. Maher Hathout performed a similar function for the Democrats. In addition, over 100 Muslims were seated as delegates at the Republican convention.

B. THE NUMBER OF MUSLIMS IN NORTH AMERICA

B1. INTRODUCTION

Establishing an accurate count of the number of Muslims in North America is no easy matter. There is no centralized membership list, and no single Muslim organization can be said to represent all of the Muslims in North America or even a majority of them. Even at the level of individual mosques, it is often the case that a majority of Muslims who worship at those mosques do not formally belong to the mosque and do not appear on the mosque's membership list. Compounding things even further, traditional polling and interview techniques via the telephone are likely to underestimate the number of Muslims in rather dramatic fashion.

B2. POLLING DATA

There are several reasons why telephone polls and interviews with regard to religious affiliation are likely to be highly suspect when it comes to reporting the estimated number of Muslims in North America. Firstly, many Muslims are suspicious of such polls and are likely to refrain from participating in them. Immigrant Muslims who are political refugees from despotic regimes learned in their countries of origin that the less information available on them, the better off they were. Secondly, some immigrant Muslims still lack the basic skills in the English language that would allow them to participate in such polls. Thirdly, in very conservative Muslim families, the wife may not be willing to answer the phone if she does not recognize the phone number of the person who is calling. Fourthly, Muslims from across the spectrum are aware that they represent a misunderstood minority within America. Having been the victims of Islam-bashing by the extreme Christian Right for many years preceding

9/11 and having to deal with the aftermath of 9/11, many Muslims are hesitant to reveal their religious affiliation to unknown and unseen pollsters on the other end of a telephone line. For all these reasons and more, telephone surveys of religious affiliation are likely to underestimate the number of Muslims in North America to a rather remarkable degree. Given the above warning about polling data seriously underestimating the number of Muslims in America, one can now turn to the published information that has come from such sources.

As early as 1991, Goldman estimated that the number of Muslims in America was 1.4 million, with fully 40% of the nation's Muslims being African Americans. His results were based on what was then billed as the largest survey of its kind to date.

In a 2001 report entitled American Religious Identification Survey 2001, Kosmin and Mayer concluded that the number of Muslims in the United States equaled only 1.1 million adults, of whom 17% were converts, and 0.7 million children. While these conclusions were based upon interviews with 50,281 Americans, the nature of the interview process suffered from all the drawbacks previously noted with regard to surveying Muslims' religious affiliation via telephone surveys.[92]

A somewhat larger Muslim population was estimated in a report by Tom W. Smith that was commissioned by the American Jewish Committee. This report, which was compiled in September or October of 2001, suggested that there were at most 2.8 million Muslims in the American population. The report concluded that a more likely figure for the number of Muslims in America was 1.4 million adults and 0.5 million children.[93]

---

92. Neibuhr G (2001); Last JV (2001); & Kosmin BA, Mayer E (2001).
93. Niebuhr G (2001).

Finally, the *World Christian Encyclopedia*, which was published in 2001, estimated that the total number of Muslims in America was 4.1 million, with 39% being African Americans.[94]

There is a great deal of variability to be found in the above estimates of the Muslim population in America. What is common to all of these estimates is that they were compiled by non-Muslims. As will be seen, the estimates compiled by Muslims have consistently been higher than those provided by non-Muslims. In part, this probably reflects the fact that Muslim researchers typically have better access to Muslims than do non-Muslims.

B3. MUSLIM ESTIMATES

One of the earliest Muslim attempts to estimate the Muslim population was conducted by the Federation of Islamic Associations in America. This study estimated the total Muslim population in the United States to be 1.2 million as of 1960. However, the estimate did not include certain Punjabi Muslims and Muslims of Turkish and Eastern European descent. Further, it must be remembered that at this early date the members of the Nation of Islam had still not been led into orthodox Islam by Warith Deen Mohammed and may have accounted for an additional one hundred thousand individuals.[95]

In 1992, Numan estimated that there were five million Muslims residing in the United States.

A 1994 survey of mosque leaders revealed a total of almost 500,000 Muslims who were directly associated with a specific mosque.[96] At first glance, this number may appear to be quite low.

---

94. Barrett DB, Kurian GT, Johnson TM (2001).

95. Ba-Yunus I (1998).

96. Bagby I, Perl PM, Froehle BT (2001).

However, it must be remembered that this number included only those Muslims who were directly associated with a mosque. Many women and children do not attend mosques, even though they are practicing Muslims. In addition, many Muslims live in areas where there is no mosque in the vicinity. Still further, the 1980s and 1990s have been an era of rapid mosque construction, and it is extremely difficult to construct an accurate listing of all mosques in America. Given considerations such as the above, the survey estimated a total of two million or more Muslims in the United States.

Using a combination of telephone polling and interviews with mosque representatives, Ba-Yunus estimated the total Muslim population in Illinois to be 320,644 in 1994, which was just less than 03% of the Illinois population at that time. (In order to insure Muslim participation in the telephone polling done in Chicago, Ba-Yunus had previously announced and explained at Chicago mosques the polling that was to be done.)

Perhaps the most ambitious Muslim attempt to estimate the number of Muslims in America was performed between March and September of 2000 by Bagby, Perl and Froehle for the Council on American-Islamic Relations (CAIR), the Islamic Society of North America (ISNA), the Ministry of Imam W. Deen Mohammed, and the Islamic Circle of North America (ICNA). The study, entitled The Mosque in America: A National Portrait, compiled a master list of 1,209 mosques in the United States. Of these, 631 mosques were randomly selected to participate in the study, and 416 of the randomly selected mosques did participate. Interviews were then conducted with the leadership of these mosques. Among the questions asked of each mosque leader was the total number of Muslims associated with his mosque. The average answer was 1,625.

Multiplying this figure by the number of mosques on the master list yielded a total of 1,964,625. The authors of the study suggested that with almost two million Muslims being associated with a mosque, it was not unreasonable to assume a total Muslim population of six to seven million Muslims in America as of 2000.

B4. GROWTH IN THE MUSLIM POPULATION

Whatever the exact number of Muslims in America, there can be little doubt that Islam is the fastest growing religion in America. For example, Ba-Yunus reported an average growth rate of 4.3% per year in the Muslim population of Illinois between 1990 and 1994, suggesting that the Muslim population would double every 16.28 years. In analyzing the results still further, Ba-Yunus determined that 44% of the growth rate was secondary to gains attributable to net migration (immigration minus emigration), 31% was due to natural growth (births minus deaths), and 25% was coming from net conversions (conversions minus apostasy).

Comparing results from almost identical studies conducted in 1994 and in 2000, Bagby et al. discovered a 300% increase in the number of Muslims associated with mosques, a 25% increase in the number of mosques, and an average increase of 235% in the number of Muslims associated with each mosque. They further reported that regular participation at mosques had increased in 77% of the mosques surveyed in 2000 and had decreased in only 05%. Consistent with what had previously been reported by Ba-Yunus, this study reiterated that the growth in the Muslim population was not just being fueled by immigration and birthrates. Bagby et al. reported that as of 2000, the average number of converts to Islam per mosque was 16.3 per year. Multiplying 16.3 converts per year times the 1,209 mosques in the study's master list yields a total of over 19,700 Americans converting to Islam each year as of 2000.

Anecdotal evidence suggests that since September 11, 2001, many Americans have begun to explore Islam for the first time, resulting in markedly higher conversion rates than those previously reported. In the wake of September 11, several different reports indicated that the number of converts to Islam increased by 100 to 300%.[97]

B5. CONCLUSIONS

As can be seen, the Muslim estimates of the number of Muslims in America are consistently and dramatically higher than the estimates offered by non-Muslims. In part, this probably reflects some hesitation on the part of many Muslims to reveal their religious identification to non-Muslims. Additionally, non-Muslims are likely to have less access to Muslims than do Muslims. Finally, it cannot be dismissed out of hand that mosque leaders may have some tendency to exaggerate the number of Muslims associated with their mosques. Given these considerations and others, Lang has suggested five million Muslims in America as a median of the estimates currently in circulation, although the estimates presently circulated by most Muslims tend to range between seven and eight million.

C. COMPOSITION OF THE ISLAMIC COMMUNITY IN NORTH AMERICA

C1. INTRODUCTION

The Muslim population of the United States currently comprises a three-legged stool. One leg is represented by the immigration of Muslims from various parts of the world, a second leg is formed by converts, and the third leg is comprised of the second generation of Muslims in

---

97. Wilgoren J (2001); Ritz MK (2001); Jimenez M (2002); & Abdeljabbar FM (2002).

America, i.e., the descendants of the first two legs. As one can well imagine, this creates a quite heterogeneous grouping of individuals, which in turn provides both an enriching diversity of cultures, ethnicities, races, nationalities, and primary languages and an opportunity for the emergence of devisiveness and discrimination.

C2. SOME DEMOGRAPHICS

In 1992, Numan estimated that 42.0% of the Muslim population in the United States were African Americans. An additional 24.4% of the Muslim population were of South Asian descent, 12.4% were of Arab descent, 5.2% were immigrants from Africa, 3.6% were of Iranian descent, 2.4% were of Turkish descent, 2.0% were of Southeast Asian descent, 1.6% were of Western European descent, and 0.8% were of Eastern European descent.

Goldman estimated that 40% of all Muslims in America in 1991 were African Americans. Barret et al. suggested that the percentage was 39% in 2001, and by 2002 Dannin reported that 90% of all converts to Islam were African Americans. Based upon his 1994 survey results, Ba-Yunus estimated that 46% of the Muslims in Chicago were indigenous Americans (almost all of whom would have been African Americans), 20% were Arabs, 19% were from South Asia, 07% were Turkish, 04% were from East Europe, and 04% were not otherwise classified.

A somewhat different approach was utilized by Bagby et al. Rather than estimating the ethnic composition of Muslims in America, this study looked at the ethnic breakdown of regular participants at the average mosque in America. Based upon interviews with the leadership of the surveyed mosques, it was estimated that regular participants at the average mosque included 33% South Asians, 30% African Americans, 25% Arabs, 3.4% African, 2.1% Eastern European, 1.6% White Americans,

1.6% Southeast Asian, 1.2% Caribbean, 1.1% Turkish, 0.7% Iranian, and 0.6% Hispanic/Latino.

C3. AN EMERGING DILEMMA

As noted in the introduction to this section, the Muslim population of the United States is diverse and heterogeneous with regard to its countries of origin, its native cultures, its ethnicities, its races, and its native languages. On the positive side of the ledger, such diversity offers untold riches to the Muslim community in America if it finds overarching unity in Islam. On the negative side of the ledger, such diversity offers ample opportunity for divisiveness and fragmentation.

Ternikar addressed the latter issue and labeled its danger as being tribalism among Muslims in America. He argued that this tribalism was built upon Muslim Americans typically tending to identify themselves according to national origins, racial similarities, and ethnic consciousness, rather than on the basis of their shared religion. He concluded that this tribalism was the root cause of disunity among Muslim Americans.

It is an unfortunate fact that one typically does not have to look very long at the Muslim community before seeing ample confirmation of Ternikar's hypotheses. Most Muslim social gatherings can be easily characterized as being African American, South Asian, or Arab in nature. Further, if the immigrant groups have a large enough population in a local area, one soon discovers that the Arabs tend to subdivide into Syrian, Palestinian, Egyptian, and Saudi groupings and that the South Asian group also fragments into separate subgroups.

Additional evidence of this fragmentation can be found in the survey of mosque leadership conducted by Bagby et al. The survey found that fully 64% of mosques in America have one dominant ethnic group, typically either African American or South Asian. An additional 31% of the mosques have two dominant ethnic groups, with the most frequent combination being South Asian and Arab. Fully 07% of the mosques were comprised of a single ethnic group, and at 24% of the mosques 90% or more of the attendees were from the same ethnic group. Finally, the survey found that 27% of mosques in America were attempting to preserve a specific ethnic or national heritage, a situation that tends to exclude Muslims who do not happen to belong to the particular ethnic or national heritage that is being preserved.

Findings such as the above give a great deal of credence to Ternikar's hypotheses. However, even more startling evidence can be gleaned by considering the data provided in the previous subsection regarding the composition of the Islamic community in North America. By and large, the various researchers have failed to make any distinction between second-generation Muslims and their parents. The American-raised children of Arab parents have been classified as Arabs, the American-raised children of South Asian parents have been classified as South Asians, etc. Such classification raises serious questions about the assumptions being made by the researchers in question.

As a clinical psychologist by training and education, let me advance a basic psychological premise that many immigrant Muslims may have some trouble accepting. The second and third generations of Muslims in America are by and large Americans. It doesn't matter where these children were born or in which country their parents were born. It doesn't matter whether their parents are immigrant Muslims or American converts. It doesn't matter whether the language spoken in the family home is Urdu, Arabic, Swahili, or English. It doesn't matter whether their names are Muhammad, Jim, Fatima, or Suzie. They have been raised in America, and their self-identity is typically going to be that of Americans.

As further support for this premise, consider the words of Yahiya Emerick, a longtime teacher in private Islamic schools and the author of an important textbook in Islamic studies for middle school students

> The most frequently voiced complaint I have heard from the youth is that they feel that their parents are trying to impose an alien and foreign culture on their American born and raised children. The youth say that they have to act in an unnatural and artificial way when they are at home, and that it is only when they are away from their parents that they are in the "real world." [98]

Unfortunately, too many immigrant Muslims fail to acknowledge and accept this all-important premise. They too often confuse their culture of origin with Islam and too often insist that their children must be Pakistani, Palestinian, etc. in order to be a Muslim. Further, they too often tend to contrast being an American with being a Muslim, and thus they help to perpetuate, perhaps even to instill, a basic psychic conflict into the self-identity of their children, who too often end up feeling that they must choose between being an American and being a Muslim. They too often feel that they must choose between America and Islam.

If the second generation is forced to link Islam with the nationalistic origins of their parents and if they are forced to choose between being an American and being a Muslim, between America and Islam, then the Muslim community in America is in for a long string of very painful disappointments. If the only option given to the second generation is to choose one or the other, then quite frankly, most of them will choose to be Americans, not practicing Muslims. This is the ultimate risk that is being run by tribalism within the Muslim community in America.

---

98. Emerick Y (1996), p. 46.

The emerging dilemma that faces the second generation of Muslims in America is how to be both American and Muslim without compromising either one. One component to the successful resolution of this dilemma is to accept, understand, and embrace the centuries-old history of Muslims in America. The importance of this cannot be overemphasized, as the ability of the second generation to resolve their dilemma will have much to say about the longterm success of Islam in America.

C4. CONCLUSIONS

Diversity of national, cultural, ethnic, racial, and linguistic heritage should be a foundation of strength for the Muslim community in America. It should enrich the entire community and provide opportunity for knowledge and deeper insight. To do so, tribalism cannot be allowed to supplant Islam as the primary building block in one's self-identity, and at some point tribal history must take a second seat to the rich and varied history of Muslims in America.

D. MOSQUES AND ISLAMIC CENTERS IN NORTH AMERICA

Just as the lack of a centralized organization that serves as an umbrella for all Muslim groups makes it hard to determine the exact number of Muslims in America, it also makes it difficult to know the exact number of mosques and Islamic centers that dot the American landscape. As such, one is once again left to rely upon estimates.

In 1992, Numan reported that there were 843 mosques and Islamic centers in the United States. Dannin reported that there were 112 mosques in the state of New York by 2002, around 40 just in Chicago, and about 1,200 nationwide. Bagby et al. were able to comprise a master list of 1,206 mosques and Islamic centers in 2000. Khan estimated the number of mosques and Islamic centers to be around 2,000 in 2002 and raised his estimate to 3,000 Islamic centers and mosques in 2005.

Part of the problem in determining the number of mosques and Islamic centers in America is that they are being created so rapidly. Bagby et al. were able to identify almost 130 mosques that were built in the 1980s and almost 120 that were built in the 1990s. With new mosques springing up at such a rapid pace and with there being no central organization to which all mosques report, it is almost impossible to keep up with the rapid growth.

E. ISLAMIC SCHOOLS IN NORTH AMERICA

In recent years, the Muslim community in America has been involved in a concerted effort to establish private Islamic schools, in order to insure proper religious instruction and the perpetuation of their children in the faith of Islam. Some of these schools are fulltime schools offering both religious education and the standard curriculum of the American public school system. Others are part-time schools that confine their offerings to religious instruction and that serve as a supplement to the public school system.

Numan reported that there were 165 private Islamic schools in the United States in 1992. Of these, 92 were fulltime schools, and 73 were part-time.

Bagby et al. found that 21% of the surveyed mosques in 2000 had a fulltime school, up from 17% in 1994, and that 71% of the mosques had part-time schools that met regularly during the weekend. If their master list of 1,209 mosques as of 2000 was correct and complete, this suggests that there were about 254 fulltime Islamic schools and about 858 part-time schools that were associated with a mosque during 2000. Using this data in conjunction with the average attendance figures reported for schools, Bagby et al. estimated that there were about 31,700 students attending fulltime Islamic schools and an additional 79,600 children attend weekend schools. (Note: this study does not take into consideration those private Islamic schools that are not directly associated with a mosque.)

Khan estimated that there were about 400 fulltime Islamic schools and an additional 800 part-time Islamic schools in America as of 2005. Based upon these estimates, Khan suggested that there were approximately two million Muslim youth in America and that about 100,000 of them attended a fulltime, private Islamic school, suggesting that fulltime Islamic schools averaged about 250 students. He offered no estimates concerning how many additional Muslim youth were attending part-time Islamic schools.

F. Islamic Organizations in North America

F1. Introduction

Over the last four decades, a variety of Islamic organizations have been established in North America. Space does not permit a complete listing of all these organizations, but the following is representative. In what follows, these organizations are presented in chronological order, according to their dates of creation.

F2. The MSA

The Muslim Student Association (MSA) of the United States and Canada is the oldest of the national Islamic organizations. In January of 1963, over 70 Muslim students from around the country gathered at the University of Illinois Urbana-Champaign to form the MSA. Most of these initial organizers of the MSA were foreign graduate students. Later in 1963, the MSA held their first national convention at Urbana-Champaign and has held a national convention every year since then.

The primary goal of the MSA has always been *Da'wah* (i.e., preaching or exhortation with regard to Islam). To accomplish that goal, the MSA established the first Muslim financial trust company (North American Islamic Trust), the first Muslim publishing company (International Graphics, which is now privately owned and is the parent company of Amana Publications) in North America, the first Muslim newsletter and magazine (*Islamic Horizons* and *Al-Ittihad*) to be issued on a regular basis, and Islamic Awareness Week as a regular part of the annual life of many American universities. Both ISNA and ICNA were founded by former members of the MSA.

F3. ICNA

The Islamic Circle of North America (ICNA) traces its history to the formation of an Urdu-speaking, Muslim organization known as Halaqa-e-Islami in 1968. Between 1971 and 1977, Halaqa-e-Islami worked within the MSA. It was renamed the Islamic Circle of North America in 1977 and held its first annual convention that same year. In 1980, the official language of ICNA was changed to English, and it became the first large-scale, national Muslim organization in America that was not limited to just college and graduate students.

ICNA's stated goal is to seek the pleasure of Allah through the struggle to establish the Islamic system of life as spelled out in the *Qur'an* and example of Prophet Muhammad. To achieve that goal, the ICNA program focuses on inviting mankind to submit to God, motivating Muslims to perform their duty of being witnesses to mankind by both their words and deeds, offering educational and training opportunities to increase Islamic knowledge, opposing immorality and oppression in all forms, supporting efforts for civil liberties and socio-economic justice, strengthening the bond of humanity by serving those in need, and cooperating with other organizations to implement this program and to unify Muslims. ICNA Relief (a Muslim organization for disaster relief and charity), the ICNA Book Service, and 877-Why-Islam (a Muslim organization for inviting non-Muslims to Islam) are among ICNA's contributions to Islamic life in North America.

ICNA's central offices are located in Jamaica, New York, and it has branch offices in Toronto, Chicago, Houston, and New Jersey. It is governed by an *Ameer* (leader or president), who is advised by a five-member Executive Council that is chosen by the *Ameer* from a *Majlis Al-Shura* (an advisory and consulting group formed from the membership of ICNA). All ICNA members are expected to read the *Qur'an* on a daily basis, to study the example of Prophet Muhammad on an at least weekly basis, study Islamic literature, and spend at least some hours each month in teaching and preaching Islam to others.

ICNA sponsors national conventions every summer and winter, which since 2002 have been held jointly with the MAS (see below).

F4. IIIT

The International Institute of Islamic Thought (IIIT) was established in 1981 and is a private, non-profit, academic and cultural institution that is concerned with general issues of Islamic thought. Headquartered in Herndon, Virginia, IIIT has branch offices in several capitals throughout the world.

IIIT is dedicated to the revival and reform of Islamic thought and its methodology. It is primarily focused on Islamic scholarship in the social sciences and on what it terms the "Islamization of Knowledge." Its stated objectives are as follows: to serve as a think tank in the field of Islamic culture and knowledge; to formulate a comprehensive Islamic vision and methodology that will serve Muslim scholars in their critical analysis of contemporary knowledge; to develop an appropriate methodology for understanding the *Qur'an* and the example of Prophet Muhammad; to establish the *Qur'an* and example of Prophet Muhammad as sources of guidance, knowledge, and civilization; to develop an appropriate methodology for dealing with Islamic legacy and contemporary knowledge, in order to draw on the experiences of both past and present and to build a better future for the Muslim community and for humanity at large; and to develop an appropriate methodology for understanding and dealing with the present situation of both the Muslim community and the world in general.

In pursuit of its aims, IIIT sponsors a variety of scholarly conferences and seminars, works in conjunction with various universities and academic institutions throughout the world, and supports a variety of researchers and scholars.

F5. ISNA

The Islamic Society of North America (ISNA) was founded in 1982 by former members of the MSA and is presently located in Plainfield, Indiana. Since its inception, it has taken on many of the functions that originally fell under the MSA. It is governed by an elected president, executive council, and board of directors (*Majlis Al-Shura*), and its daily activities are administered by a secretary general.

As presently constituted, ISNA serves as an umbrella organization that coordinates and unifies the efforts of many other Islamic organizations. Its mission statement is to provide a common platform for presenting Islam, supporting Muslim communities, developing educational, social and outreach programs, and good relations with other religious communities and with civic and service organizations. Its strategic goals are to provide *Imam* training and leadership development, propogate youth involvement, promote a positive public image of Islam, build coalitions and interfaith understanding, and promote community development.

ISNA sponsors a national convention every summer and numerous smaller conventions every year.

F6. MPAC

The Muslim Public Affairs Council (MPAC) was established in 1988. It is a public service agency that works for the civil rights of Muslim Americans, the integration of Islam into American pluralism, and a positive and constructive relationship between Muslim Americans and their representatives. In pursuit of this agenda, MPAC actively promotes an American Muslim identity, grassroots organizations, and an accurate portrayal of Islam and Muslims in the mass media and popular culture.

F7. MAS

The Muslim American Society (MAS) was founded in 1992 and maintains its central offices in Falls Church, Virginia. Its stated objectives are as follows: to present the message of Islam to Muslims and non-Muslims and promote understanding between the two groups; to encourage Muslim participation in building a virtuous and moral society; to offer a viable Islamic alternative to many of society's prevailing problems; to promote family values in accordance with Islamic teaching; to promote such Islamic values as brotherhood, equality, justice, mercy, compassion, and peace; and to foster unity, cooperation, and coordination among Muslims and Muslim organizations. MAS sponsors joint national conventions with ICNA every summer and winter.

F8. IANA

The Islamic Assembly of North America (IANA) was formed in 1993 to represent those Muslims who identify with a more restrictive and exclusionist interpretation of Islam that is various known as *Ahl Al-Sunnah Wa Al-Jama'ah* and *Salafi*. It is a principle of IANA that correct Islamic methodology is to be derived from the *Qur'an* and example of Prophet Muhammad as understood and applied by the first few generations of Muslims after Prophet Muhammad. In pursuit of its aims, IANA is actively involved in the propogation of Islam (i.e., *Da'wah* activities) and sponsors conventions and a bookstore.

F9. CAIR

The Council on American-Islamic Relations (CAIR) was established in 1994 as a grassroots civil rights and advocacy group. Its central offices are in Washington, DC, but it also has branch offices throughout the United States and Canada. CAIR defines its mission as being to enhance understanding of Islam, encourage dialogue, protect civil liberties, empower American Muslims, and build coalitions that promise justice and mutual understanding.

F10. THE MOSQUE CARES

The Mosque Cares is an Islamic association under the leadership of *Imam* W. Deen Mohammed. It is an outgrowth from W. D. Mohammed's earlier organization, the American Society of Muslims, and represents a large portion of the African-American Muslims in America.

G. ISLAMIC PUBLICATIONS IN NORTH AMERICA

Numan reported that there were 89 Islamic publications in the United States in 1992. While many of these publications were probably little more than newsletters, the last few decades have seen an enormous upswing in the number of Islamic publications in North America.

At the present time, Islam is represented by at least four weekly newspapers and three monthly magazines in the United States. The weekly newspapers include *Muslims Weekly* out of Jamaica, New York, *The Muslim Observer* out of Farmington, Michigan, the *Mirror International* out of Greenpoint, New York, and the *Muslim Journal*, which evolved out of the old *Muhammad Speaks* newspaper of the Nation of Islam, which is primarily associated with the Islamic ministry of W. D. Mohammed and which is published out of Chicago, Illinois. In addition to the above newspapers, there are several monthly magazines that represent the Islamic community in North America. Among these one can list *Islamic Horizons* (the official magazine of ISNA), *The Message International* (the official magazine of ICNA), and *Al Jumuah*.

Over the years, a number of different Islamic publishing houses have arisen to serve the needs of the Muslim community in North America. Both through the translation of Arabic and Urdu texts into English and through the publication of original works in English, these publishers have played a crucial role in educating and expanding the Muslim community. At the forefront of these publishing houses is Amana Publications, a subsidiary of International Graphics, which was originally established by the Muslim Student Association. Amana publishes a wide range of original works in English (several of which have been translated into other languages), 'Abdullah Yusuf 'Ali's highly regarded translation of the *Qur'an* into English, and English translations of a few classic works of Islamic thought. Other Islamic publishers include Kazi Publications, Darussalam, IQRA' International Educational Foundation, Al-Basheer Company for Publications and Translations, American Trust Publications, the International Institute of Islamic Thought, and Khatoons, Inc.

The extent and success of Islamic publishing in North America can be illustrated by the fact that it is currently estimated that more Islamic texts are presently being published in English than in Arabic.

H. ISLAMIC STUDIES IN HIGHER EDUCATION

One indication of the growing prevalence of Islam in America can be found in the number of Islamic studies programs that have been incorporated into the curricula of American colleges and universities. In a survey of American institutions of higher learning, Bukhari identified 225 different Islamic studies programs. While these programs attest to the growing influence of Islam on the American consciousness, unfortunately many of them are completely staffed by non-Muslim faculty members.While Muslims are frequently members of the faculties in a number of different scientific, medical, and technical disciplines within American academia, they remain poorly represented in what should be their center of strength, i.e., Islamic studies programs, in American colleges and universities.

I. CONCLUSIONS

Islam is currently the fastest growing religion and, according to most estimates, the second largest religion in North America. Its growth in population, mosques, schools, organizations, and publications speaks to Islam's remarkable success in the latter half of 20th-century America. However, those successes are still marked by a couple of discrete failures. One failure has been the Muslim community's inability or unwillingness to rise above a tribalism defined by ethnicity, race, and cultural, national, and linguistic origins. A second failure is reflected in the number of sec-ond-generation Muslims who are no longer actively practicing their religion. Both failures speak to the need for Muslims in America to establish a self-identity that is both fully Muslim and fully American. (It must be quickly added that this does not mean accepting every whim, fad, and deviancy that becomes part of American popular culture, nor does it mean agreeing with every policy issuing forth from the government. After all, the right to dissent is part of the American identity.)

With regard to establishing a self-identity that is both fully Muslim and fully American, it is hoped that this volume's presentation of the history of Muslims in America provides a heritage and legacy that may help formulate such a self-identity.

Bibliography

Abdelhabbar FM: Islam gains Hispanic adherents in Hudson. *The Jersey Journal*, February 1, 2002.

Abdullah AA: In search of my brothers. *The Message* 21: (1), 19, 1996.

Abiva H, Durkee N: *A History of Muslim Civilization: From Late Antiquity to the Fall of the Umayyads: Vol. 1*. Skokie, IQRA' International Education Foundation, 2003.

Abraham A: The Amistad revolt: An historical legacy of Sierra Leone and the United States http://usinfo.state.gov/products/pubs/amistad/

Abun-Nasr JM: North Africa, history of: From the Islamic conquests to 1830. In --- (ed.): *Encyclopaedia Britannica 2003*. ---, Encyclopaedia Britannica, 2003.

Ahariof MA: The Islamic community in the United States: Historical development. http://www.islamfortoday.com/historyusa2.htm.

Ahmed Z: *Islam: Africa to America*. Rancho Palos Verdes, Islamic Research and Publications, 2003.

Akbar N: *Breaking the Chains of Psychological Slavery*. Tallahassee, Mind Productions & Associates, 1996.

Al-Azdi SA (*Abu Dawud*): *Kitab Al-Sunan*. In Hasan A (trans.): *Sunan Abu Dawud*. New Delhi, Kitab Bhavan, 1990.

Al-Bukhari MI: *Kitab Al-Jami' Al-Sahih*. In Khan MM (trans.): *The Translation of the Meanings of Sahih Al-Bukhari*. Madinah, ---, undated.

Al-Hafez MA, Rabia JAA, Dirks DL, Dirks JF: From Syria, with love: A letter from the grandson of Sheykh Akmet Hafez. *Arabian Visions* 11: (1), 39-40, 1994.

Al-Hafez MA, Rabia JAA, Dirks DL, Dirks JF: The life and times of Sheykh Ahmad Al-Hafez. *Arabian Visions* 11: (3), 36-42, 1994.

Al-Qushayri MH (*Muslim*): *Al-Jami' Al-Sahih*. In Siddiqi 'AH (trans.): *Sahih Muslim*. ---, ---, 1971(?).

Al-Tirmidhi MI: *Sahih Al-Tirmidhi*. In --- (trans.): *Alim Multimedia CD Rom*. ---, ISL Software Corporation, ---.

'Ali 'AY: *The Meaning of the Holy Qur'an*. Beltsville, Amana Pub., 1992.

Ali ND: *Moorish Literature*. ---, ---, ---.

Ali Z: Return to roots. *Islamic Horizons* 34: (4), 17-36, 2005.

Amatullah-Rahman AA: A history of Islam among African Americans. In Lin PL (ed.): *Islam in America: Images and Challenges*. Indianapolis, University of Indianapolis Press, 1998.

Armento BJ, Cordova JM, Klor de Alva JJ, Nash GB, Ng F, Salter CL, Wilson LE, Wixson KK: *Across the Centuries*. Boston, Houghton Mifflin Company, 1999.

Armstrong K: *A History of God: The 4,000-Year Quest of Judaism, Christianity and Islam*. New York, Ballantine Books, 1993.

Armstrong K: *Holy War: The Crusades and their Impact on Today's World*. New York, Anchor Books, 2001.

Austin AD: Tracing early African Muslims in America: Some barely tapped and possible sources: Let the search go on. Paper presented at the Islam in America Conference, DePaul University, September 29, 1995.

Austin AD: *African Muslims in Antebellum America.* New York, Routledge, 1997.

Bagby I, Perl PM, Froehle BT: *The Mosque in America: A National Portrait.* Washington, Council on American-Islamic Relations, 2001.

Baird R: UVa-Wise biologist unveils Melungeon genetics study. *Coalfield Progress,* June 25, 2002.

Barnard WC: Hi Jolly and the U.S. Camel Corps. http://www.scvhisto ry.com/scvhistory /hijolly-ap.htm

Barrayn LA: Higher learning: Muslim students organize at historically Black colleges and universities. *Islamic Horizons* 34: (4), 28-29, 2005.

Barrett DB, Kurian GT, Johnson TM: *World Christian Encyclopedia.* New York, Oxford University Press, 2001. As referenced in Dannin R (2002).

Ba-Yunus I: Muslim population of Illinois: Preliminary findings. In Lin PL (ed.): *Islam in America: Images and Challenges.* Indianapolis, University of Indianapolis Press, 1998.

Berggren JL: Mathematics, history of: Mathematics in medieval Islam. In --- (ed.): *Encyclopaedia Britannica 2003.* ---, Encyclopaedia Britannica, 2003.

Beruni KR: Give me that old time religion: Searching for God. In Dirks DL, Parlove S: *Islam Our Choice: Portraits of Modern American Muslim Women.* Beltsville, Amana Publications, 2003.

Bewley A: *Glossary of Islamic Terms.* London, Ta-Ha Publishers, 1998.

Bokser BZ: Maimonides, Moses. In --- (ed.): *Encyclopaedia Britannica* 2003. ---, Encyclopaedia Britannica, 2003.

Bracewell CW: Croatia: History. In --- (ed.): *Encyclopaedia Britannica* 2003. --- (ed.), Encyclopaedia Britannica, 2003.

Bukhari Z: The state of Islamic studies in American universities. Paper presented to the Islam in Higher Education Conference, United Kingdom, January 30, 2005.

Campbell H: The Powhatan remnants. http://www.melungeons.com/baber/articles/ powhatanremnants.htm.

Cox H: What the mad knight was seeking. *Harvard Divinity Bulletin* 33: (1), 87-89, 2005.

Curiel J: Muslim roots of the blues: The music of famous American blues singers reaches back through the South to the culture of West Africa. *San Francisco Chronicle*, August 15, 2004.

Curtin PD: *Africa Remembered: Narratives by West Africans from the Era of the Slave Trade.* Madison, University of Wisconsin Press, 1968.

Dannin R: *Black Pilgrimage to Islam.* Oxford, Oxford University Press, 2002.

Day GE: Letter to the editor (about the Amistad Africans). *New York Journal of Commerce*, October 10, 1839.

De Graft-Johnson JC: Musa. In — (ed.): *Encyclopaedia Britannica* 2003. — (ed.), Encyclopaedia Britannica, 2003.

Diouf SA: *Servants of Allah: African Muslims Enslaved in the Americas.* New York, New York University Press, 1998.

Dirks DL, Dirks JF: *An introduction to Davenport Arabians. Arabian Horse Country* 4: (9), 40-81, 1987.

Dirks DL, Dirks JF: *The Davenport importation. Arabian Horse Country* 4: (10), 60-85, 1987.

Dirks JF, Dirks DL: *The Bani Sham Source Book.* Kiowa, Bani Sham Association, 1996.

Douglas K: Remnant Indians of the Southeast. In Douglas K (ed.): *American Indian Melungeon* at http://www.angelfire.com/tn3/youngeagle/AMERICAN_ INDIANbook. htm, 2002a.

Douglas K: Racial realities, *American Indians and Melungeons.* In Douglas K (ed.): American Indian Melungeon at http://www.angelfire.com/tn3/youngeagle/ AMERICAN_INDIANbook.htm, 2002b.

El MAR: Digging for the red roots. *The Message* 21: (1), 23, 1996.

El-Badry S, Shabbas A: The Arab Americans. http://www.mepc.org/public_asp/ workships/arabamer.asp, 2002.

Emerick Y: Just what are the youth thinking anyway? *The Message* 21: (1), 45-46, July, 1996.

Entienne-Gray T: *Black Seminole Indians.* http://afgen.com/black_seminoles2.html.

Ertan SZ: Amerika'daki Turklerin Tarihi (A history of Turks in America). In Guzel HC, Cicck K, Koka S (eds.): *Turkler.* Ankara, Yeni Turkiye, 2002.

Fausets A: *Black Gods of the Metropolis*. Philadelphia, U. of Pennsylvania Press, 1971.

Fayer S, Bagwell O: *Malcolm X: Make It Plain*. Boston, WGBH Boston & Blackside, Inc., 1994.

Flint VIJ: Columbus, Christopher. In --- (ed.): *Encyclopaedia Britannica* 2003. --- (ed.), Encyclopaedia Britannica, 2003.

Gines JV, Viguera MJ: Spain: History: Muslim Spain. In --- (ed.): *Encyclopaedia Britannica* 2003. --- (ed.), Encyclopaedia Britannica, 2003.

Goins J: Examining Melungeon history and genealogy. In Douglas K (ed.): *American Indian Melungeon* at http://www.angelfire.com/tn3/youngeagle/ AMERICAN_INDIANbook.htm, 2002b.

Goldman A: Portraits of religions in U.S. holds dozens of surprises. *New York Times*, Section A, page 1, April 10, 1991. As referenced in Dannin R (2002).

Gomez MA: Muslims in early America. *Journal of Southern History* 60 (November, 1994), 671-709.

Griggs K: *Slavery and Freedom in Islam*. Bridgeview, Sound Vision, 2002.

Haddad YY, Smith JI: *Mission to America: Five Islamic Sectarian Communities in North America*. Gainesville, University Press of Florida, 1993.

Hagy JW: Muslim slaves, abducted Moors, African Jews, misnamed Turks, and an Asiatic Greek lady: Some examples of non-European religious and ethnic diversity in South Carolina prior to 1861. *Carologue* 9: (1), 12-13 & 25-27, 1993.

Haley A: *Roots*. Garden City, Doubleday & Company, 1976.

Harrison RJ: Spain: History: Pre-Roman Spain. In --- (ed.): *Encyclopaedia Britannica* 2003. --- (ed.), Encyclopaedia Britannica, 2003.

Hathout H: *Reading the Muslim Mind.* Burr Ridge, American Trust Publications, 2002.

Hauser T: Ali, Muhammad. In --- (ed.): *Encyclopaedia Britannica* 2003. --- (ed.), Encyclopaedia Britannica, 2003.

Haywood JA: Masudi, al-. In --- (ed.): *Encyclopaedia Britannica 2003.* ---, Encyclopaedia Britannica, 2003.

Hellie R: Slavery. In --- (ed.): *Encyclopaedia Britannica 2003.* ---, Encyclopaedia Britannica, 2003.

Hickman M: *Homer, the Country Boy.* Salem, Micky Hickman, 1986.

Hirschman EC: *Melungeons: The Last Lost Tribe in America.* Macon, Mercer University Press, 2005.

Huot L, Powers A: *Homer Davenport of Silverton: Life of a Great Cartoonist.* Bingen, West Shore Press, 1973.

Irving TB: Islam and Columbus' America: Lessons we can learn from the fall of Islamic Spain. http://salam.muslimsonline.com/~aza hoor/irving1.htm

Jardine K: Mum, I've decided I want to follow Allah. *The Herald,* March 8, 2002.

Jenkins BL: The Black Seminoles' long road to freedom. http://www.ccny.cuny.edu/ library/News/seminoles2.html, 1998.

Jimenez M: New Muslims. *National Post,* January 19, 2002.

Jwaideh W: Idrisi, ash-Sharif al-. In --- (ed.): *Encyclopaedia Britannica 2003.* ---, Encyclopaedia Britannica, 2003.

Kaba L: Americans discover Islam through the Black Muslim experience. In Koszegi MA, Melton JG (eds.): *Islam in North America: A Source Book.* New York, Garland, 1992.

Kappler CJ (ed.): *Indian Affairs: Laws and Treaties. Vol. II (Treaties).* Washington, Government Printing Office, 1904.

Katz WL: *Black Indians: A Hidden Heritage.* New York, Simon Pulse, 1997.

Kennedy NB: The Melungeons, An Untold Story of Ethnic Cleansing in America. *Islamic Horizons,* Nov./Dec., 1994.

Kennedy NB: Saga of the Melungeons. *Georgia Journal,* Winter, 1994b.

Kennedy NB: An Update on Melungeon Research. ---, ---, 1997.

Kennedy NB, Kennedy RV: *The Melungeons: The Resurrection of a Proud People.* Macon, Mercer University Press, 1997.

Kennedy NB: A new path. In Douglas K (ed.): American Indian Melungeon at http://www.angelfire.com/tn3/ youngeagle/AMERICAN_INDIANbook.htm, 2002.

Kennedy NB: Background. In Scolnick JM, Kennedy NB: *From Anatolia to Appalachia: A Turkish-American Dialogue.* Macon, Mercer University Press, 2003a.

Kennedy NB: Acceptance speech. In Scolnick JM, Kennedy NB: *From Anatolia to Appalachia: A Turkish-American Dialogue.* Macon, Mercer University Press, 2003b.

Khan MAM: *American Muslims: Bridging Faith and Freedom.* Beltsville, Amana Publications, 2002.

Khan MAM: Struggling for the souls of Islamic schools. *San Jose Mercury News,* July 3, 2005.

Koenigsberger HG: Spain: History: United Spain under the Catholic monarchs. In --- (ed.): *Encyclopaedia Britannica 2003.* ---, Encyclopaedia Britannica, 2003.

Koenigsberg HG: Spain: History: Spain under the Habsburgs. In --- (ed.): *Encyclopaedia Britannica 2003.* ---, Encyclopaedia Britannica, 2003.

Kosmin BA, Mayer E: American religious identification survey 2001. http://www.gc. Cuny.edu/studies/aris_part_two.htm., 2001.

Koszegi MA, Melton JG (eds.): *Islam in North America: A Source Book.* New York, Garland, 1992.

Lang J: *Losing My Religion: A Call for Help.* Beltsville, Amana Publications, 2004.

Last JV: Seven million American Muslims? *The Daily Standard,* December 11, 2001.

Lincoln E: *The Black Muslims in America.* Westport, Greenwood Press, 1982.

Linder DO: Salvaging Amistad. *Journal of Maritime Law and Commerce* 3: (4), October, 2000.

Lo M: *Muslims in America.* Beltsville, Amana Publications, 2004.

Lotfi A: *Muslims on the Block: Five Centuries of Islam in America.* Ifrane, Al Akhawayn University Press, 2002.

Lowe S: Hi Jolly: Camel driver's dream lives on in Quartzsite. In *The Arizona Republic*, November 1, 1999.

MacLeod MJ, Ferguson JA: Haiti: History. In --- (ed.): *Encyclopaedia Britannica 2003*. ---, Encyclopaedia Britannica, 2003.

Malhotra P: Islam's female converts. Newday.com, February 16, 2002.

McCloud AM: *African American Islam*. New York and London, Routledge, 1995.

McElwainT: Melungeon memories. In Douglas K (ed.): American Indian Melungeon at http://www.angelfire.com/tn3/youngeagle/AMERICAN_INDIANbook.htm, 2002b.

McEvedy C, Jones R: *Atlas of World Population History*. New York, Facts on File, 1978.

McKee S: Warith Deen Muhammad. http://home.att.net/~spmckee/people_ muhammadwd.html.

Mroueh Y: PreColumbian Muslims in the Americas. www.sunnah.org/history/precolmb. htm, 1996.

Muhammad A: Impact of a Nation on 20th-century America. http://www.finalcall.com/national/ saviorsday2k/noi_impact.htm.

Muhammad ANA: *Muslims in America: Seven Centuries of History* (1312-2000). Beltsville, Amana Publications, 2001.

Muhammad ANA: Mothers of resolve: Remembering the early Muslim matriarchs of the African diaspora in America. *Islamic Horizons* 34: (4), 22-23, 2005.

Niebuhr G: Studies suggest lower count for number of U.S. Muslims. *New York Times*, October 25, 2001.

Numan FH: American Muslim history: A chronological observation. www.islam101. com/history/muslim_us_hist.html, ---.

Numan FH: The Muslim population in the United States. http://www.islam101.com/ history/population2_usa.html, 1992.

Nyang SS: Islam in the United States of America: A review of the sources. In Koszegi MA, Melton JG (eds.): *Islam in North America: A Source Book*. New York, Garland, 1992.

Nyang SS: *Islam in the United States of America*. ---, ABC International Group, 1999.

O'Callaghan JF: Spain: History: Visigothic Spain to c. 500. In --- (ed.): *Encyclopaedia Britannica 2003*. --- (ed.), Encyclopaedia Britannica, 2003.

Parrish L: *Slave Songs of the Georgia Sea Islands*. Athens, University of Georgia Press, 1992.

Peck D: Original Seminoles. *Florida State Times,* September 13, 2000.

Plestina D: Croatia: The People. In --- (ed.): *Encyclopaedia Britannica 2003*. --- (ed.), Encyclopaedia Britannica, 2003.

Quick AH: *Deeper Roots: Muslims in the Americas and the Caribbean from before Columbus to the Present*. London, Ta-Ha Publishers Ltd., 1998.

Raboteau AJ: *Slave Religion: The "Invisible Institution" in the Antebellum South*. New York, Oxford University Press, 1980.

Rashad A: *Islam, Black Nationalism & Slavery: A Detailed History.* Beltsville, CWriters, 1995.

Rashid S: Blacks, the WOI theory, and hidden transcripts. *American Journal of Islamic Social Studies* 21: (2) 55-76, 2004.

Richardson JS: Spain: History: Roman Spain. In --- (ed.): *Encyclopaedia Britannica* 2003. --- (ed.), Encyclopaedia Britannica, 2003.

Ritz MK: More in Hawai'i turn to Islam. *The Honolulu Advertiser*, November 11, 2001.

Rosenthal EIJ: Averroes. In --- (ed.): *Encyclopaedia Britannica* 2003. ---, Encyclopaedia Britannica, 2003.

Savannah Unit of the Georgia Writers Project of the Works Project Administration: *Drums and Shadows: Survival Studies among the Georgia Coastal Negroes.* Athens, University of Georgia Press, 1986.

Scolnick JM, Kennedy NB: *From Anatolia to Appalachia: A Turkish-American Dialogue.* Macon, Mercer University Press, 2003.

Shah T: The Islamic legacy of Timbuktu. http://users.erols.com/gmqm/timbuktu.html

Shaw SJ: Ottoman Empire: (1) The Ottoman state to 1481: The age of expansion; (2) The peak of Ottoman power, 1481-1566; (3) The decline of the Ottoman Empire, 1566-1807. In --- (ed.): *Encyclopaedia Britannica* 2003. ---, Encyclopaedia Britannica, 2003.

Shelton MS: African Muslims in the Americas. http://us.f409.mail.yahoo.com/ym/ShowLetter?MsgId=4376_61520_5493_1862_7218_0_1

Shubert A: Spain: The people. In --- (ed.): *Encyclopaedia Britannica* 2003. --- (ed.), Encyclopaedia Britannica, 2003.

Siddiqui AH: *Life of Muhammad.* Des Plaines, Library of Islam, 1991.

Simpson GE: *Black Religions in the New World.* New York, Columbia University Press, 1978.

Skybova A, Hroch M: *Ecclesia Miltans: The Inquisition.* New York, Dorset Press, 1990.

Smallwood AD: A history of Native American and African relations from 1502 to 1900. *Negro History Bulletin*, April-Sept., 1999.

Stevens ME, Allen CM (eds.): *Journals of the House of Representatives, 1789-1790.* http://foclark.tripod.com/gypsy/journal.htm.

Suleiman MW: Arab-Americans: A community profile. In Koszegi MA, Melton JG (eds.): *Islam in North America: A Source Book.* New York, Garland, 1992.

Tappan L: Letter of September 9, 1839. As found at http://www.law.umkc.edu/faculty/ projects/ftrials/amistad/AMI_LTR.HTM

Ternikar FB: Tribalism in Muslim America. In Lin PL (ed.): *Islam in America: Images and Challenges.* Indianapolis, University of Indianapolis Press, 1998.

Umar KB: Leading a nation. *Islamic Horizons* 34: (4) 40-44, 2005.

Uotila UA, Garland GD: Earth: The figure and dimensions of the earth. In --- (ed.): *Encyclopaedia Britannica* 2003. ---, Encyclopaedia Britannica, 2003.

Vincent-Barwood A: Columbus: What if? http://users.erols.com/gmqm/columbus.html

Virk S: Concordia students tell of their conversion to Islam. *The Link*, February 5, 2002.

Wadstrom CB: *An Essay on Colonization, particularly applied to the Western Coast of Africa*. London, Darton & Harvey, 1794.

Ward J, Brown M (eds.): *Muhammad Ali—Through the Eyes of the World*. Universal City, Universal Studios, 2001.

White VL, Jr.: *Inside the Nation of Islam: A Historical and Personal Testimony by a Black Muslim*. Gainesville, University of Florida Press, 2001.

Whittell G: Allah came knocking at my heart. *The Times*, January 7, 2002.

Wilgoren J: Islam attracks converts by the thousands, drawn before and after attacks. *New York Times*, October 22, 2001.

Winkler W: About the Melungeons. http://www.melungeons.org/?BISKIT=4076367959 & CONTENT=cat&cat=10005. 2004a

Winkler W: *Walking Toward the Sunset: The Melungeons of Appalachia*. Mercer U. Press, 2004b.

Yahya H: *Islam Denounces Terrorism*. In Rossini C. Evans R (trans.): *Islam Denounces Terrorism*. Bristol, Amal Press, 2002.

Zahoor A: The Melungeons. http://salam.muslimsonline.com/~azahoor/define.htm. 1998.

---: Abdul-Jabbar, Kareem. In --- (ed.): *Encyclopaedia Britannica* 2003. ---, Encyclopaedia Britannica, 2003a.

---: Ali, Muhammad. In --- (ed.): *Encyclopaedia Britannica* 2003. ---, Encyclopaedia Britannica, 2003b.

---: *Amistad* mutiny. In --- (ed.): *Encyclopaedia Britannica* 2003. ---, Encyclopaedia Britannica, 2003c.

---: Andalusia. In --- (ed.): *Encyclopaedia Britannica* 2003. ---, Encyclopaedia Britannica, 2003d.

---: Attucks, Crispus. In --- (ed.): *Encyclopaedia Britannica* 2003. ---, Encyclopaedia Britannica, 2003e.

---: Bahia. In --- (ed.): *Encyclopaedia Britannica* 2003. ---, Encyclopaedia Britannica, 2003f.

---: Battani, al-. In --- (ed.): *Encyclopaedia Britannica* 2003. ---, Encyclopaedia Britannica, 2003g.

---: Biruni, al-. In --- (ed.): *Encyclopaedia Britannica* 2003. ---, Encyclopaedia Britannica, 2003h.

---: Boston Massacre. In --- (ed.): *Encyclopaedia Britannica* 2003. ---, Encyclopaedia Britannica, 2003i.

---: Cinque. http://www.law.umkc.edu/faculty/projects/ftrials/ amistad/AMI_BCIN.HTM

---: Cordoba. In --- (ed.): *Encyclopaedia Britannica* 2003. ---, Encyclopaedia Britannica, 2003j.

---: Farrakhan, Louis. In --- (ed.): *Encyclopaedia Britannica* 2003. --- (ed.), Encyclopaedia Britannica, 2003k.

---: Hi Jolly's tomb. http://www.scvhistory.com/scvhistory/1w2161c.htm.

---: Huelva. In --- (ed.): *Encyclopaedia Britannica* 2003. ---, Encyclopaedia Britannica, 2003l.

---: Inquisition. In --- (ed.): *Encyclopaedia Britannica* 2003. ---, Encyclopaedia Britannica, 2003m.

---: Iroquois. In --- (ed.): *Encyclopaedia Britannica* 2003. --- (ed.), Encyclopaedia Britannica, 2003n.

---: Islam, Nation of. In --- (ed.): *Encyclopaedia Britannica* 2003. --- (ed.), Encyclopaedia Britannica, 2003o.

---: Islam way south of the border. *The Message*, November, 1997.

---: Kano. In --- (ed.): *Encyclopaedia Britannica* 2003. ---, Encyclopaedia Britannica, 2003p.

---: Khwarizmi, al-. In --- (ed.): *Encyclopaedia Britannica* 2003. ---, Encyclopaedia Britannica, 2003q.

---: Latitude and longitude. In --- (ed.): *Encyclopaedia Britannica* 2003. ---, Encyclopaedia Britannica, 2003r.

---: Macro-Algonquian languages. In --- (ed.): *Encyclopaedia Britannica* 2003. --- (ed.), Encyclopaedia Britannica, 2003s.

---: Malcolm X. In --- (ed.): *Encyclopaedia Britannica* 2003. --- (ed.), Encyclopaedia Britannica, 2003t.

---: Morisco. In --- (ed.): *Encyclopaedia Britannica* 2003. ---, Encyclopaedia Britannica, 2003u.

---: Muhammad, Elijah. In --- (ed.): *Encyclopaedia Britannica* 2003. --- (ed.), Encyclopaedia Britannica, 2003v.

---: Newspaper accounts of the Amistad case. http://www.law.umkc.edu/faculty/projects /ftrials/amistad/AMI_NEWS.HTM

---: On the good red path. *The Message* 21: (1), 6, 1996.

---: Osman I. In --- (ed.): *Encyclopaedia Britannica* 2003. ---, Encyclopaedia Britannica, 2003w.

---: Pinzon, Martin Alonso; and Pinzon, Vicente Yanez. In --- (ed.): *Encyclopaedia Britannica* 2003. ---, Encyclopaedia Britannica, 2003x.

---: Reconquista. In --- (ed.): *Encyclopaedia Britannica* 2003. --- (ed.), Encyclopaedia Britannica, 2003y.

---: Seminole. In --- (ed.): *Encyclopaedia Britannica* 2003. --- (ed.), Encyclopaedia Britannica, 2003z.

---: Seminole Wars. In --- (ed.): *Encyclopaedia Britannica* 2003. --- (ed.), Encyclopaedia Britannica, 2003za.

---: Siouan languages. In --- (ed.): *Encyclopaedia Britannica* 2003. --- (ed.), Encyclopaedia Britannica, 2003zb.

---: Sketches of the Amistad captives. http://www.law.umkc.edu/faculty/projects/ftrials /amistad/AMI_SLAV.HTM

---: Slave rebellions. In --- (ed.): *Encyclopaedia Britannica* 2003. ---, Encyclopaedia Britannica, 2003zc.

---: The Amistad case: A chronology. http://www.law.umkc.edu/faculty/projects/ftrials/ amistad/AMI_CHR.HTM

---: Vandal. In --- (ed.): *Encyclopaedia Britannica* 2003. --- (ed.), Encyclopaedia Britannica, 2003zd.